GEORGIAN ENGLAND

THE SMOAKING CLUB.

From a coloured aquatint by Robert Dighton.

" A club there is of Smokers, dare you come
To that close, clouded, hot, narcotic room?
When midnight past, the very candles seem
Dying for air and give a ghastly gleam:
When curling fumes in lazy wreaths arise,
And prosing topers rub their winking eyes."

CRABBE.

GEORGIAN ENGLAND

A Survey of SOCIAL LIFE
TRADES, INDUSTRIES & ART
from 1700 *to* 1820

By

A. E. RICHARDSON

F.S.A., F.R.I.B.A.

Author of "Monumental Classic Architecture in
Great Britain," Joint Author of "The Smaller
English House," "The English Inn,"
"London Houses," etc.

CLASSIC EDITIONS

This edition digitally re-mastered and
published by JM Classic Editions © 2008
Original text © AE Richardson 1931

ISBN 978-1-906600-00-6

All rights reserved. No part of this book subject
to copyright may be reproduced in any form or
by any means without prior permission in writing
from the publisher.

PREFACE

In the following pages an endeavour has been made to present an intimate picture of life, work, and the arts in England between the years 1700 and 1830. The book does not pretend to be a work of criticism or of detailed historical description or analysis. Its purpose is to record the more salient features and characteristics of the age, and at the same time to present some other of its aspects which are probably less familiar to the student and general reader. Thus, I may be criticised for devoting considerably less space to the fine arts than to the decorative crafts, and in the same way my section on building crafts and materials almost equals in bulk that on architectural design ; but the course of architecture and painting during the eighteenth century are both fairly familiar, while the crafts of building and decoration, with their resultant influence on design, are practically, it may be said, a closed book to the ordinary reader. Again, accounts of the course of political history and statesmanship can be found in any reliable text-book, so that it has been thought advisable here only to refer to these incidentally. I have, however, taken the opportunity of including a chapter on some of the varied aspects of sport, which formed so important a factor in eighteenth-century life.

Of necessity the book can neither be encyclopædic nor complete. It has been necessary to sift and sift again the mass of material at hand, to include only that which has a direct bearing on the development of Georgian England and the Georgian Englishman throughout the century. An effort, however, has been made to illustrate the book largely from contemporary sources, of which a great wealth exists. If, from the resulting narrative, the reader finds in his mind a clearer picture of this great epoch in history, of vital importance after a lapse of two centuries ; or if it aids him to appreciate and trace more clearly the thread of a great tradition of which we are to-day still the heirs, I shall be more than content.

The genesis of this book was a series of Lectures on eighteenth-century art and life in England, delivered some little time since before the University of Bristol, but the matter has been rewritten, rearranged, and considerably extended. I wish to convey my appreciation of the kind reception accorded to the Lectures at their delivery.

I have to thank several friends for criticism and advice, including my friend and late colleague, Mr Oswald M. Doughty, LL.D. Particulars of varied indebtedness in the matter of illustrations will be found in the Note of Acknowledgment which follows.

A. E. R.

AMPTHILL, *January* 1931.

NOTE OF ACKNOWLEDGMENT

The subjects on Plates LXXXI. (1) and LXVII. (1) are from the collections of H.M. the King and H.R.H. the Prince of Wales, respectively, by whose gracious permission they are reproduced. For other subjects reproduced from private collections, the author must express his indebtedness to His Grace the Duke of Richmond and Gordon for Plate I., the Right Honourable the Earl of Durham for Plate XCIII. (2), the Lady Desborough for Plate XCII. (1), Charles Wade, Esq., for Plate X. (3), and Mr Jules S. Bache of New York for Plate LXXXII. (2). Plate LXXI. (4) is reproduced by permission of The Governor and Directors of the Bank of England.

A number of subjects are reproduced from public collections, including Figs. 2 and 3, and Plates XV. and XXI. (2) from the Guildhall Library, London; Plate LXXIX. (2) from the Soane Museum, London; Plates III. and XXXIV. (2) from the Science Museum, London; and Plate LXXXI. (2) from the Wallace Collection, London. A number of other subjects are also included from the Victoria and Albert Museum, the British Museum, and the National Gallery, London.

The subjects on Plate XLVII. are from fine originals in the possession of the Marylebone Cricket Club at Lord's Ground, by whose permission they are reproduced, and by courtesy of the Secretary, Mr William Findlay. The frontispiece is from a rare print in the Bodleian Library, Oxford, and is included by courtesy of Bodley's Librarian.

I must acknowledge my indebtedness to Messrs Rimell & Sons and Messrs Walford Bros. for their kindness in placing their large and valuable illustration material at my disposal for reproduction. Also to Mr J. L. Douthwaite, of the Guildhall Library, for his valuable aid and advice in selecting illustration material.

The illustrations on Figs. 51, 52, and 53 are reproduced by courtesy of Messrs Rushworth & Dreaper Ltd., Organ Builders, Liverpool, from their fine permanent collection of antique musical instruments. I am also indebted to Messrs Basil Dighton Ltd. for Plates LXVI. (2 and 3), LXVII. (2 and 3); Messrs F. Frith & Co. Ltd., of Reigate, for Plate LXXXVII. (1); H. Nelson King, Esq., for Plate LVI. (2); H. W. Lane, Esq., of St Albans, for Plate LV. (1); Messrs Bedford Lemere & Co., for Plate XIII. (2); and to Messrs Valentine & Co. Ltd., of Dundee, for Plates XLVIII. (1), LIII. (2).

The remainder of the illustrations are reproduced from the author's and publishers' collections.

CONTENTS

CHAPTER		PAGE
	PREFACE	v
	NOTE OF ACKNOWLEDGMENT	vii
I.	TRADITION AND CHANGE	1
II.	THE SOCIAL SCENE	14
III.	THE NAVY, THE ARMY, AND THE CHURCH	37
IV.	TRADE AND INDUSTRIES	61
V.	SPORT, PASTIME, AND RECREATION	74
VI.	THE ARCHITECTURAL BACKGROUND	97
VII.	THE BUILDING CRAFTS	116
VIII.	INTERIOR DESIGN	130
IX.	THE DECORATIVE ARTS	134
X.	PAINTING, FROM LELY TO CONSTABLE	158
XI.	SCULPTURE, FROM GRINLING GIBBONS TO FLAXMAN	170
XII.	PLAYS AND PLAYERS, FROM CONGREVE TO SHERIDAN	174
XIII.	MUSIC AND MUSICAL INSTRUMENTS	178
XIV.	LITERATURE, FROM THE RESTORATION TO ROMANTICISM	187
	INDEX	195

PLATE I.

Views of London in the Early Eighteenth Century. (*Above*) Whitehall, with the Holbein Gate House (now demolished) and Banqueting Hall. (*Below*) The River Thames, looking towards St Paul's, from the gardens of old Somerset House.

GEORGIAN ENGLAND

CHAPTER I

TRADITION AND CHANGE

IT would seem particularly wrong in an account of life, art and industry in Georgian England to restrict the survey to the stretch within two arbitrary dates, those of the accession of the first of the Georges in 1714 and of the death of George IV. in 1830. Manners and traditions develop by so slow a progress of transition, and the life of one period is so closely interwoven with that of the period preceding it, that it is impossible, except in a general way, to determine the exact beginnings of any one epoch in history. Thus, in treating of architecture, it is necessary constantly to refer back to the innovations of Inigo Jones and the important work of Wren in London following the Great Fire, which belong to the previous century; while a bare account of Georgian manners and customs would be impossible without some reference to the circumstances of the previous century from which they developed. This applies in equal respect to almost every aspect of the age reviewed in this book.

In the same way the Georgian tradition survived into the next century, in many spheres up to the accession to the throne of Queen Victoria in 1837. But here the spirit of a new age was also apparent, and an account of such tendencies as belong properly to the nineteenth century has not been attempted. In the present work an effort has been made to trace the inception, maturity and decline of the Georgian tradition as it affected English social conditions, art, crafts and industry, and its scope may be said to correspond roughly with the span of the eighteenth century.

We are probably now only just beginning to see the England of the eighteenth century in its true perspective, as an age linking up our own epoch with the mediæval past. There were in it, as might be expected, many traditional survivals of the spirit of the old feudalism, and much that predicted the modernism of to-day. It was a period of exciting transition, which saw the culmination of the old order of things and the inception of new ideas and methods that went to form the nucleus of another epoch. Yet at the same time it possessed, perhaps, a more distinct identity of its own than any other age in English history. The new currents of progress and ideas for a long time hardly seemed to ruffle the face of the waters.

It was an age of political excitement, national expansion and scientific exploration ; but in the crowded events of its history we have been apt to overlook the tenor and temper of a Society which, however unsettled the times, generally contrived to retain its calm individualism, its reasonable, unperturbed humanism. English life and work throughout the reigns of the Georges developed by careful methodical stages till, in the early years of the nineteenth century, the seed sown by a few remote pioneers produced its astonishing harvest. The dogged determination to resist continental aggression of half a century before developed suddenly into the beginnings of an Imperial policy ; the restrained humanism of the arts blossomed into the early rapture of the Romantic movement ; and, more alarming still, conservative tradition was faced with the formidable prospect of an age of scientific democracy. The new steam railroad began to cut its grimy track through smiling acres of private park land. Chimneys began smoking in earnest in the North.

Up to the opening years of the eighteenth century England had been principally an agricultural country. Feudal conditions had been replaced, the absolute rule of the monarchy checked, and the people were enjoying the first-fruits of political freedom ; but the main mass of the population lived calmly enough, mildly observing ancient semi-feudal ordinances under a squirearchy and landed gentry responsible to the Crown. It was an almost automatic system which, under the conditions existing, worked well enough. But the span of a century was to see its almost complete abolition.

In this early, formative period, social conditions were sharply defined ; yet never so sharply as when, a hundred years later, with rumours of Political Reform in the air, the aristocracy was fighting with its back to the wall to retain its ancient privileges. At both times, and throughout the reigns of the Georges, the population fell into its three divisions of the aristocracy, " middling " people and working masses. But whereas in the early period there was an intimate, instinctive connection between these three classes, at the close

THE RISE OF INDUSTRIALISM

of it each represented an isolated section of the community, jealous of its own privileges or of those of the class above it.

The administrations of Sir Robert Walpole and of the elder Pitt had added enormously to the national prosperity. At the same time, rivalry with France and Holland had by the opening of the century opened the eyes of the nation to the importance of its power on the high seas. By the close of the century England was supreme at sea, and the intervening period is not only one marked by long and exhausting wars, but also by colonial expansion and an immense increase in overseas trade. What was at the beginning of the period a small island kingdom with a few colonies was transposed within the span of a century into a vast empire.

This increase in the national wealth produced as a direct result a prosperous and powerful new middle class; but at the same time its effect on the masses was to spread a poverty and squalor even more dreadful than that existing at the beginning of the period. Town life was developing by strides; we find London spreading out its tentacles, Bristol developing into a great seaport, and Birmingham growing up into the first of the new manufacturing towns. The rural population, slow to move at first, became increasingly attracted to these new centres of commercial activity. With the protracted Napoleonic wars, the price of corn rose to meet an abnormal taxation, and the value of land and property rose in consequence; and thus the position of the landowners was consolidated, while the distress of the masses became even more acute. The rise of industrialism afforded any amount of employment for the working classes, but pay was by no means proportionate to the cost of living, and bread riots and agrarian outrages were an almost inevitable result (see Plate IV.). The slums in the growing towns were filled with teeming, insanitary warrens into which whole families were miserably herded. Crabbe's lines sketch, doubtless, no exaggerated picture, and also indicate the wretched state of the streets and lanes, and the lack of any organised system of handling waste and rubbish:—

> Farewell to these; but all our poor to know,
> Let's seek the winding lane, the narrow row,
> Suburban prospects, where the traveller stops
> To see the sloping tenement on props,
> With building yards immix'd, and humble sheds and shops;
> Where the Cross-Keys and Plumber's-Arms invite
> Laborious men to taste their coarse delight;
>   *   *   *   *   *   *

> Here is no pavement, no inviting shop,
> To give us shelter when compell'd to stop ;
> But plashy puddles stand along the way.
> Fill'd by the rain of one tempestuous day ;
> And these so closely to the buildings run,
> That you must ford them, for you cannot shun ;
> Though here and there convenient bricks are laid,
> And door-side heaps afford their dubious aid.

Among the various branches of home industry which encroached on the ancient occupation of farming, we find the cotton trade, scarcely remarked in the days of George I., occupying almost the whole of Lancashire at the close of the century. In Scotland and northern Ireland the progress of the linen industry was almost as pronounced, and both Belfast and Glasgow were growing into large and important cities. In the Potteries, the industry established by Wedgwood had risen to enormous proportions. Birmingham, already established as the home of braziers and metal workers in the reign of Queen Anne, had become a hive of industry for every kind of hardware. The colliery districts were being further developed, and ore smelting works were springing up at Carron and in Warwickshire. The woollen trade had now migrated from East Anglia and Devonshire to Yorkshire. To every country in the world English goods were being carried in English ships.

The victory of the machine was complete. King's invention of the flying shuttle, Hargreave's spinning jenny, and Arkwright's water-frame in turn produced Crompton's famous " Mule " (Plate III.). The machine had been made to spin ; but workers were agape when Cartwright devised a machine to weave. Soon the hand-loom persisted in only a few out-of-the-way places, and as invention succeeded invention and patent patent, the whole aspect of the country in the Midlands and the North began to change. Villages became towns, the roads were improved, and a system of canals linked up the incipient spoliation. Huge wealth accrued to the masters, but the by-industries were doomed.

The rise of the middle classes towards the middle of the century has already been noticed, but at the same time, by the year 1800, the character of the aristocracy had itself partially changed, largely owing to the liberal creation of new peers under the younger Pitt. These new peers represented the accumulated wealth of England. The House of Lords now included among its numbers members of the merchant and middle classes, lesser landowners, bankers,

PLATE II.

River Transport by Horse and Sail in the Middle of the Century.
An engraving by Boydell.

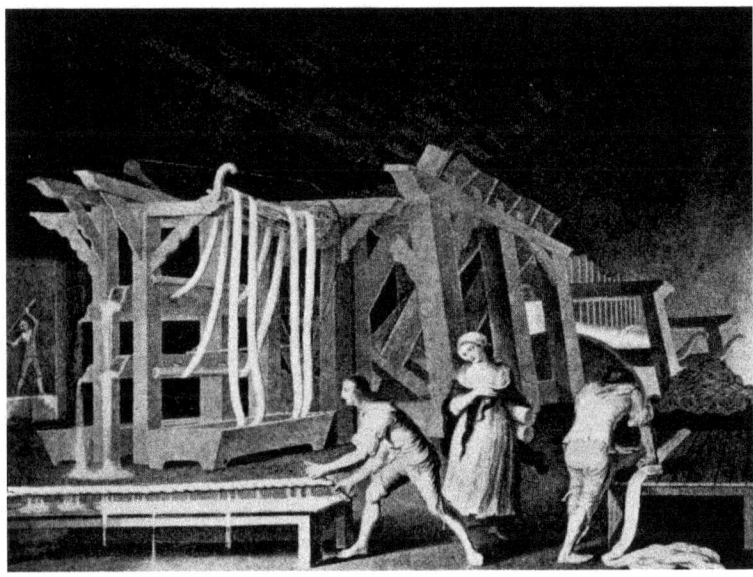

A Belfast Flax-spinning Plant at the close of the Century.
From an engraving by W. Hincks.

PLATE III.

"The victory of the machine was complete."
Some early pioneers : (*Above*) Crompton's "Mule" Spinning Frame, 1774-79;
(*Below*) Hargreave's Spinning Jenny, 1750-57.

PLATE IV.

A Riot. The destruction of Newgate by the mob in 1780.
From a contemporary print.

A Fight between Two Women. A typical illustration of slum life at the close of the century.
From Rowlandson's " Miseries of London."

PLATE V.

The more sordid reflection of London life in the Early Georgian Period. "Night" and "Morning," by William Hogarth.
From Cook's engravings.

lawyers, admirals, generals and so on. While the aristocracy was being levelled in one sense, at the same time the newer creation was as jealous of its position and dignity as the older. With the increase in wealth, living in these circles was elevated in some cases to a height of luxury hitherto unknown.

A hundred years had, then, produced, practically unnoticed, an almost complete transformation in manners, ideas, and economic organisation in England. But throughout its course the Georgian period is remarkable for its contrasts. We have only to read some of the early novels, say Defoe's "Moll Flanders" or Fielding's "Tom Jones," to find an accurate picture of the squalor that went hand in hand with fastidious elegance, cultured humanism or solid comfort during the early part of the century. At this time the Evangelical Revival had still to be accomplished, and all classes of society were, it must be remembered, case-hardened to a misery which seemed only a natural, if regrettable, aspect of a rational society. Moll Flanders is at once thief, pickpocket, professional bigamist and harlot, yet she obviously engages the author's sympathy as a typical and quite usual product of her generation ; and we shut the book with the feeling that her ultimate moral regeneration is a rather hasty piece of whitewashing. Pity is evoked for the *personal* plight of this engaging heroine when she is sentenced to death for pilfering, but no horror or indignation is expressed for the savage ferocity of the sentence. The horrors of Newgate are presented with stoical exactitude, but there is no suggestion that such a state of things could be remedied.

Some of Hogarth's pictures, "Night," for instance, illustrated, with its companion, "Morning," on Plate v., contrive to crowd into a few square feet of canvas the whole abject misery of this aspect of town life at the period. The tipsy watchman and his companion, the street bonfire, the broken-down coach with its profane occupants, the crudeness (to say the least of it) of the sanitary methods depicted, and the poor woman with her baby huddled beneath a stall for shelter—all this under a wild and stormy sky produces an effect of accumulated sordidness hard to equal. It sets us thinking of the ferocity of the law and the corruption of its officers, the cruelty of popular amusements, the bestial drunkenness prevalent amongst those who could afford it, the passion for dicing and speculation, the scandalous sanitary conditions which would have shamed a Roman city, the illiteracy and boorishness of the masses. We almost forget to look at the reverse of the picture.

Amongst the privileged classes, a craving for culture, fostered by the habit of the "Grand Tour," had begun to make itself felt. The achievement of Italy was dawning on an aristocracy whose appetite had been whetted by the innovations of Inigo Jones and Vanbrugh. Palladio was everywhere cited, and Vitruvius dug from obscurity to teach columnar architecture to eighteenth-century Englishmen. Italy was ransacked for paintings and sculpture, and the

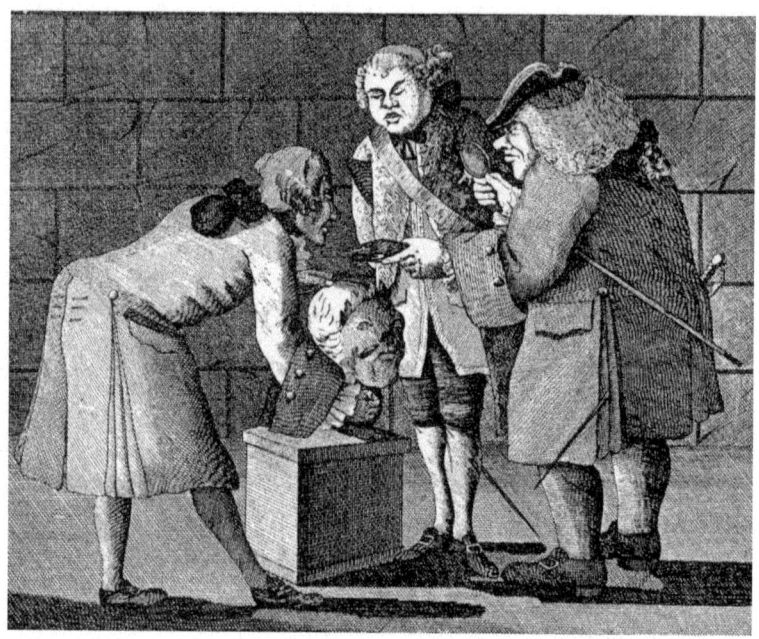

Fig. 1.—"The Connoisseurs."
A caricature by Mathew Darly.

early part of the century saw the inception of many of our greatest private collections. Lord Burlington and his group of "Amateurs" made the fine arts, and that particularly of architecture, an occupation for the man of fashion (see Fig. 1). The authors of antiquity were the oracles of taste, and a good repertoire of classical tags an integral part of the fashionable equipment.

Pope, with his erudition and mockery, did much to spread the appetite for culture. His Augustan talent established a poetical idiom for more than a generation, and his influence was one of the most remarkable in the history of English letters. The seed of culture had fallen on good ground, and before the middle of the century architects such as Gibbs, Hawksmoor, and Kent, and writers such as Pope, Fielding, Addison, Swift, and Johnson, had subscribed to its achievement. The great school of painters was to follow later.

These influences, and the habit of the Grand Tour, were at the same time introducing a rarefied elegance into English manners, an elegance which we find personified in such men as Bolingbroke and Chesterfield, which was to produce in its turn Horace Walpole and Beckford, the dilettanti *par excellence*. English gentlemen thought less of their horseflesh and appetites, and more of the elegance of their establishments in town and country, the neatness of their conversation, the elaboration of their dress, together with every other point of social equipment. They pulled down their " barbarous Gothick " abbeys and Tudor palaces, and erected vast Palladian piles, vying with one another in the sumptuousness of their furnishings and decorations. No splendour could be splendid enough for men who had dawdled a little at the Versailles of Louis XIV. and Louis XV.

The two extremes that have been sketched, however, had little bearing on the trend of ordinary middle-class and professional life. The tradesman, parson, attorney, and small squire enjoyed a solid enough comfort, aping the manners of the rich as far as they were able, and generally turning a rather callous ear to the complaints of the less fortunate. The Squire Westerns of the remoter counties hunted prodigiously, ate and drank prodigiously, and were content enough with their small world. The cleric responsible for man's spiritual welfare was usually ill-informed and contemptible in his cringing to authority ; though the academical diversions of some bishops and the zeal of the early dissenters must not be forgotten. There was always, however, plenty of scope for the young man of real talent, and a large majority of the artists, architects, generals, admirals, and even politicians famous at the time owed their success to their unaided personal efforts. The opposite path, too, was fatally easy ; at a time when cards and speculation were the rage, such a history as Hogarth's " Rake's Progress " was of quite common occurrence.

In the country, a considerable class of yeoman and tenant farmers employed the mass of the labouring folk, other than those who farmed strip holdings. But as the land came to be enclosed, pauperism increased the nomadic population, and it is little wonder that the stocks and whipping-posts were rarely empty. Each village and hamlet was a self-contained settlement where the man of property and the parson had almost patriarchal authority. The ordinary villager or small townsman, anchored to the spot by the necessity of earning a bare pittance, was thrown back on his own limited resources for amusement; in fact almost the sole place of entertainment open to him was the village inn and alehouse.

Except for those few whose affairs took them to the market towns, there was little occasion for travel among the rural population. Though the main routes of the Roman roads were still the principal lines of communication, the centuries had produced a network of lanes and by-tracks, intersecting the highways, winding between villages, branching to farms, and often ending in mud. There were few milestones and fewer signposts. In summer the wayfarer advanced through clouds of dust, in winter he plunged through marshy depths, often held up by floods and dilapidated bridges. It is easy to understand Dr Johnson's distaste for the country.

The turnpike system had come into force, and tolls were levied for road maintenance. These arteries, such as they were, were anathematised. At the beginning of the century stage coaches were advertised to run between London and York, Coventry, Ipswich, and a score of places within fifty miles of London. Stage wagons (see Plate vi.) descended upon the metropolis from all parts and held picturesque station at Southwark and Smithfield. At bi-weekly intervals carriers' carts entered and departed from London, together with wagons bringing farm produce and building materials. This heterogeneous collection of vehicles churned the roads in fine weather or foul.

The growth of the newspaper is one of the first signs of the improvement in communications about the country. In 1690 there were nine London newspapers published weekly. By 1709 this number was increased to eighteen, the only daily paper being *The London Courant*. During the next reign the number was three daily, six weekly, and ten published three times a week. As a contemporary versifier puts it in 1785 :—

> For, soon as morning dawns with roseate hue,
> The Herald of the morn arises too;
> Post after Post succeeds, and, all day long,
> Gazettes and Ledgers swarm, a noisy throng.
> When evening comes, she comes with all her train
> Of Ledgers, Chronicles, and Posts again.

PLATE VI.

A Stage Coach passing through Dunstable.

From an original drawing by Rowlandson.

A Carrier's Wagon on the Open Road.

From an aquatint by Pyne.

PLATE VII.

"Towards the end of the century, public opinion began to view the wretched condition of prisoners with some concern." This *macabre* sketch by Rowlandson shows Charitable Ladies giving Alms to Debtors at the special box for this purpose in the Fleet Prison.

By the half-century the number of copies published annually throughout England had increased to seven and a half millions. Finally, in 1808, twelve million printed copies were issued to the public. With the improvement in the roads and in mail-coach communication (see Plate VI.) reliable news and information was thus dispensed regularly throughout the entire population — a marked contrast to the haphazard diffusion of inaccurate and equivocal news of a century earlier. By the middle of the century the public was kept in accurate touch with the current of national and political events and the social movements of the times.

With these improvements came some effort towards the amelioration of the conditions of prisoners and paupers. In 1732, General James Oglethorpe had founded the colony of Georgia as a means of securing employment and support for members of the English poor and for persecuted Protestants of other countries. The religious revivals inspired by the great itinerant preachers, John and Charles Wesley, and George Whitefield had a widespread effect. A large mass of the public was converted to an active and definite form of faith, and the Established Church began to bestir itself to resist the encroachments of "Enthusiasm," as any vigorous manifestation was reproachfully called. It was thanks to these and other reformers that, towards the end of the century, public opinion began to view the wretched condition of prisoners with some concern, herded together as they were under filthy conditions (Figs. 2 and 3), whipped in public, and

FIG. 2.—" Prisoners were herded together under filthy conditions." The interior of a debtor's prison. " Debtors and hoggs together feeding ! "

FIG. 3.—" A debtor drag'd in a hurdle cal'd the Gaoler's Coach."

deprived of any kind of medical attention. It was mainly due to John Howard of Bedford that any reform in prison administration was effected. But though Howard secured the enforcement of proper discipline, hygiene, and other matters, his viewpoint did not comprehend, even at the end of the century, the wider issue of improving the criminal himself. Prisons were certainly better places, but the period under review never saw a proper reform in the administration of justice. The village "cages" remained under the control of unintelligent parish officers, and many punishments for trivial offences were still barbarous in their severity. Even long after the close of the century a hanging was a popular diversion.

Meanwhile London and other great cities were expanding, and the century was leaving a mark of congruity on their streets and squares. First it was an age of brick, with squared windows and a lacing of white paint; and this was followed by an extensive use of stucco which lasted well into the next century. The University cities encouraged the prevalent taste in building, and the projectors of the new Bath, one of the most exquisite building schemes ever accomplished in the country, perfected an ordered convention of street architecture in stone (Plate VIII.). In England we can still feel an intimacy with the eighteenth century through its background of street architecture.

The second half of the century is architecturally remarkable for its preoccupation with the works of classical antiquity, and its application of classical ideas to contemporary building needs. The year 1760 may be said to mark the close of the formative period of the academic phase in eighteenth-century architecture. The men who succeeded the great masters of the early period respected the conventions the latter had established. In spite of its professed antipathy to French mannerisms, English thought at this time was nevertheless susceptible to foreign influence, though this had less effect on architecture and painting than on minor crafts such as silver work and engraving. In the later years of the reign of George III. we find English art gaining appreciably in the prestige of the world, and English reticence beginning to react on French minds. But whereas the best works of architecture in England were in most cases produced by private enterprise, in France, no matter how solicitous society might be for its own comfort, there was always a desire present to create great civic and national monuments. This was less evident in England, where this civic sense was never fully developed.

Other influences were also at work to organise the artistic

PLATE VIII.

" . . . Bath, one of the most exquisite building schemes ever accomplished in this country." A contemporary view of the Entrance to the Pump Room.

John Wood, architect.

"Fashion, with the First Gentleman in Europe as its arbiter." The Prince Regent presiding at a Banquet at his Pavilion at Brighton.

From a contemporary aquatint by Nash.

talent of the country. " The Society for Promoting Arts and Commerce " was founded in 1753, and the Royal Academy, with Sir Joshua Reynolds as its first president, incorporated in 1768. Gay is succeeded by Sheridan in the great school of English comedy, and Dr Johnson, with his obedient and talented coterie, became the unofficial pontiff of literary taste.

FIG. 4.—The Learned Antiquarians Puzzled (by an English Epitaph).
A caricature by Mathew Darly.

Gibbon, one of the few cosmopolitan Englishmen of letters, established an international reputation, while the enterprising members of the Dilettanti Society scoured the earth in search of archæological treasure, and architects and artists were no less busy among the ruins of Rome and Athens. With the support of the Academy, painting advanced by strides from the work of a handful of minor artists to the splendid achievements of the English school at the close of the century. But the efforts of such men as Gray, Walpole, Beckford, Blake had fallen on fertile ground. Just as classicism seemed most secure and at the height of its prestige, taste became suddenly affected by a craving for Romanticism, a craving which was to sweep the whole art of the next century before it, and, in architecture at any rate, finally to obliterate the tradition evolved through three centuries.

The great increase in the national wealth which produced a prosperous new middle class and often fabulously enriched the aristocracy has already been noticed. Disraeli's young Duke of St James, with his acres and castles all over the country, his vast rent roll and mining interests, is quite typical of the state in which a number of noblemen found themselves at the close of the century. Those such as Lord Hertford, with his enormous hereditary possessions, and the Duke of Bridgewater, an aristocrat of the new school, kept court like princes in their London mansions and on their vast country estates. Fashion certainly, with the First Gentleman in Europe as its arbiter (see Plate VIII.), was now less concerned with culture than with cockfights, the prize ring and the set of a coat ; while vast fortunes often changed hands over the card table. The aristocracy was becoming exclusive and jealous of its privileges, while the great middle class, always eager to climb a step in the social ladder, occupied itself with the real business of the country and was well enough rewarded. The miserable condition of the poor at this time has already been touched upon. The first stage of the Industrial Revolution had been accomplished and by the year 1820 England was embarking on a new era.

* * * * * *

Whatever transformations may occur in social conditions, Englishmen appear to adjust themselves easily enough to new ways without much loss of national individuality. The Georgian Englishman was of sturdy enough breed, necessarily, if he was to survive the appalling medical and sanitary conditions under which he had to live. Generations of open-air life had produced a good stock, and good stock was needed to man battleships and fill the ranks of the army. These very conditions, and even, perhaps, the general callousness which has already been remarked, case-hardened men to endure the horrors of the cockpit and battlefield. English seamen and English troops were probably the best in the world at this time.

There was still a nucleus of earnest, unpretending devotion

and practical faith, if the Church showed much worldly slackness and suffered from flagrant abuses. If a vague deism was rife, there was, except in a narrow circle, an absence of scepticism or definite "free thought." It was an ordered existence; till late in the period the privilege of the governing classes was unquestioned, and the humbler sort, though of course finally emancipated from feudal conditions, took their lot for granted and envied the more fortunate their luck. And so the tradesman envied the small gentleman, and the small gentleman envied the great gentleman who, in his turn, paid his respects to whichever stolid Hanoverian occupant of the throne might be reigning.

Among the cultured classes, the preoccupation with classical art and literature was by no means mere pedantry; nor was the art of the eighteenth century, for that matter, mere plagiarism. The almost religious veneration with which classical antiquity was regarded was, perhaps, exaggerated; but at the same time, up to the very close of the century, it was the aim of artists and architects to base their work on it for inspiration, and not for mere slavish imitation. Palladianism operated in Architecture throughout this period as a lively purge against the neo-classic temptation to which architects only finally capitulated in the early years of the nineteenth century.

As in its art, so in its moral characteristics the century was stimulated by classical ideals of heroism, dignity, and fortitude. If humanity was often lacking, so it was in classical times, but fixed ideals of justice and loyalty, and a firmly rooted conviction in the justification of the age were always present. We have only to make a superficial study of minor Georgian literature to find that humbug, hypocrisy and cant were quite as rampant then as to-day; but this cannot disguise the fact that the ideals just noted were a very potent factor in the composition of the national character.

The age was a little over-given to pomposity, rhetoric and heroics, perhaps, but never has wit been more keen, or conversation glittered so sharply. That it was definitely less humane than our own there can be no doubt; but then, in the history of Europe, humanity is a rather modern invention. It was, however, unlike our own, an age of settled and progressive tradition despite the somewhat turbulent course of its events. The suddenness with which this tradition was snuffed out and a new era inaugurated is only fresh evidence of the fact that in this life the existence of traditions and social organisations is a sadly transitory one.

CHAPTER II

THE SOCIAL SCENE

In all ages of civilisation the same general rules have applied. Life in the eighteenth century was no exception; its course, in fact, was much the same as that of the preceding century and not dissimilar from our own to-day. Society was modelled on the example of the rich and powerful, and this imitation of customs deemed fashionable and usual was carried in some degree into every sphere of life, whether it was that of the country gentleman, the merchant, the shopkeeper or even the humble workman.

The child when born was submitted to a swaddling process (see Plate IX.) that would be deemed fatal to-day; and throughout its life encountered sanitary arrangements which were rudimentary to say the least, a poor water supply, and a constant prevalence of fever. Smallpox, particularly, was rampant till the introduction of vaccination at the end of the century. If the child ailed or was fretful, it was dosed at one period with a concoction known as " Daffy's Famous Elixir Salutis," and at another with " Dr James's Powder " (see Plate X.) — a well-known specific unhesitatingly recommended by Horace Walpole, which seems to have polished off Oliver Goldsmith in 1774. Its active principle was antimony.

Quacks flourished mightily and their nostrums, impudently puffed and restrained in no way by the law, attained a wide circulation and doubtless did infinite harm, as the contemporary comment suggests:—

> Void of all honour, avaricious, rash,
> The daring tribe compound their boasted trash—
> Tincture or syrup, lotion, drop or pill;
> All tempt the sick to trust the lying bill;
> And twenty names of cobblers turn'd to squires,
> Aid the bold language of these blushless liars.

It is small wonder that infant mortality was common, though a famous doctor, Pechy, made the diseases of infants

PLATE IX.

"The child when born was submitted to a swaddling process that would be deemed fatal to-day." A Christening, from an early Georgian print.

"Private academies existed, including day and boarding schools for both sexes." The Prospectus of a Boarding School for Ladies of the mid-Georgian Period.

PLATE X.

Children's Toy Wagons. The subject above is part of a print by Rowlandson.

An Advertisement for "Dr James's Powder," bearing a picturesque rendering of the Scene of the Good Samaritan.

and children his special study, and prescribed for such various complaints as measles, teething, fits and worms. Still, apart from such discomforts, there were always in the nursery dolls, cardboard windmills, toy wagons (see Plate x.) and horses, whips, drums, trumpets and tops, which were treasured as they are to-day; and among the forgotten literature of the time are a variety of books published especially for children.

Private academies existed for the children of parents who could not afford tutors or governesses, including both day and boarding schools for both sexes (Plate IX.), and in London and other cities there were a few free schools for the poor. In the better schools education centred almost entirely upon the classics, for it was considered that every gentleman should be a fair classical scholar. For a long time the works of the immortal Cocker sufficed for mathematics, and great pains were taken with caligraphy, the writing instruments varying from crow quills to brass pens. There were also a few special schools for the teaching of cookery. Finally there were the universities to complete the education of boys schooled at St Paul's, Westminster, Winchester, Harrow or Eton.

In the eighteenth century marriage usually took place at an early age. Irregular marriages were a crying evil in spite of efforts to stop them, and there is on record the case of a clergyman at the Fleet Prison who carried on a remunerative business in marriages of this sort from 1709 to 1740, when measures were taken to suppress the illegal system. But deprived of the advantages of a Fleet marriage, many couples who could afford the expense had recourse to the journey to Gretna Green. The ordinary marriage customs are also of interest, and for a long time these continued to follow the traditions of the seventeenth century described so intimately by Samuel Pepys.

With the poverty of medical science, over-eating and over-drinking were prevalent with their disastrous effects, as was also a malady described as "the spleen" in men, and "the vapours" in women. Still, the majority of people lived to a ripe old age. Childbirth, however, took a heavy toll of young mothers, for the midwives and nurses who assisted were miserably incompetent and dirty. Funerals, when they occurred, were the excuse for lavish display and not a little ingenuity on the part of the undertaker (Plate XI.). Hatchments were hung on the front of the houses, and a whole company of mutes were stationed from the top of the stairs to the hall door, often overflowing into the street. The cards issued by the undertaker depicted corpses, skulls and coffins, and contained eloquent warnings of the brevity of human life. Some among this fraternity acted as brokers and appraisers, and all, without exception, called attention to their reasonable rates of burial. Such was the importance attached to a respectable burial that the poor had their own burial clubs and societies to which they subscribed regularly during lifetime.

We of the present day have learnt to appreciate the handsome houses of the Georgian period and the restrained elegance of their interiors. In the early part of the century, rents were not too high. Some houses were let by agreement and in other cases the leases were sold. In Queen Anne's time, the leases of five houses in Pall Mall were offered for sale, their total rental being £200 per annum. Gentlemen's houses near London, with coach-houses and stabling, could be had at a rent varying from £40 to £50 a year. At Mortlake, a good brick house was going for £6. 10s. a year, and when Swift lodged in London he paid 8s. a week for a dining-parlour and bedchamber in Bury Street, which he considered "plaguey deep, but I spend nothing on eating." Towards the end of the century, £200 per annum for a first-class town house was thought high, and houses in the country of decent size could be had for £100 a year.

The danger from fire in town and country was very considerable. This, and memories of the Great Fire, may have caused the passing of the Act in the sixth year of the reign of Queen Anne "for the better preventing of mischiefs that may happen by fire." At certain shops it was possible to buy rope ladders and other means of facilitating escape from blazing houses, but the opening of the century saw stronger measures being taken against the material, as well as the personal, danger in the founding of the first Insurance Companies. These included "The Phœnix" with offices at the Rainbow Coffee House in Fleet Street, "The Friendly Society" in Palgrave Court without Temple Bar, and "The Amicable Contributors" at Tom's Coffee House in St Martin's Lane. As the century developed other companies came into prominence, including "The London Assurance," "The Royal Exchange," "The Royal," "The Sun," and "The County." All the fire insurance companies employed their own liveried firemen (Plate XI.) who, trundling one of Bristowe's fire engines over the cobbled streets of the cities, can be imagined to have added to the picturesque confusion.

As has previously been remarked, the sanitary arrangements were deficient, and water could be obtained only from pumps and conduits. Innumerable wells were sunk in the vicinity

PLATE XI.

A Funeral Cortege. From an early engraving by Hogarth done for one of the undertaker's invitations referred to.

Eighteenth-century Fire Engines.
Drawn and etched by W. H. Pyne.

PLATE XII.

"A dining-room was considered amply furnished by a table and eight chairs, a side table and a wine cooler." The Dining-room at Holkham, Norfolk (1734).

By William Kent.

of cesspools and churchyards, so that the water was often far from healthy. At a later date water was laid on direct to houses from the New River, and one of the attractions of the houses in Stratford Place was that there was a direct water supply from the Hampstead ponds. Water for houses in the city was obtained from the Thames by means of a huge water-wheel at London Bridge. In the country, people had either to rely on well water or to store rain-water in lead cisterns ; and at the close of the period slate tanks began to be used.

Houses were warmed in winter by coal brought by sea and delivered to most towns and villages by river or canal. If no such waterway existed, it was carted by road from the nearest wharf. If we examine the development of the basket-fire grate of the period, we find that it gradually diminishes in size except in large houses where the scale of the rooms demanded good-sized fires. Coal was inferior in quality and expensive, and was usually bought in small quantities from itinerant hawkers by people of moderate means.

In the eighteenth century, no matter which period we study, we always find the houses to be sparsely furnished. Contemporary paintings and engravings give an authentic idea of interiors, movables and the general disposition of rooms. What might be termed the rich simplicity of the interior architecture did not require elaborate appointments ; a dining-room in 1740 was considered amply furnished by a table and eight chairs, a side table and a wine cooler (see Plate xii.). This furnishing scheme had varied very little thirty-five years later. In 1775, typical parlour furniture consisted of a flat harpsichord pianoforte, considered to be an improvement on the spinet, a table in the centre, half a dozen chairs, a fauteuil sofa and an armchair. There was also, perhaps, a bracket clock and an escritoire. The walls had two or three oil-paintings, and the mantelshelf was singularly free of ornaments. The floors were frequently covered with Turkey rugs, and later with printed oilcloths.

People took a considerable pride in the character of their needlework and velvet chair covers, their upholstery, and their window curtains. By the middle of the century the carpets in the best rooms were richly woven ones from Axminster, or London made, but they did not extend beyond the centre of the room. In the later eighteenth century these carpets were often plain in design, a woven hearthrug being placed in front of the fireplace.

Before the manufacture of English china was brought to perfection, China ware was imported by the East India

Company, and many bargains of broken or damaged goods could be obtained. Only the rich could afford the porcelain from Bow, Lambeth, Vauxhall, Derby and the other factories, but Staffordshire pottery was manufactured in large quantities in the days of Wedgwood. People of all classes had great respect for rare chinaware, and objects of art from China were placed in cabinets and recesses; but for ordinary use, even in good houses, there were family services of pewter.

Returning to the furnishings, it is interesting to note that the best pieces were reserved for the bedrooms. The liking for a good bed had remained from the seventeenth century, and the tradition was continued throughout the Georgian period. The heavy four-posters of the Queen Anne period, with their wrought-cloth canopies, gave place to the mahogany beds of Chippendale, Manwaring, and Sheraton. The hangings and curtains were of heavy stuffs and rendered the bed almost airtight; and indeed people were in dread of draughts and fearful of even a little fresh air in their bedrooms. Beside the bed stood the night commode, and as the beds of the time stood high, this was sometimes treated with a short flight of steps as a means of approach. The other movables included a tall-boy, a writing bureau, a small chest of drawers, a dressing-table draped with stuff, and a swing looking-glass (see Plate XIII.). There were also usually two or three chairs. Washhand-stands were exceptionally small, and there were usually two of these, one for the mistress and one designed also to serve as a wig stand for the master. Another accessory was the tin rushlight canister pierced with holes.

One of the means of recognising social status was by the number of male servants employed, and in these can be traced a distant survival of the mediæval system of retainers. In the house of a nobleman of the time of George I. there would be first a page, who wore livery more costly than that of the first footman, as is seen in the painted model on Plate XIV. He had served his apprenticeship as "a little foot boy," and as the relation between master and page was something akin to that which had existed between knight and squire, it was only natural that in time he should become a steward to the household. The page is seen in contemporary illustrations attending his master's carriage, and Steele, referring to the custom in the days of Queen Anne, says: "I know a man of good sense who put his son to a blacksmith, tho' an offer was made him of his being received a page to a Man of Quality!"

In houses where it was not possible for the master to afford

PLATE XIII.

An Early Georgian Parlour-hall.   "Finchcocks," Goudhurst, Kent.

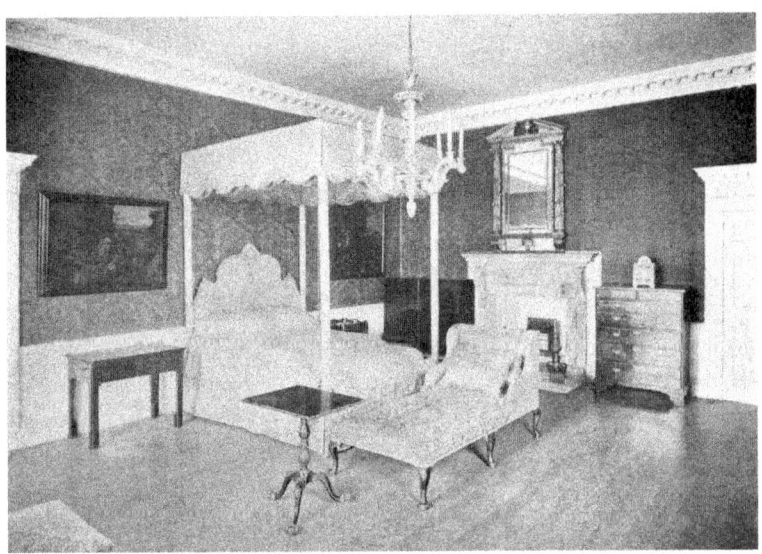

A Georgian Bedroom at the Treasurer's House, York.

PLATE XIV.

The Black Page was considered an integral feature in any fashionable household. Notice also the Monkey, a popular pet at this period.

From an engraving by Hogarth.

Painted figures of servants were often used as fire-screens. These two examples show a typical Serving Woman and a Page.

(In the possession of the Author.)

a page, a small painted figure of a boy in livery often stood by the fireplace as a fire-screen (Plate XIV.). Footmen in the Georgian period were a butt for satirists, as indeed they still were at the time of Thackeray's "Yellowplush Papers." At the beginning of the period no man of fashion dared dispense with his "Sett of Genteel Footmen," but as the century matured, the number of footmen in private families decreased. As a class they had a good time, receiving heavy "vails" for the slightest of services, and in addition a salary of from £6 to £10 a year; but at the same time they were often treated like dogs by their masters and caned unmercifully. In the second half of the century the footman's livery became more gorgeous, but the valet was almost inevitably a Frenchman, an Italian or a Swiss. Addison refers to the time when "well bred Country Women kept their Valets de Chambre because, forsooth, a man was much more handy about them than one of their own Sex."

Another class of servant was the black slave, for, strange as it may appear, the sons and daughters of Ham were in bondage in England until the days of Wilberforce. Needless to say, these black servants were always running away; and you will see from the engraving after Hogarth shown on Plate XIV., or, later, from some of Rowlandson's drawings, what an integral factor in a household they had become. A French cook was also usually employed in the larger houses, but the country gentry were generally content with a woman cook, two scullery-maids, four chamber-maids (see Plate XIV.), and a dairymaid for the female staff. Then there was a butler, two footmen, and black boy. The garden staff naturally varied with the size of the pleasure-gardens, but for a garden of ten acres, four gardeners and two boys were usual. The stable staff included the coachman and his family, three grooms and an ostler.

Of daily life there is so much to record that we must be content with a summary. The majority lived in towns, and during the first half of the century only the very rich could afford to travel in comfort. Journeys by road were, to say the least, hazardous, and a ride from London to Exeter, to York or to Norwich, was always accompanied by some degree of risk. After 1770 matters began to improve, however.

The suburbs of London were, at the beginning of the century, on the immediate fringe of the city, and included Bloomsbury, Mayfair, Kensington and Chelsea. The villages of Hampstead, Highgate, Leyton, Woodford, Kew and Richmond were looked upon as rural retreats. The fields between these and the inner suburbs were given over to dairy-farming and allotments, and while the rich took the air in Hyde Park or St James's Park, the people living in Bloomsbury enjoyed walks as far as Tottenham Fields or St Pancras. On Sundays, the tradespeople with their families and apprentices journeyed to the tea-gardens of Islington, Highgate or Hampstead, or the more adventurous took horse to Epsom or Epping. Towards the close of the century, Sunday trips were taken farther afield, and excursions were made by coach to Greenwich, Windsor, Richmond, Edmonton and Ware.

In the eighteenth century the pursuit of pleasure among the upper classes, as it is shown in most contemporary paintings and prints, is nearly always marked by a studied dignity of posture (Plate xv., *below*), which, however, a closer searching of contemporary records shows not always to have distinguished the gatherings of the elect. It is true that the older families preserved in public a decent dignity that was often enough lacking in their personal associations; but the routs at fashionable assemblies and bachelor drinking-parties (Plate xv., *above*) were often riotous enough affairs, and the women were not always such models of feminine virtue as they might appear to be in their portraits by Reynolds or Romney. Indeed feminine vigour of language among the upper classes at the close of the period has, it is believed, never been equalled.

The fashionable world sought every kind of distraction, and although class distinctions were rigid, the rich attended public amusements with the masses. In early Georgian times, Bath, Epsom, Tunbridge Wells and Clifton formed the circle of inland spas to which wealth and fashion flocked, but later on, when George III. had made sea-bathing popular, Margate, Weymouth, Scarborough and Brighton became fashionable as watering-places. After the year 1780, Cheltenham, Leamington and Harrogate increased the number of inland spas.

We must return to London for a record of the town pleasure-resorts of the period. Vauxhall Gardens (Fig. 5), Spring Gardens and Ranelagh head the list, other public gardens and places of amusement including Apollo Gardens, St George's Fields, Spa Gardens, Bermondsey, Marylebone and Kensington Gardens, and the Bayswater Tea-Gardens. But even when such minor resorts as the "Adam and Eve" St Pancras, Bagnigge Wells, Canonbury House, Islington Spa, the "Temple of Flora" Lambeth, and the White Conduit House, Islington, are included, we are only mentioning a limited number of the many pleasure and tea gardens which were very popular throughout the century.

Among the middle classes, the domestic virtues were encouraged and highly extolled, and the care of the house and the production of needlework were deemed the most suitable occupations for the womenfolk. But among the wealthy, the primary occupation of women was to entertain and to be entertained. Addison writes at the end of the seventeenth century that : "ladies received visitors while in bed or at their toilette," whilst the " English Lady's Catechism," dated

Fig. 5.—Vauxhall Gardens. A contemporary view.

1703, gives an amusing account of the day of a lady of fashion from which we may quote briefly :—

> " How do you employ your time now ? "
> " I lie in Bed till Noon, dress all the Afternoon, Dine in the Evening, play at Cards till midnight ! "
> " How do you spend the Sabbath ? "
> " In chit chat ! "
> " What do you talk of ? "
> " New Fashions and New Plays ! "
> " How often do you go to Church ? "
> " Twice a year or oftener, according as my Husband gives me new Cloaths ! "
> " Why do you go to Church when you have new Cloaths ? "

"To see other People's Finery, and to shew my own, and to laugh at those scurvy, out of fashion creatures that come for Devotion!"

"Pray, Madam, what Books do you read?"

"I read lewd Plays and winning Romances!"

"Who is it you love?"

"Myself!"

"What, nobody else?"

"My Page, my Monkey, and my Lap Dog!"

"Why do you love them?"

"Why, because I am an English lady, and they are Foreign Creatures, my Page from Genoa, my Monkey from the East Indies and my Lap Dog from Vigo!"

FIG. 6.—A London Street Scene.
From an engraving after Hayman.

What is true of the indolent life of some fashionable women at the opening of the period also applies very well to the later stages of the reign of the Georges. They breakfasted on chocolate or tea and bread and butter, interviewed the mantua-maker, enjoyed a slight "nuncheon" between eleven and twelve, drove to the silk mercers between one and half-past two, returned and dined between three and four. After dinner till midnight there was the play, calls at drums and assemblies, cards, scandal, and home in a sedan-chair. The chief recreation of men and women in this age of candle-light was cards, and Pope has described the game of "Ombre" in "The Rape of the Lock." It was played by two, three or five people, its name being derived from the Spanish "Yo Soy L'Hombre"—*I am the man.* Other popular card games were Picquet, Basset, Whisk, Brag and Lanterloo. The cards were rather smaller and thinner than those in use to-day, and were often embellished with scenes of topical interest. The Kings, Queens and Knaves are shown with feet.

Men and women indulged their passion for gambling often

PLATE XV.

"Bachelor drinking parties were often riotous enough affairs."
A print by Rowlandson (1805).

A more dignified Bachelor Assembly. The Court of Equity, La Belle Sauvage Yard.
From a contemporary print.

PLATE XVI.

"Speculation and risk were a passion sought for and found in such forms as the South Sea mania and fire and life insurance." Notice the Coffee-house Interior in the top right-hand corner of this print of 1720.

without any regard of the consequences. From the days of Addison to those of Charles James Fox entire fortunes were sometimes staked on the turn of a card or a throw from a dice-box. Gangs of tricksters and swindlers frequented the " Academies " where fortunes were improved or lost, and some of these gentry became very rich indeed. The passion for gambling was apparent in every order of society, and the lower classes were as inveterate as the rich. Whatever debts a man or woman incurred were thought of small account compared with a debt of honour, and it was an unwritten law that losses at cards should be paid at once. Fox once won about £8,000 at Brooks's, and one of his bond-creditors, hearing of his good luck, asked for payment. " Impossible, sir ! " replied Fox, " I must first discharge my debts of honour." He then asked for the bond, tore it in pieces, and threw the fragments into the fire. " Now, sir," he said, " my debt to you is a debt of honour," and immediately paid him.

Speculation and risk were a passion sought for and found in such forms as the South Sea Mania (see Plate XVI.), and fire and life insurance, and this is responsible for the steady increase in the number of the Assurance Societies. Another form of speculation was the lottery, which was legalised by the Government in 1709 ; and from then until 1824 no year passed without Parliament sanctioning a Lottery Bill.

Examining the minuter details of social life, we find both sexes indulging in snuff-taking, though only the men were allowed to smoke. We hear of ladies drinking cordial waters and spending their money on all sorts of choice perfumes— Spirit of Ambergris, Otto of Roses, Aqua Mellis, and Cordova Water. The soaps included Joppa, Genoa, Irish, Bristol, Windsor, Black and Liquid, and the craze for wash-balls, which dated from the reign of Queen Anne, never entirely died out. So we go on to items of lip salves, tooth powders, patches, false teeth " so fine and exact as to be eat on," and " methods of darkening the colour of the hair." The spectacle-makers furnished wares ranging from those in silver frames to the horn-rimmed type, and varying in price from one to thirty shillings a pair.

Costume in Georgian times forms not one of the least fascinating studies that the period offers. The characteristics of an age are always broadly reflected in its costume, and the development of dress throughout the epoch corresponds in a remarkable manner to its changing phases. We can form an amusing analogy between costume and architecture in comparing the scarlet coats and white stockings of the opening phase of the century with its red brickwork and white paint, while the black silk costumes and white cravats of the period of George III. tell of plainer buildings of stone and brick.

Surviving examples of old costumes are comparatively scarce,[1] for it is obvious that in the eighteenth century all but the wealthy were forced to alter and adapt clothes to suit successive changes of fashion. From a study of the dresses that do remain, we may form the opinion that men and women were on the whole smaller than they are to-day, the women slighter in build and the men more stocky.

At the beginning of the eighteenth century the fashion in Holland, Germany and England was largely influenced by that of the Court of Louis Quatorze. A universal style was already apparent in Western European dress, with certain modifications due to national traits. In the early Georgian period, English costume became much plainer than it had been during the reigns of Charles II. or William III. Ladies were beginning to hide their shoulders and to favour looped skirts and panniers to give fullness to the hips. At the theatre they wore black masks with embroidered falls, and embroidered pinafores gave a slightly domestic air to the well-dressed woman (Plate XVII., *above*). Male costume had also lost many of the frills of late Stuart times. The gentry were adopting long, braided coats with big sleeve cuffs, and waistcoats reaching to the knees (Plate XVII., *above*). The breeches buttoned at the knee above black silk stockings and buckled shoes.

The costume of the *beau* of this time came, however, direct from the French Court. Misson describes these *beaux* as " Creatures compounded of a Periwig and a Coat laden with Powder as white as a Miller's, a face besmear'd with snuff, and a few affected airs." Colley Cibber describes one of them as follows : " One that's just come to a small Estate and a great Periwig—he that sings himself among the women—he won't speak to a Gentleman when a Lord's in Company. You always see him with a Cane dangling at his Button, his breast open, no Gloves, one Eye tuck'd under his Hat, and a Tooth pick." So the eighteenth-century fashion began.

The ladies of Queen Anne's time wore hoods and capes above their feathered head-dresses, called *Commodes* or

---

[1] Perhaps the most representative collection of English costumes is that on view at the Victoria and Albert Museum, London. A smaller collection, but one of supreme interest, is that formed by Mr Charles Wade at Snowshill Manor, Worcestershire.

PLATE XVII.

"Building houses with cards." A print after Francis Hayman, showing Costume of the Mid-eighteenth Century.

"The Allemande Dance." A print after Baudoin, showing the Costume of 1770.

PLATE XVIII.

Ladies' Dress (*left*) of the Later Part of the Century ("July," by R. Dighton, from a series of the "Seasons") and (*right*) of the Middle Period. These examples from the Victoria and Albert Museum are of French brocade, silk and muslin, decorated with feathers.

Fontanges, owing to their having been introduced by Mademoiselle Fontange. Sometimes they were also called " heads " or " top knots." They wore quilted petticoats of rich quality beneath full skirts looped up, and thin, V-shaped bodices with delicately worked stomachers. They had little muffs for outdoors of the type satirised in *The Spectator*, and dresses " flounced and furbelowed from head to foot, with every ribbon wrinkled, and every part of her garments in curl."

In the reign of George I., these dresses were succeeded by the " sack - back " type, with full short sleeves, a fan of lace enriching the wrists and one of the round hoops which set out the skirt. Men's coats became short-skirted, and they wore breeches with six buttons at the knee and the capes which are to be seen in Hogarth's drawings. The *beau* of George II.'s reign next appears, with his little hat, short coat with capes and high walking-stick. The change from the mode of the preceding reign is very slight.

Fig. 7.—The *Beau* of 1745.
From an engraving by Gravelot.

From a study of these costumes in the museums it is evident that the silk weavers and textile manufacturers of the period used the best materials. The silk merchants imported direct from Lyons, and the needlewomen belonged to a guild that can never be revived. The exquisiteness of the " Braid stitch, cross-and-change, pinking, pointing, and filling "—in fact all the methods used in the Spitalfields industry which produced the brocades, voluminous skirts and purled sleeves—has passed. In the reign of George II. there was a craze for floral patternings which embroidered the coats and waistcoats of the men as well as the skirts of the women. Here is a description of the Duchess of Queensbury's Court costume in the year 1741 :—

> They were of white satin embroidered, the bottom of the petticoat as brown hills covered with all sorts of weeds, and every breadth had an old stump of a tree that ran up almost to the top of the petticoat, round which twined nasturtions, ivy, honeysuckle, periwinkles, convulvuluses, and all sorts of twining flowers which spread and covered the petticoat ; vines with the leaves variegated as you have seen them by the sun, all rather smaller than nature, which makes them look very light ; the robings and facings were little green banks with all sorts of weeds, and the sleeves and the rest of the gown loose, twining branches of the same sort as those on the petticoat. Many of the leaves were finished with gold, and part of the stumps of the trees looked like the gilding of the sun.

The hoop petticoat, which was a revival of the great farthingale of Queen Elizabeth's reign, developed from the graceful pannier type worn by Lavinia Fenton into an immense floating tent. These hoops, however, disappeared early in the reign of George III., when the enormous coiffures that we see in the portraits of the period came into vogue.

So we pass to the simpler and more restrained costume of the second half of the century. Flowered silks and brocades continued in fashion, but the mode from 1775 to 1790 allowed for grace without extravagance. Dresses made of brown or plain silk, worn with a lace fichu over a quilted petticoat (Plate XVIII., *left*), and an apron of gold embroidery, came into fashion. They consisted of bodices and skirts, slightly hooped, of Spitalfields silk. Those graceful, sack-back dresses of *eau-de-nil* silk must also be mentioned.

The period of fashion which is familiar to us through the paintings of Romney, Reynolds and Gainsborough (see Plate LXXXI.) reflects the prevalent style of the Court of Louis Seize. French brocades (see Plate XVIII., *right*) were much sought after, but at the same time, for outdoor wear and for riding and travelling, ladies affected a somewhat masculine style between the years 1780 and 1795. The final phase is seen in the classical mode of 1790 to 1810 in which *Directoire*, Empire and revived Greek fashions from Paris were assiduously copied.

A keen rivalry existed between the cheap clothiers of Monmouth Street, the vendors of second-hand suits, and those merchants in Birchin Lane who boasted that they could

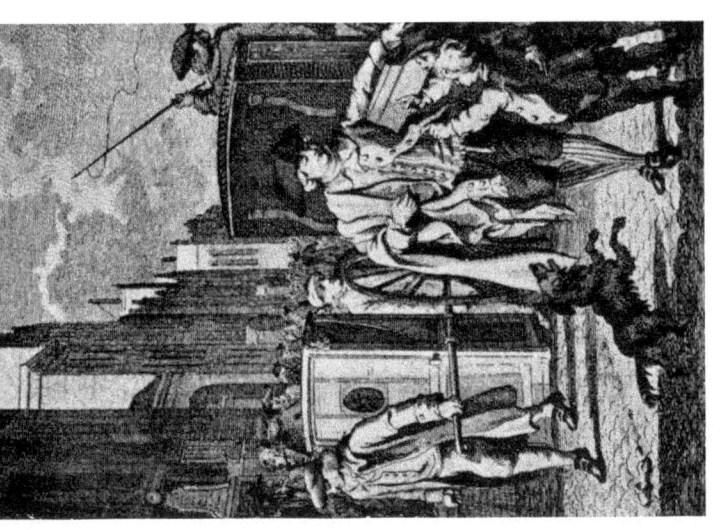

The London Streets. (*Left*) An Itinerant Seller of Prawns on her Rounds. An original water-colour in the manner of Wheatley. (*Right*) A Busy Street Scene. Notice the sedan chair with carriers, the private coach, and the footman returning with his master's purchases, accosted by begging urchins.

PLATE XX.

Contemporary Model Figures of a Travelling Clock Repairer and a Jewish Pedlar. The left-hand figure is in reality a clock.

The Milkmaid.
From an aquatint by Pyne.

supply new goods at the same price. A large trade was also done in ready-made clothes, especially for children. Shoes could be bought ready-made, but it was more usual to have them made to order.[1] Early in the period, shoes with red heels were in favour, these being adjusted with steel or silver buckles. Boots were used only for riding, so that owing to the foulness of the gutters and the uneven pavements, boot-blacks did a thriving trade, using either " Fucus " or the more famous " Spanish Blue King," until at the end of the century " Day and Martin's " was in general use.

Owing to the difficulties of travelling by road, it is not surprising that fashions continued in country places a long time after they had altered in London and other cities. Breeches for men, however, did not change very much in cut. These were of cloth, knitted wool, thread and silk. According to the type of dress adopted, the breeches of fashionable men were of the same stuff as the coats, but black silk was the distinguishing wear of the merchant, the professional man and the wealthy citizen. Black silk stockings were also worn with those of other colours to match costumes.

We have seen how the Georgian Englishman lived and took his pleasures, and have examined the appointments of his house and his dress. The next point to be considered is that of his food and his drink. England has never been noted for good cooking, though the diet of the country has always been plain and plentiful. In the early eighteenth century a dinner was never of more than two courses, and it was not until the period was drawing to its close that " soup, fish, and game " families gained the respect of local tradesmen. Dinner was the principal meal of the day, the chief dishes being roast beef, roast mutton, boiled beef or pork, with puddings and vegetables. In addition there were such variants as fowls, tripes, tongues, rabbits, hares, pigeons and venison. In the days of George I., ordinary people dined at two o'clock, and fashionable people between three and four. By the end of the century the time had changed to five o'clock. Breakfast and luncheon were eaten as secondary meals and supper was occasionally taken.

The national dish was the pudding, which was a compound of steak, kidney, larks and oysters. In London and other ports, fresh fish could be obtained daily, but in the country, except for barrels of oysters, people were dependent upon fresh-water fish. Billingsgate market was, as now, the dis-

[1] There is an excellent exhibition of period shoes in the museum at Northampton.

tributing centre for fish in London. Oysters were very cheap and were sold from wheelbarrows in the streets; and the drawing on Plate XIX., in the manner of Wheatley, shows prawns being hawked in this way. Bread was made the subjects of Acts of Parliament. The large number of farmhouses on the fringe of London assured a plentiful supply of dairy produce (Plate XX. shows a typical London milkmaid), and vegetables could be had from the gardens of Lambeth and Nine Elms or the orchards of Chiswick. Then, as now, Covent Garden was the chief fruit-and-vegetable distributing centre for London.

The number of small tradesmen dealing in supplies increased enormously with the spread of the city. These retailers included dairymen, butchers, bakers, fishmongers and chandlers. Their business was to buy from the distributing centres and to deliver the food to regular customers. Some greengrocers acted as footmen in neighbouring houses. Itinerant vendors of food — pie-men, muffin-men, vendors of asses' milk and hawkers of fruit and vegetables, walked the poorer streets with their trays, baskets and barrows.

Beer was considered a drink fit only for the poorer and middle classes; the porters and chairmen had a light ale of their own which came to be known as "Porter." There were local breweries in London and in almost every town of size throughout the country. Hard drinking among the richer classes was prevalent, as has already been noticed, but their taste was for foreign wines, including French claret, sherry, Marsala and port. French wines were easily obtainable, except during the wars, but it was considered more patriotic, more fitting, to drink "Good Solid Edifying Port." Champagne was imported in large baskets containing from ten dozen to two hundred bottles each, and in consequence of the brisk trade, the wine merchant became almost as important a figure as the brewer. The retailers had, as now, to take out a licence to sell wines.

Foreign wines reached England at London (see Plate XXI.), Bristol, King's Lynn or Topsham, from whence they were forwarded by road. Meanwhile every large house had its still-room for the concocting of liqueurs and cordials which included orange-flower, cherry-brandy, sloe-gin, and elderberry wine. Bottled cider could be obtained in the West of England for about 7s. a dozen, and another drink which was popular for after-dinner potations was rum, which was introduced about 1714. Unintoxicating drinks were also popular at table, among them ginger beer, lemonade, and barley water, and tea, coffee and chocolate were in great demand. With the introduction of tea, chocolate drinking went largely out of favour, though some still preferred to start the day with a cup of chocolate and proceed to tea and toast. For a long time tea was regarded as a luxury for the well-to-do, and we have only to study the tea-caddies of the different reigns to appreciate in what small quantities it was purchased, and how carefully it was ladled out with a silver spoon for each meal.

In London there were a large number of shops devoted to the sale of tobacco and snuff, which did a good business among the frequenters of coffee-houses and taverns. In the West of England it is on record that even the women smoked, and this prevalence of the habit was probably due to the proximity of Bristol and Bideford, to which ports the tobacco was shipped from Virginia. It came over in barrels, was twisted into a kind of rope and made up into rolls. Tobacconists sold handsome boxes for tobacco and snuff, besides pipes, long and short, and lighting spills. At Bideford, disused hogsheads were first used as dustbins for street refuse.

At the beginning of the Georgian period the coffee-house [1] was an established institution, and had reached the height of its popularity as a centre for the latest news, and a meeting-place for idlers, business men and wits. The club had come into being in the previous reign. In *The Spectator* for the 10th of March 1711 there is reference to the Beefsteak and October clubs. Addison used the Bedford Head as a rendezvous for himself and his associates. The Rumpsteak, or Liberty Club first met at the King's Arms in Pall Mall on the 15th of January 1734, its members foregathering to oppose Walpole's government. Other clubs of a political nature included the Saturday Club and the Brothers' Club, from which sprang the famous clubs of St James's, of which White's, Brooks's and Boodle's remain to the present day. Whole volumes could be devoted to the story of each of these famous clubs. White's began as a chocolate-house; Brooks's, which was started as a speculation by Almack, was closely associated with it, as many of the members belonged to both clubs. Almack's club was founded in 1764 in Pall Mall. Brooks's was built in 1778, and after this Almack appears to have severed his connection with it. This club was always associated with the Whig party, Charles James Fox, Selwyn, Sheridan, Whitbread and the

---

[1] Contemporary illustrations of coffee-house interiors are rare, but the top right-hand corner of Plate xvi. depicts one of them, and the bottom subject of Plate xv. gives something of their atmosphere.

Duke of Bedford being prominent members of it at the time of the Regency.

Boodle's club, designed by Crunden, was completed in 1765. Among the many lesser clubs of the period was the Literary Club, founded by Sir Joshua Reynolds and Dr Johnson in 1764. This club for some years met on Monday evenings at seven, but in 1773 the day was changed to Friday, and the next year the membership was enlarged from twelve to twenty members. Boswell, in his "Life of Johnson," gives some entertaining accounts of these gatherings.

The first coffee-house in England, opened in 1650, was due to the enterprise of a Jew. The first in London also belongs to the time of the Commonwealth, and was opened by a foreigner, Rosa Pasquie, in 1652. By the beginning of the eighteenth century there were nearly three thousand coffee-houses in London alone, and Steele, in No. 87 of *The Spectator*, gives an interesting account of the company. "Every man about him," he writes, "has, perhaps, a News Paper in his Hand; but none can pretend to guess what step will be taken in any one Court of Europe." News was indeed the great attraction, news and gossip; and as the news sheets contained nothing but bald statement, there was plenty of scope for speculation among the *habitués*. Here are a few of the more famous coffee-houses : Anderton's in Fleet Street, Batson's in Cornhill—a meeting-place for gentlemen of the gold-nobbed cane, Button's, a favourite of Addison's, and Child's, in St Paul's Churchyard, much frequented by doctors of the College of Physicians and members of the Royal Society. In St Martin's Lane was the Camisards; Garraways took its name from its original owner, one Garway, a tobacconist and coffee-man at the time of the Restoration. Jonathan's and Baker's in Exchange Alley were stock "jobbers" houses. Lloyd's, then in Lombard Street, was a mercantile house. Here began a sale of wines and ships, and to this address mercantile information was sent, forming the basis of the great institution that now bears its name. It was here, also, that the custom of selling goods by candle came into vogue, and all through the eighteenth century selling and letting by candle continued to be practised, the last bidder before the candle went out being the successful one.

At the beginning of the Georgian period road travel had greatly increased in volume since the time of the Stuarts. The travellers of the seventeenth century described by Fynes Morrison had made their journeys on horseback, on foot, or in lumbering carriages, and even when stage coaches began

PLATE XXI.

Foreign Wines being Unloaded at the Port of London. Notice the Tower in the background.

"In Southwark the old inns of the seventeenth century were for the most part intact."

A water-colour drawing of one of them by Schnebellie.

PLATE XXII.

Three Illustrations of Postchaises, drawn and etched by W. H. Pyne. Notice the uncommon open type for a large party.

A Stage Coach, drawn and etched by W. H. Pyne. Note the basket attachment for carrying extra passengers.

to ply, the going was poor enough. It was not until the end
of the reign of Queen Anne that any signs of real improvement
became noticeable. Better intercommunication between towns
was desired, and a regular service of public vehicles, main-
taining a speed of four miles an hour on the indifferent roads,
was added to the stream of carriers making periodical journeys
to and from London. The nobleman of the reign of George I.,
like his predecessor of the seventeenth century, travelled in
state in his family coach, attended by liveried servants and
outriders. He was followed by his steward in another carriage,
and yet another vehicle containing servants with the baggage.
The smaller gentry travelled in their own carriages with at
least two attendants to keep guard. Many gentlemen rode
their own horses, whilst others took advantage of the posting
system then established. By the year 1719 the mail service
was well regulated, and the horses unrivalled for their staying
powers. Another means of travel was to make the journey by
sea from one English port to another, or to make use of the
" fly boats " which plied on the navigable rivers.

The number of vagrants increased considerably during
this reign, and we have seen how the highways teemed with
disbanded soldiers, gipsies and sturdy beggars of both sexes.
No traveller could be certain of a safe ending to his journey,
but the rough-and-ready justice of the time dealt relentlessly
with cases of assault or even of vagrancy.

From 1720 to 1760 the public coaches were of two classes
—*i.e.*, " Flying Coaches " that would travel sixty miles in one
day, and others more leisurely that performed long journeys
by easy stages. Carriers' wagons were used both for the
conveyance of goods and of the humbler sort of travellers ;
and as evidence of the wretched state of some of the roads,
the pack-horse train survived until quite late in the century.
We must look to Georgian London for a description of the
inns and taverns which formed the termini of travel at this
time. All traffic from the southern counties made for the
Borough, and here for countless generations the carriers of
Kent, Sussex, Surrey and Hampshire had assembled. In
Southwark the old inns of the seventeenth century were for
the most part intact (Plate XXI.), and continued to serve
as stations for coaches, wagons, passengers and goods until
the invention of steam transport. On the northern edge of
London, St John's Street, Clerkenwell, was the recognised
centre for carriers from Hertfordshire, Bedfordshire, Huntingdon, Northamptonshire and Nottinghamshire. Carriers from
the west country came to the Oxford Arms in Oxford Street,

near St Giles' Pound, and also to Warwick Lane, under the shadow of St Paul's. Other carriers frequented the inns at the top of Holborn Hill, from Gray's Inn Lane to Ely Place.

In the early part of the century, coaches for the north still began their journeys from Holborn, as we may see from Pepys' Diary as well as from the many curious advertisements which remain, one relating to a four days' stage coach between London and York, which left on Mondays, Wednesdays and Fridays from the Black Swan in Holborn. Some towns, such as Ipswich, had the advantage of a fast coach which made the journey to London in one day. The traffic from East Anglia centred upon the inns of Bishopsgate and Aldgate. In 1725 the journey to Bristol took two days and to Exeter four. In the early days of coaching there was no accommodation for outside passengers, but as Hogarth has shown in one of his engravings, there were adventurous spirits who preferred the roof of a coach to the basket. It was not until 1750 that a prejudice that was felt against travelling by coach on Sundays was removed.

With the increase of trade and prosperity, quicker travel was everywhere demanded, with the result that in 1740 some coaches were scheduled to travel by night. The coaches of the early Georgian period were cumbersome and odd-looking enough. They were constructed of timber covered with dull black leather thickly studded with black, broad-headed nails. In some coaches the upper panels had four oval windows with heavy frames painted red and leather curtains within. The names of the towns between which they plied were painted on the doors.

The construction of the sedan-chair was almost similar (see Plate XIX.). It was used for short journeys from door to door, but it is recorded that one invalid lady travelled in one the whole distance from London to Bath, because she feared the fatigue of a carriage. Towards the end of the century both the coaches and the roads were enormously improved, and in the year 1775 eight passengers were carried inside and ten on top. In that year no less than four hundred road machines and seventeen thousand four-wheeled carriages were licensed. The success of Palmer's mail coach, which became established in 1784, brought further improvements in its train; night travelling now became general, and riding outside became the fashion among the better sort of passengers (see bottom picture on Plate XXII.). This was a period of great improvement in coach-building, as is evidenced by the numerous patents for axles, wheels, hubs, springs, and interior reading-

PLATE XXIII.

A Party Arriving by Postchaise at an Inn, "The Sugar Loaf," at Dunstable.
From an original drawing of Dunstable by Rowlandson.

The Obsequious Host and Hostess Ushering in a Rich Guest. Notice the names "Ram" and "Union" over the doors in the customary tradition of naming the rooms.
From a cartoon by Robert Dighton.

PLATE XXIV.

Late Georgian Inns. The "Swan" at Market Harborough and the "George" at Buckden. Notice the fine wrought-ironwork of the sign on the left.

lamps. Very few of these old vehicles have survived, but Hogarth has shown us the types of carriages of the earlier part of the century, while from the coloured prints of James Pollard we can gain an accurate idea of the crack coaches of the Regency period.

Travelling in late Georgian times seems to have been one long round of excitement. The start was accompanied by farewells from friends, the last efforts of ostlers to turn out the team, the raucous cries of itinerant merchants selling diaries and snuff-boxes, and the shouts of the mob that collected to share in the general pandemonium. This scene was repeated at every stage of the journey. On the road were encountered

FIG. 8.—" During the whole period the highwayman was the terror of the traveller."
A contemporary engraving.

private carriages, post-chaises and horsemen, to say nothing of droves of cattle and flocks of geese *en route* for the London markets. Then there were the wandering humans to be met with, the casual labourers, outcasts, footpads and runaway apprentices who infested the highways. Unemployment seems to have been considered a necessary evil, and hence the increase in the floating criminal population which called for the strongest methods of repression. During the whole period, the highwayman was the terror of the traveller (Fig. 8) and the hero of the mob. The environs of London and other large cities were notoriously unsafe, and travellers from the North would often prefer to stay the night at Barnet rather than undergo the risks of Finchley Common ; while the inns of Slough or Colnbrook claimed the travellers from Bath who dared not cross Hounslow Heath in the dark. The ostlers and hangers-on who frequented the inn yards were often enough in league with the " high toby men," and kept them posted on the movements of goods and passengers out of town. Old letters and diaries are eloquent on such adventures, as, for instance, that which befell Sir William Chambers, the architect, who was robbed on his way to his seat at Whitton. Travellers to Dover or to Exeter had occasion to fear Blackheath or Bagshot respectively in the daytime ; but the age that produced Turpin, Shepherd and MacHeath had naturally enough its counter-host of thief-takers, from " that truly great man " Jonathan Wild to the urbane Townshend of Bow Street. A study of the Newgate Calendar or a reference to contemporary newspapers reveals a criminality that was both audacious and brutal ; and it was small wonder that a hanging formed a popular diversion or that the cross-road gibbets were looked upon as a usual part of the scenery.

The Georgian inn, both in town and country, reflected the architecture of each reign (see Plate XXIV.). In its architectural character it was half official and half domestic. Some of the brick-fronted inns bear the bucolic character that stamps the reigns of the first and second of the Hanoverian kings, whilst examples built after 1780, such as the " George " at Grantham and the " George " at Aylesbury,[1] have something of the refinement and dignity that marks the buildings of the period. Tradition had decreed the arrangement of the plan. There was the courtyard with its arched or beamed entry, at first low when coaches carried no outside passengers, but loftier after 1760. The hall was the chief internal feature, and this held the main staircase with the coffee-room to the right and the dining-parlour to the left. In addition there were private rooms, each known by a name such as " Sun," " Star," " Moon," " York," " Union," " London," " Mitre," " Paragon," etc. (see Plate XXIII.). Many of the later Georgian inns had few architectural features, their external quality being determined by the plain statement of sashed windows and broad surfaces of brick or stone, as in the right-hand example on Plate XXIV.

With the increase in travelling, the old class distinctions of the road were bound soon to disappear. The nobleman may have scorned to travel by the public stage and sought his night accommodation in the houses of his friends, but the ordinary traveller of almost every rank looked upon the inn as his temporary home (see Plate XXIII.). It must also be remembered that many of the earlier inns were altered and

[1] Now closed.

made more comfortable to accommodate the increase of passengers in later Georgian times. Road travel was also enlivened by the signs which projected from the fronts of inns or swung gibbet-wise across the highway. The making of these signs employed the painter, the carver, the blacksmith and the carpenter, while even the coach-builder and the artist were sometimes called upon to help in their manufacture. Cipriani devised a Turk's head, and Samuel Wale painted a Shakespeare and a Falstaff; whilst it is recorded that George Morland left a freshly painted sign in payment of a tippling score.

To an inn of the times the sign was as important a feature as a figurehead to a sailing-ship (see Plate xxiv.). They fall under many headings as to subject, or under a combination of any three of them. They are in turn historic, heraldic, humorous, prophetic, religious, threatening, appealing, war-like, peaceful, nautical, amorous, pagan or ecclesiastical. In Georgian times, every political event was drawn upon as a subject for one of them, and a minor history could be written from their study.

It now remains to give some impression of the state of the English countryside that formed the background for wayfaring and travel. When the Georgian period opened, farming was in much the same condition as it had been in for centuries, except for the new system of intakes and enclosures. By 1750, waste-lands, heaths and commons began to be absorbed by wealthy landowners and converted into farm-land. This development was viewed with alarm, for it meant the end of the smallholders who, hitherto, had found means of support from the farming of a few acres, and it is to this cause that can be traced the gradual disappearance of the yeoman class, dating from about this time. Open fields and strip cultivation gave the small man a chance to compete with those who farmed on a large scale, but the enclosing of land expedited the ruin of the small farmer who, in many cases, migrated to the industrial towns and was absorbed in the working classes. Arthur Young, the agricultural enthusiast who travelled in France at the time of the Revolution to study French farming, was an advocate of the large farm, and sought to prove the superiority of the English farmer who worked on a large scale. The English gentry, however, were the first to see the advantages of investing capital in land and encouraging farming. There is no better example of this kind of enterprise than the drainage of the Bedford Level by Francis, fifth Duke of Bedford, and similar experiments were made by the Duke of Grafton, Lord Townshend and Lord Rockingham, which met with equal success. At the end of the century, Sir Thomas

Tyrwhitt and some others attempted to reclaim parts of Dartmoor for farming.

The advance of farming to the status of a scientific profession belongs, therefore, to the third quarter of the eighteenth century. Farming implements were improved, wheat drills, such as that invented by Salmon, sometime surveyor to Francis, Duke of Bedford, were patented, and the old wooden implements,[1] such as the plough shown in Pyne's illustration on Plate xxv., were succeeded by ploughs, harrows, and rollers from Sharp's manufactory at Southwark. More attention was given at the end of the century to stock-breeding, and the name of Robert Bakewell must here be mentioned for his enterprise in this direction.

The revival of agriculture first determined by the acquisition of further land by the wealthy, in turn brought about a minor architectural revival. The tilling of the soil and the breeding of cattle meant the further employment and adequate housing of the peasantry. In the West of England, the Duchy of Cornwall farmed out the land on leases to small farmers. In Bedfordshire, the Duke of Bedford and Samuel Whitbread began to organise their estates on a liberal scale, recognising the status of the independent farmer. Between the years 1790 and 1830 these great landowners built cottages and farm-houses which, even to-day, are models of appropriate accommodation and artistic distinction. The Bedfordshire cottages were built of brick or of timber-framing covered with lathing and roughcast. Roofs were thatched, windows leaded, and pumps and wells constituted the water supply. Many such houses can be seen in Bedfordshire, in the neighbourhood of Woburn, Ridgmont, Southill and Cardington. The farm-houses on a larger scale included excellent outbuildings and sheds for cattle.

Here is the first evidence of a revival which in turn gave place to the ornamental cottages, rustic lodges and dairies which became fashionable during the Regency (see Plate xxv.). What had been engaged upon as a pastime by the ladies of the Court of Louis XVI., had become a serious study with the English nobility, squirearchy and country gentlemen.

---

[1] Miss Gertrude Jekyll has formed a most interesting collection of these at Guildford.

PLATE XXV.

The Old Type of Wooden Plough.   *From Pyne's "Microcosm."*

A Georgian Farmhouse and Yard.   *From an engraving by C. Middleton.*

"... A revival which in turn gave place to the ornamental cottages, rustic lodges, and dairies, which became fashionable during the Regency." One such at Puckaster, Isle of Wight.   *From an aquatint by W. Westall.*

PLATE XXVI.

A Military and a Naval Engagement of the Time of Marlborough.
(*Above*) The Battle of Bonn.   (*Below*) The Taking of Gibraltar.

From engravings by P. Decker.

CHAPTER III

THE NAVY, THE ARMY AND THE CHURCH

I. THE NAVY: ITS SHIPS AND ORGANISATION

THAT the English navy in the eighteenth century achieved the magnificent results that it did and grew into so tremendously effective a striking force is somewhat remarkable when it is considered what drawbacks and defects had always to be contended with. The captains were not seldom haphazard in their methods, and no systematic scheme of battle tactics was worked out until the end of the period under review. Opportunities to press home an advantage were, it must be admitted, often let slip, as by Bridport and Hotham after more than one Channel action, and by Jervis after Cape St Vincent. There was sometimes a complete lack of co-ordination between one squadron and another through half-heartedness or mere incompetence, a shocking instance of this occurring in the West Indies in 1702 when nearly all Benbow's captains refused to engage the ships of de Casse with anything like vigour, or at all. The suggestion on this occasion was that most of the disaffected captains were Jacobite in their sympathies.

Les autres certainly needed a measure of the *encouragement* which Voltaire suggested might be supplied by the shooting of the unfortunate Byng in 1756 after his failure to retain Minorca with the totally inadequate forces allotted to him. The predicament in which he found himself in this action was somewhat similar to that of Cradock off the South American coast in 1914, and the ferocity of his sentence was meant to appease a public whose anger was directed more against the pusillanimity of naval policy at this time.

As the century advanced, the old method of attack by fireships grew obsolete, and the efficacy of blockading tactics became increasingly manifest. By these means the French fleet was usually rendered impotent, though detached squadrons often enough managed to evade the blockade and get through—either in or out. But naval policy had, especially in the early part of the century, a good deal of the casual and happy-go-lucky about it. Gibraltar was taken more with the idea of having some tangible accomplishment to show in response to the urgings of the King of Portugal and the Archduke Charles that the navy should do something, rather than in the pursuance of a thought-out plan (see Plate XXVI.). Once in English hands, however, it was gradually manned, stored and fortified, and withstood several determined sieges. An instance of the ingenuity of a commander is that of Cornwallis who in 1795 extricated himself by a clever ruse from an awkward situation. Attacked by Villaret-Joyeuse in superior force, he detached a frigate to signal to him, in a code which the French were known to have captured, that the Channel Fleet was about to rejoin him. The results of this trick were eminently satisfactory.

The crews of English battleships were largely manned by jailbirds, the alternative of "prison or navy" being quite common. The pressgang mostly roped in young fellows without much family responsibility and accustomed to seafaring in some form; its harshness has possibly been exaggerated, though there were undoubtedly cases of great hardship, as that of the son of the Canadian magistrate for whose release, after two years' service, Nelson's personal intervention was sought.

But it was the fine class of professional sailors, "prime seamen," with a pride in their craft, who supplied the backing; and the indomitable spirit of the men was frequently shown in desperate exploits of "cutting-out" boat attacks on armed ships well manned and ready to give a hot reception. Generally the human element was superior to the French, as was the handling of the ships and their gunnery, though the latter often had the advantage in the vessels themselves, which were usually faster, larger, and easier handled. As in Tudor days, English ship-designers lagged behind. At St Vincent (1797) the Spaniards had the largest ship in the world, the four-decker "Trinidad" of 130 guns. As for heavy guns, in 1798 the East Indiaman "Glatton" was armed with 68-lb. and 42-lb. carronades. On the way out she beat off, single-handed, six French frigates with ease, but the lesson was not taken to heart. The "big" ship time and again showed her ability to stand heavy punishment and come off without serious damage. In 1794 the 100-gun "Revolutionnaire" gave a creditable account in the Atlantic in combat with six British 74's.

But the actual size of ships increased scarcely at all during the century; and it is curious to think that the dimensions were mostly determined by the length of the trees which could

PLATE XXVII.

Lord Howe in the "Queen Charlotte" Breaking the Enemy Line. The "Glorious First of June," 1794.

From " The Naval Achievements of Great Britain."

A Patrolling Squadron.

From the engraving by Boydell after Brooking.

PLATE XXVIII.

Examples of the Ornamental Stern-work of Warships at the close of the Seventeenth Century. (*Left*) A French Second-rater.
(*Right*) The "Royal Charles." *From engravings after Vandervelde.*

be grown. The naval gun also remained practically unchanged throughout the century. The British practice was to aim at firing crippling broadsides into the enemy at comparatively short range ; and the closeness at which ships fought is well illustrated in the top picture on Plate xxvii. In his fight with a Spanish treasure-ship off South America, Anson, in the " Centurion," from shortage of crew, ordered individual firing, and as it was the Spanish practice to lie down till a broadside had been fired, this measure caused deadly execution among

FIG. 9.—A Twelve-pounder Carronade.
From the engraving by E. W. Cooke.

them. The French method of firing at the rigging resulted in much damage, but had its own drawbacks : a vessel could not be disabled or sunk unless its hull had been badly knocked about.

In connection with the improvement of dockyards, the work must be recalled of General Bentham, who returned from the Russian navy, and, in the face of opposition, installed steam machinery at Devonport in 1798.

It is curious that uniform was by no means a settled thing during most of this century ; much depended on the captain's own feeling and taste—for instance, Anson had his men finely togged out for his calls on the Viceroy at Canton during his romantic sail round the world by South America in 1741-44. Floggings were of course brutal and often inflicted for comparatively trivial causes, but little was thought of them, for savage punishments were equally the rule ashore. The food was frequently disgusting—weevilly or maggotty biscuit and stinking cheese were common fare, but the cause was often not so much carelessness or dishonesty as the system by which the oldest stuff had to be consumed first; the policy of cheese-paring economy showed its baleful effects in many ways. That the same troubles were rife early in the century is shown by the following extract: "Whereas it is presented to me that there is two butts of stinking beer with a small quantity of damnified vat-meal and cheese on board H.M. Ship 'Adventure' you are directed to take a strict and careful survey of the same, etc." (Sir John Norris, Vice-Admiral of the Blue Squadron, 30th December 1707, *B.M.Add MSS.* 20056).

The quantity for the men was intended to be lavish, and liquor was also plentiful. The rum-and-water ration was introduced about 1745 by Admiral Vernon, who, from his habit of wearing a Grogram coat, bore the nickname of "Old Grog," hence the familiar term "grog" for the liquor. But skinflint methods were apparent in the medical equipment; and nothing could exceed the horrors of the cockpit during a fleet action, when terribly wounded cases were flung overboard and the surgeons hurried their rough-and-ready amputations with instruments sometimes borrowed from the carpenter. As may be imagined, an insufficient issue of sponges for a large number of cases was followed by distressing consequences of infection. Illness was terribly rife in the crowded, mephitic, lower deck, but the adoption of a system of windmill and other ventilation, devised by Dr Hales in 1753, caused a much-needed improvement. On foreign expeditions sickness swept away more lives than the enemy, as with Nelson at Nicaragua in 1780. Generally speaking, it is difficult to explain or condone the country's marked and callous neglect of and indifference to the welfare of the sea-fighting men, who deserved well at its hands.

The amounts distributed in prize-money were immense in the case of captains and officers, and quite considerable even for bluejackets. This undoubtedly served as a fighting inducement and a compensation for many privations and hardships, though there were always waiting sharps, pimps, and harpies of all sorts to relieve Jack of his gains as soon as he stepped ashore. Numerous rich Spanish treasure ships were captured, as by Anson in 1741.

The man who tightened up the discipline of the Mediterranean Fleet was Lord St Vincent (Admiral Jervis), though his efforts were by no means regarded with favour by the officers of the Channel Fleet. Almost everything depended on the discretion, or tyranny, of the individual captain. There was never any trouble in Nelson's ships; like St Vincent, he was assiduous in providing lemons as a specific against the scourge of scurvy, which only too often followed an uninterrupted diet of "salt horse." Nelson even went so far as to arrange theatricals for the men. Against this must be set the practice of a brute like Pigot of the "Hermione," who indulged in the charming custom of flogging the last man or two down from a job aloft. It is little to be wondered that the exasperated crew mutinied and took the ship over to the Spaniards. There were other instances of disaffected crews going over to the enemy with their ships.

Of the important mutinies which occurred in 1797 those at Spithead and Plymouth were quite gentlemanly affairs, conducted with much restraint and having the character of a strike for better conditions—" More humanity to the wounded," was one of the points advanced. But the mutiny at the Nore, May to June 1797, was a far more serious affair, and had a distinctly political complexion, the ringleader, Richard Parker, who was afterwards hanged, being a sort of early Bolshevik. The mutinous fleet actually blockaded the Thames, leaving Admiral Duncan with very few ships; and an attack by the enemy then might have had grave results. On other occasions England was left open to invasion, as when, in 1780, against sixty-four French and Spanish ships, Sir C. Hardy had only thirty-seven English vessels, and these sailed away westward. Only aimless wanderings on the part of the allies then saved the country, which was menaced by a navy of double the English strength, and an army of 40,000 men. There are other instances of a similar danger averted owing more to luck than anything else. Doubtless it was ignorance of the other side's position and movements that led to the loss of vital opportunities. What would now be called "naval intelligence" was in a remarkably backward state.

The British merchant navy suffered severely and continuously at the hands of the French privateers who infested the Channel. One hundred corsairs were captured in 1760 and eighty-seven in 1800. The losses were considerable because of the amount of sea-borne traffic reaching these shores, while the proportion of captures remained small—somewhere about two to three per cent. Ships in an escorted convoy were usually safe, if they did not hurry on to arrive early to make a large profit on their cargoes. That French losses were insignificant was due to the virtual extinction of her sea-carrying trade.

The Wooden Walls

To study the development of the wooden walls we must return to the beginning of the eighteenth century, at the

FIG. 10.—The Stern of H.M.S. "Asia." A 74-gun ship.
From the engraving by E. W. Cooke.

time when Peter the Great was living at Deptford and receiving instruction in naval architecture from Sir Anthony Deane. England then possessed about one-third of the whole naval power of Europe—France and Holland together having practically the same amount. Owing to the increase of the British navy, an order was given in 1703 for diminishing the expenses in building and rebuilding ships of war. This order related to the decoration customary for internal and external embellishment. The display of ornamental work had increased, but now it was ordered " that the carved work

PLATE XXIX.

(*Above*) Deptford Dockyard.   *From an engraving by T. Milton.*
(*Below*) The New "Royal George," 1800.   *From an engraving by G. Stables.*

PLATE XXX.

The Convict Hulk in Portsmouth Dockyard.

From an engraving by E. W. Cooke

The "Royal George," a first-rater of 100 guns, launched 1756; lost with Kempenfeldt in 1782.

An engraving after T. Bastin.

should be diminished, and that the ornaments at the head should consist of only lion and trailboard, with mouldings instead of carved brackets placed against the timbers; and that the excessive ornamental work of the stern should be discontinued and only a taffrail and four quarter-pieces used instead of the brackets between the lights of the stern galleries."

If reference is made to the " twenty-two prints of several of the Capital Ships of His Majesty's Royal Navy, with a variety of other sea pieces after the drawings of T. Bastin," no great change is observable in the general lines of the ships belonging to the first quarter of the century, which follow the traditions of Sir Anthony Deane's regime. It is, however, recorded that the general inferiority of British ships of war, in comparison with those of France, led to the ordering of a new establishment in 1719 for the dimensions of ships. One step in the direction of improvement was made when the " Princessa," a Spanish ship of 70 guns, was captured in 1740. This vessel was taken as a model for the " Royal George," which was laid down at Woolwich in 1746, launched ten years later, and lost with Kempenfeldt on board at Spithead in 1782 (Plate xxx.). The decorative attributes of the " Royal George " appear to have followed contemporary architectural ornament. Such features as the door and hood moulding to the gangway, with balcony and wrought-iron railing, the stiff pilasters to the divisions of the stern galleries, and the carved terms finishing the ramps from the beak are of decided interest.

In 1747 the capture of the " Invincible " of 74 guns from the French led to an increase of dimensions in British ships of the same class, such as the " Triumph," " Mars," " Thunderer," and the " Canada."

Scale Models

The scale models of old-time warships in the Royal United Services Museum and at the Naval Museum, Greenwich, supplement in a very realistic manner the series of line engravings and working drawings contained in contemporary volumes. At the United Services Museum the model of the line-of-battleship of the year 1650 of the Hanseatic League is reticent in the treatment of the poop. There is an interesting model of the " Victory," a ship of 100 guns, immediately preceding Lord Nelson's " Victory," which was not built till 1765. The earlier ship was built in 1735 and served until 1744, when she was lost in a violent storm near the Race of Alderney. A view showing the lines of the stern and the decoration of the poop enables us to imagine the aspect of the ship as she stood in dock prior to her launching. The end tiers of windows are grouped vertically into towers, with two open-balustraded galleries above the lower storey connecting the decorated quarter-pieces.

There are many other models which should be studied in detail, including the "Lion," built at Deptford in 1738, a 64-gun ship of the 1720 period, the "Dryad," a model belonging to Nelson when a boy, the "Mars," of 74 guns, built in 1794, which played no unimportant part at Trafalgar, the "Cornwallis," a third-rater, built in 1812, at Bombay, by Jamsetjee Bomajee, the model built simultaneously with the ship by the son of Jamsetjee; and several fine models of English ships made by Breton sailor prisoners, from bones. From a study of these miniature examples it is possible to trace the gradual development in design from the seventeenth to the early nineteenth centuries, to understand how the pomp of the officers' quarters at the poop gave way to extreme simplicity, how the "tumble home" of the walls of the ship was reduced almost to the vertical lines of the Indiamen, and how increased speed resulted when the design of hull and rigging was elevated to a science.

Another model of an English ship belonging to the late eighteenth century of decorative interest is the "Boyne," launched in 1790, showing an advance in naval design.

Among specimens of carving in the United Services Museum is the clock face taken from the poop of the French "Ville de Paris" in Lord Rodney's action on the 12th of April 1782; the hand was turned by the sentinel every hour; the carving is of the Louis Seize period. The second group consists of the figurehead representing George III., and six caryatides from the stem of the yacht "Royal George," built at Deptford in 1814-17, and remarkable for her exceptional sailing qualities.

Dockyards

At the close of the eighteenth century the English dockyards comprised the following: Deptford (Plate xxix.), established in the reign of Henry II.; Chatham, where some of the noblest wooden ships were constructed, from Charles II. to Nelson's day; Sheerness, used chiefly for the repair of ships slightly damaged in action; Portsmouth, which became a serious rival to Chatham at the end of the seventeenth century; Plymouth Dock, projected in the time of King William III., when Vanbrugh was engaged to build a wharf and storehouses;

and Pembroke, which, although offering deep and ample anchorage, was very seldom used. A minor dockyard existed at Harwich.

Between the years 1760 and 1790 many fine warships were launched at Plymouth. The following description is part of a contemporary account: "The launch of the 'Royal Sovereign,' of 100 guns, was preceded by that of the 'Glory,' almost as fine a vessel, with 98 guns, and the 'Cæsar,' a superb third-rater, with 74 guns. The last named carried the head of Julius at the fore, the warrior grasping his sword and advancing his shield on his nervous right arm, his eye darting lightning on the foe." The three-deckers were painted with black and yellow alternation, and the figureheads were appropriately treated in colour. These ships had majestic figureheads,[1] and such symmetry that no one could fail to be impressed with their beauty and grandeur. At this period Dickerson, the famous dockyard sculptor, was employed at Plymouth, and several of his original designs are extant. Even a small sixth-rater, the "Narcissus," carrying only 21 guns, boasted an elaborately carved poop. Although naval emblems are not found on contemporary buildings, Robert Adam introduced the prow of the "Royal George" into the tympanum of the south pediment of the Admiralty screen.

Napoleonic Ships and Decoration

Among the work of French designers for the new ships of the Napoleonic epoch are ambitious designs by P. Ozanne for the ornamental prows of 80-gun ships, inspired by classic themes. In one, a gigantic sea-conch follows the lines of the beak, and supports two Tritons driving spirited sea-horses; in the other a Fame, carrying a flag and blowing a trumpet, heads the stem, seaweed masking the junction of the upper and lower lines of the prow.

The underlying spirit is throughout military rather than naval. The general lines of French warships of this period were excellent and often superior to the English. There is, for example, the famous "Implacable," lately refitted at Devonport.

English Warships from 1780 to 1850

From 1780 to the Regency began the second great period of timber warship construction, when fighting power and seaworthiness received first consideration. Steam power was

---

[1] The museum at Devonport contains many examples.

introduced into the dockyards, labour-saving devices employed, and the whole establishment was placed on a scientific basis. These precautions were wisely ordained, for, from the time of the loss of the American dependencies to the battle of Navarino, the work of the British Navy demanded every resource. The painting by Clarkson Stanfield of the Battle of Trafalgar is interesting, as are the drawings by Turner, which show the lines of English fighting ships of Nelson's time.

Lighthouses

The story of British Lighthouses is bound up with the Corporation of Trinity House, which was founded in Tudor days. Thence, through the sixteenth, seventeenth, and eighteenth centuries, the care of guarding shipping from dangerous rocks became more and more the business of the Trinity Brethren. On the summit of St Agnes, the principal of the Western Islands in the Scillies, stands one of the earliest of the more important works erected by Trinity House. This was built of brick and was finished in 1681. It is said that it was owing to the dimness of this light that Sir Cloudesley Shovell met disaster in 1707. All sorts of patents were originally granted to private individuals for building lighthouses; some were accepted and others apparently fell through. In 1695 Henry Winstanley began work on the Eddystone with his perfect specimen of ludicrous ingenuity (Fig. 11). He was on it during the terrific gale in 1702 which swept edifice and occupant into a raging sea. Smeaton, referring to the destruction of the lighthouse and the model, shrewdly observed, "This, however, may not appear extraordinary if we consider that the same general wind that blew down the lighthouse near Plymouth might also blow down the model at Littlebury." After Winstanley came John Rudyard, a mercer of Ludgate Hill, who put up a simple timber tower (Fig. 12). The base was strengthened by courses of Cornish granite. This work was completed in 1709 and stood until 1755, when it was destroyed by fire. The owner of the patent obtained by Winstanley then employed John Smeaton to construct a new lighthouse (Fig. 13). Smeaton formed the opinion that stone was the best material, though the Trinity Brethren favoured wood; Smeaton eventually gained his point. In 1757 Smeaton surveyed the rock, made a model, and, after obtaining Admiralty approval and the patentees', began operations. On the night of 16th October 1759 the light was first shown. In 1807, when the lease expired, Trinity House took over the manage-

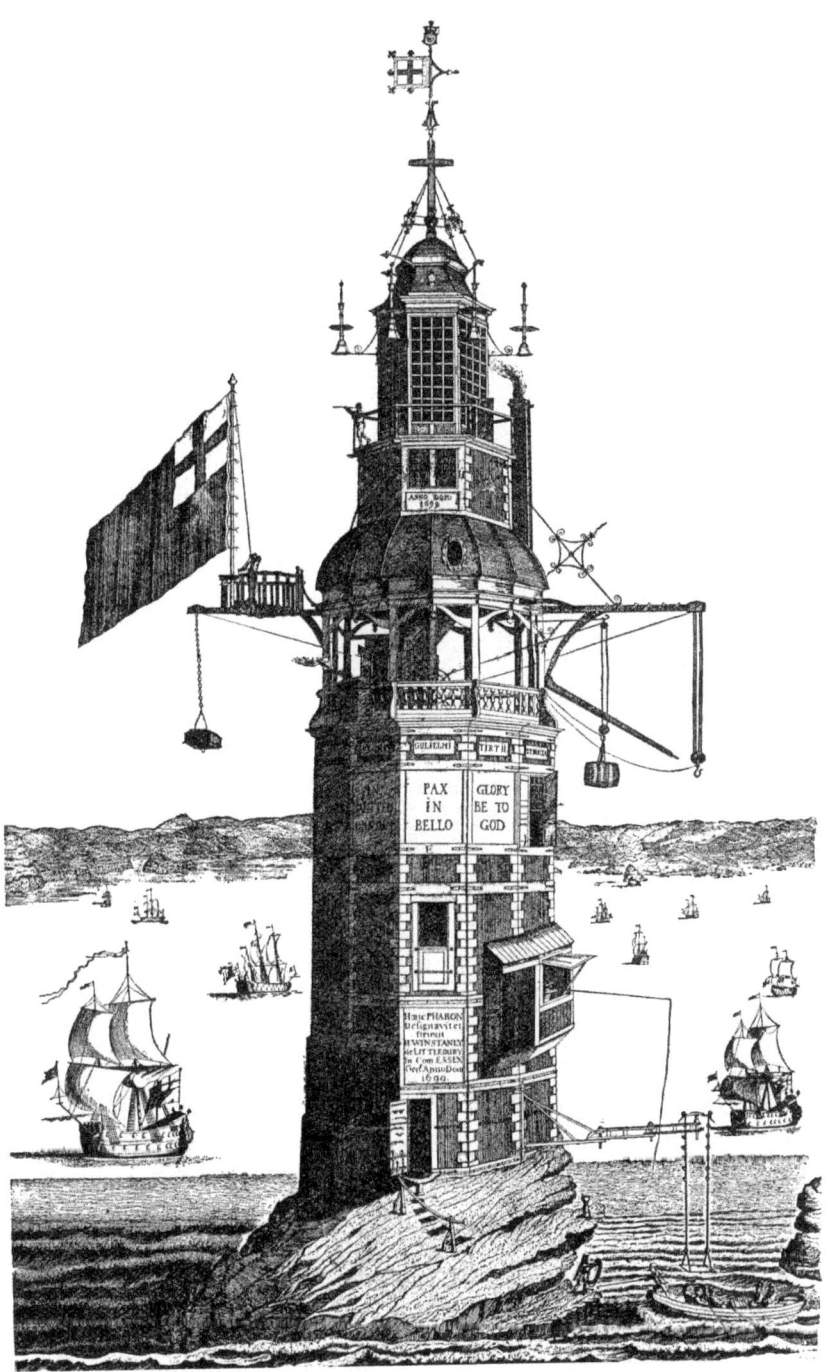

Fig. 11.—The First Eddystone Lighthouse, designed by Henry Winstanley (*not* by Heath Robinson). Built in 1695, it was swept away with its inventor in a great gale in 1702.
A contemporary engraving.

ment. Seventy-one years later the fourth lighthouse was erected, not by reason of any fault in Smeaton's work, but because of the undermining of the rock by the sea. Smeaton, in his original treatment, completely changed opinion regarding the building of lighthouses. He was engaged on many works, such as the harbour of St Ives and its diminutive light tower, as well as the original works at Ramsgate.

In Smeaton's time candle-lighting replaced the burning of wood or coal in an iron brazier, but as the glass prevented the light from being seen at a distance, sperm-oil lamps were introduced in 1790. The Goodwin Sands had long menaced navigation, and various attempts were made to erect lighthouses on the treacherous shoals. In 1795 the Trinity Brethren moored an old hulk on the North Land's End as a lightship, and thus began the series which continue to this day. The lights on the North Kent coast date from the late seventeenth century. In 1719 the first lighthouse at Cromer was built on Foulness Point, some 220 feet above sea-level, the keepers being two young women, who received £1 per week for wages with perquisites. Very few of the eighteenth-century lighthouses now remain, and it is fortunate that Smeaton's masterpiece has been re-erected on Plymouth Hoe.

FIG. 12.—Rudyard's Eddystone Lighthouse, 1709-55.

Fig. 13.—Smeaton's Eddystone Lighthouse.
From an engraving by E. Rooker and S. Wale, 1759.

II. The Army

On the military side, the eighteenth century begins with Marlborough (1650-1722) and ends with Wellington (1769-1852). The military qualities of both these generals were remarkably outstanding, though of very diverse types. Both rendered supreme service to their country and were admirably suited to the tasks with which they were faced—Marlborough, as the daring and brilliant strategist, could crush the plans of aggressive ambition, and Wellington, as a steady, cautious fighter, could wear down doggedly a superior force.

The period opens with the Wars of the Spanish and Austrian Successions, and then passes to the Jacobite risings, the Seven Years' War, and the War of Secession in America, till finally we come to the struggle with Napoleon. In addition, there were interludes such as the military expeditions in which certain regiments co-operated with the navy, and the conquest of India by the generals in the employ of the East India Company. During the hundred-odd years which separate Marlborough from Wellington there were many able and distinguished generals, such as Wolfe and Sir John Moore, besides hundreds of officers of lesser rank, who achieved distinction. But the period as a whole did not offer opportunities for campaigns on the grand scale.

There is no denying the military genius of Marlborough. In the annals of the British Army no other figure, with the solitary exception of Wellington, in any way approaches his power as a commander. He had all the attributes of a great captain, combining organising power with brilliant audacity and rare imagination. As a strategist he favoured the teachings of Turenne, and these theories he followed when he shattered the supposed invincibility of the French Army on the field of Blenheim. Yet Marlborough reached ripe middle age before he found scope for his genius as a leader of fighting men. The mere list of his great battles is trifling: Blenheim, Ramillies, Oudenarde, Malplaquet, are but the culminating actions of campaigns conceived and maintained on a vast scale.

Not on the battlefield alone was he brilliant, but in the sphere of diplomacy, when quarrels among the allies threatened to destroy plans of campaigns ready to mature. No man ever had to struggle against more mountains of heart-breaking difficulties—the jealousy or vain claims of associated commanders, on occasion insubordinate defiance, and the stubborn, narrow-minded, cautious timidity of the Dutch. By no one could those difficulties have been more successfully surmounted. He fought over the well-known Flemish ground, and places familiar through the Great War figured in his ten hard campaigns, which broke the threatening domination of Louis XIV. Mons and Lille were taken by him; he fought at Ypres, Tournai, Cambrai, Douai, and had designs on Arras. Then he showed by his patience that he could wear down opposition without giving offence to his co-operators. His greatest achievement was the march from the Lower Rhine to the Upper Danube, when he effected a junction of forces with Prince Eugene and beat the French. His final scheme, had the war been continued, was to break down all the French fortresses between Maubeuge and Paris and to dictate peace in the French capital. The generals who fought with him were pigmies by comparison. Neither Ormunde nor Cutts had minds suited to slow campaigning—although Cutts at least was a fighter and had distinguished himself at Venloo. The most able man on the Duke's staff was Cadogan, to whose administrative ability much of the success of the campaign which finished at Blenheim was due.

At the opening of the century there was the usual lack of machinery for raising forces. The English contribution for the allied forces was 40,000 men—18,000 British and the rest mercenaries—later, 10,000 were added. Acts were passed to release debtors from their dreadful and often hopeless imprisonment to serve with the forces; these were supplemented by criminals and enrolments from the large vagrant class in the parishes. These devices are amusingly lampooned by G. Farquhar in his play "The Recruiting Officer" (1705). Sergeant Kite, a pothouse bravo, suggests that a coal-miner is eligible as, his work being underground, he has "no visible means of livelihood."

Indeed, Marlborough's forces needed miners for the desperate struggles in the Flanders fortifications, and Marlborough complains of the weakness of his engineering branch. Similarly, the engineers were weak and badly equipped at the close of the period, and lack of efficient co-operation caused fearful loss of life at some Peninsular and Indian stormings.

But the slow promotion offered little encouragement to join the specialist services, and the home direction was often utterly defective. Lt.-Col. Rowe, in Spain, was supplied with shells that did not fit the guns furnished: fortunately the navy was able to provide cannon to fire the shots. Blind cavalry horses were sent out: he had to use oxen in their place.

From the first quarter of the eighteenth century we pass

to the days when George II. took the field at Dettingen during the War of the Austrian Succession. The command of the British Army was given to the Earl of Stair, but this general was hampered by the presence of his sovereign. In this reign the Duke of Cumberland, then twenty-four years of age, became Commander-in-Chief, and although he suffered defeat at Fontenoy, and was abused for his brutality in Scotland, he was acknowledged to be a brave soldier. His chief work was the reorganisation of the army and the drafting of a much-needed code of discipline.

The greatest soldier in the middle Georgian period was Wolfe, who entered the army as an ensign at the age of fourteen. At twenty he was a major, and at twenty-three a lieutenant-colonel. When he was appointed to command the British Army in Conquest of Canada he was thirty-two. His lack of experience, in spite of his enthusiasm for soldiering, led him to engage in minor enterprises which placed the fall of Quebec outside the realm of success until he conceived the idea of scaling the "Heights of Abraham," followed by his victory and death. While the defeat of the French in Canada provided a brilliant facet to the star of British military prestige, the campaign against the rebellious colonists in the War of Secession cast a cloud over the nation.

In this campaign many experienced soldiers were engaged, such as Howe, Clinton, Burgoyne and Cornwallis. There was, however, lack of co-ordination between the generals, as well as inability among those in office, from the king downwards, to appreciate the circumstances and the nature of the operations. It was actually attempted to direct the war from Whitehall, in the same way that the Admiralty, prior to the days of Hawke, had prescribed the tactics to be followed in line of battle.

The loss of America, therefore, can be ascribed not so much to the generals entrusted with the conduct of the war as to incapable ministers at home. George III., in his bid for autocracy, was never so ill-served as he was by the Secretary of State for the Colonies, Lord George Germaine.

From 1785 until the ill-fated Walcheren Expedition, save for military achievements in India against native troops, the British Army entered upon a period of ordinary routine. Reform, however, was at hand, and the Napoleonic wars changed the whole aspect of soldiering. The Duke of York had no claim to be ranked as a leader, but he was an able organiser, and he, at least, appreciated the enterprises of Sir John Moore, who invented "light infantry."

PLATE XXXI.

(*Above*) Landing the British Troops in Egypt under Sir Ralph Abercrombie in 1800.   (*Below*) The Battle of Salamanca, 1812.

From a rare colour-plate book, " *The Martial Achievements of Great Britain.*"

PLATE XXXII.

The Church and the Free Church. (*Left*) Service at a City Church. (*Right*) A Presbyterian Conventicle.

The Staff College was established at High Wycombe in 1799, with a junior branch at Marlow. A good knowledge of French was essential, as the lectures were delivered in that language, among others by General Jarry, a French *emigré*.

Mention should be made of the effective operations round Alexandria by Abercromby, and after his death by Hutchinson, early in 1801, by which the French were entirely cleared out of Egypt.

Like British statesmen subsequently, Pitt (in 1792) anticipated a settled peace directly before a mighty and protracted war, and made substantial reductions in the army. In popular estimation, service in the army did not rank nearly as high as on board ship, but far fewer criminals went to the colours, and it was contemptible to assert that all the soldiers had joined for the sake of drink. This came from Wellington, who never showed any consideration to the men who served him magnificently. The officers were largely out of touch with their men, and the prolonged floggings were barbarous. The conditions on troopships were appalling, and epidemics decimated the expeditionary forces, especially in tropical countries.

By the Napoleonic wars the purchase of commissions had been put on a regular basis; an ensign's appointment could be purchased, often for a boy of sixteen, for 300 guineas. Promotion was often a matter of purchase; without it officers grew grey in the weary wait for vacancies.

At the beginning of the nineteenth century the regular forces amounted to some 140,000 men, scattered over various theatres of war, 53,000 being in Great Britain. There were coloured troops in the West Indies—that white man's graveyard—and Indian regiments were also coming into use; there was even a body from New South Wales. The militia, amounting to over 38,000 men, recruited by county ballot, was a force of importance and a fine feeder for the army. Beyond that were the Yeomanry, and various bodies of " Loyal Volunteers," of greater spirit, probably, than military merit.

It is interesting to observe the changes of uniforms which had taken place from the time of Marlborough to the period of the gaitered and mitred Hanoverian soldiers or the heavy-horsed dragoons and the shakoed infantry of the campaigns in the Peninsula (Plate XXXI.). It is a curious detail that at the end of the century the pigtails of British soldiers were limited to six inches!

It can be said that the culmination of eighteenth-century military science was the day on which veterans, and the raw recruits from behind the plough, withstood the shock of the French cavalry with the massed attack of the Old Guard at Waterloo. But the way to victory had been prepared by the reforms of Cumberland, of Sir John Moore, and the ripe experience of Wellington during the campaigns in India and the Peninsula.

III. The Church

The dullness and apathy of the Church during most of the eighteenth century had its effect in the almost heathen ignorance of the people generally. Deism—a general belief in God—was common among the upper classes, and the message of the pulpits was largely a vague morality without any distinctively Christian doctrine. There is the tale of a clergyman who apologised for mentioning Christ in his sermon as it was Christmas Day, but promised that the allusion should not be repeated till the next anniversary. In this age of rife latitudinarianism the High Church party continued its distinctive tenets under Bishop Horsley (1733-1806), eminent also as a scientist. But the great religious awakening came through the Evangelical Revival, and the work of John (1703-91) and Charles Wesley (1708-88) and George Whitefield (1714-70).

The Wesleys were sons of the Rector of Epworth, in Lincolnshire, where John was born in 1703. They had formed the " Holy Club " at Oxford, and had preached unsuccessfully in General Oglethorpe's colony in Georgia. But their new spiritual impulse had come from their association with the Moravians, and especially Peter Böhler. The start of the movement did not take place till 1738, when John Wesley underwent a spiritual transformation by hearing, very unwillingly, Luther's " Preface to the Epistle to the Romans " read at a meeting in Aldersgate Street. George Whitefield's mother kept the Bull Inn at Gloucester ; he had been associated with the brothers at Oxford and in Georgia. Excluded from the churches, they turned to open-air preaching, where Whitefield's histrionic gifts had terrifying effect upon the listening multitudes ; though he was undoubtedly one of the greatest preachers of all time in his riveting eloquence. Crabbe's none too sympathetic sketch of this type of evangelist is intensely graphic :—

> Soft women fainted, prouder man express'd
> Wonder and woe, and butchers smote the breast ;
> * * * * * *

> The stubborn spirits by his force he broke,
> As the fork'd lightning rives the knotted oak :
> Fear, hope, dismay, all signs of shame or grace,
> Chain'd every foot, or featured every face ;
> Then took his sacred trump a louder swell,
> And now they groan'd, they sicken'd, and they fell ;
>
> * * * * * *
>
> And thus in triumph took his glorious way,
> Through scenes of horror, terror, and dismay.

The print (Plate xxxiii.) bears the title " Enthusiasm Displayed," the word being then synonymous with rabid fanaticism. A church bell cast during the eighteenth century bears the motto, " Hurrah for the Church of England and down with Enthusiasm."

The evangelistic preaching of John and Whitefield was effectively seconded by the many hymns of Charles ; and a reference to any standard hymn-book will show a number of his which are sung to-day after a lapse of nearly two hundred years. The eighteenth century was on the whole a prolific period in hymn-writing, and produced much sound work if little of outstanding power. Charles's son, Samuel, was a church composer of considerable merit. The campaigns of the evangelist fathers of Methodism parallel the apostolic labours of St Paul, especially as regards " in journeyings oft " ; neither the hardships of eighteenth-century travel, nor persecution—which included mob riots and bitter opposition by the upper classes—could prevent their evangelising, from the colliers of Newcastle to the Cornish miners. John Wesley died in harness in 1791 after fifty-three years' labourings, during which he had preached 42,400 sermons ; and his followers at his death numbered 500,000.

One little touch which shows the fame of John Wesley is seen in the number of china busts which are now extant of the preacher, dressed in black with white hair falling on his shoulders.

The brothers' chief associates ranged from John Nelson, stonemason, to Selina, Countess of Huntingdon, who built numerous chapels and founded Trevecka College, Wales, in association with Howell Harris ; later, Rowland Hill joined the movement. Warm supporters in the Church included John Berridge, who wrote his own epitaph :—

> Here lies the earthly remains of John Berridge, late
> Vicar of Everton, and an itinerant servant of Jesus Christ,

who loved his Master and his work, and after running on His errands many years was called to wait on Him above

and John Newton, the former naval cadet, seaman, and slave captain, Vicar of St Mary Woolnoth in the City, and later Rector of Olney, long associated with the poet William Cowper, whose dark melancholy he possibly intensified rather than lightened. The two collaborated on the " Olney Hymns," which include some current to-day. The chequered history of Newton's strange passionate soul may be followed in his Autobiography.

The *Evangelical Magazine* of 1807 quotes the testimony of an unfriendly naval officer on the " Victory," regarding " A set of fellows called Methodists " in that ship. " These men never wanted swearing at. The dogs were the best seamen on board." They had a separate mess and were allowed to be by themselves.

Few who pass the large drab church of St Bartholomew, Gray's Inn Road, realise that it was built as New Providence Chapel by William Huntington, S.S., a converted coal-heaver, the degree-like initials standing for " Sinner Saved." The revival under the Wesleys chiefly affected the peasants and labouring strata of society, but the upper and middle classes were greatly influenced by a work by Samuel Wilberforce in 1797, which drew a contrast between the usual religious practice current in high society and a vital, active Christian faith.

With a great proportion of the livings under £100 a year, the majority of the clergy had to do something to supplement their incomes, the more so as the bitterness of the anti-tithe feeling frequently led to their being cheated. Many were associated, as to-day, with schools and teaching; others farmed in various ways, and it is suggested that the baser sorts were not averse to a little poaching; as Squire Worthy says of Parson Hairbrain :—

>I often wished his neck he'd break
>Or tumble drunk into the lake.
>So you must know the poaching hound
>Fulfilled one wish, for he is drowned—
>Unfit for preaching or for praying
>His merit lay in cudgel-playing
>And he preferred to saying prayers
>The laying springes for the hares.

THE CASUAL PARSON

Crabbe limns the casual parson intent on a good time, and indifferent and neglectful of his flock :—

> A jovial youth, who thinks his Sunday's task
> As much as God or man can fairly ask ;
> The rest he gives to loves and labours light,
> To fields the morning, and to feasts the night ;
> None better skill'd the noisy pack to guide,
> To urge their chase, to cheer them or to chide ;
> A sportsman keen, he shoots through half the day,
> And, skill'd at whist, devotes the night to play.

Some of the clergy were addicted to drink ; others frequented alehouses or were habitués of the theatre, but many were ordinary good fellows enough, whose besetting weakness was, as Crabbe depicts, a timid servility towards anyone of an influential position. Many of the Church pastors,

FIG. 14.—" A pillar of the Church."
A caricature by Mathew Darly.

58 THE NAVY, THE ARMY AND THE CHURCH

however, lived lives of unflagging devotion and manifold service to their flocks, like the epitaph quoted in "Doctor Syntax":—

> "For fifty years the pastor trod
> The way commended by his God,
> For fifty years his flock he fed
> With the divine substantial bread.
> His wide, his hospitable door
> Was ever open to the poor.
> Thus, the commands of Heaven his Guide,
> He lived, and then in peace he died."

The greatest abuse in the Church was the system of holding a plurality of livings by an absentee vicar, who employed a curate at a meagre wage to carry out the duties of the cure; sometimes the bishops were tarred with the same brush. The hardships of the starveling curate and his bitter complaint are frequently sketched in contemporary literature, as in "The Tour of Doctor Syntax," and other works.

FIG. 15.—"The curate on a visit."
A caricature by Mathew Darly.

Of Church-preferment he had none,
Nay, all his hope of that was gone.
He felt that he content must be
With drudging in a curacy,
Indeed on ev'ry Sabbath-day,
Through eight long miles he took his way
To preach, to grumble and to pray;
To cheer the good, to warn the sinner,
And, if he got it, eat a dinner,
Thus were his weekly journeys made,
'Neath summer suns and wintry shade;
And all his gains, it did appear
Were only thirty pounds a year.

* * * * * *

E'en birch, the pedant master's boast,
Was so increas'd in worth and cost
That oft, prudentially beguiled
To save the rod, he spar'd the child.

—"Syntax," Canto I.

Nothing can be more mordant than this comment:—

Better, apprenticed to a humble trade,
Had he the cassock for the priesthood made,
Or thrown the shuttle, or the saddle shaped,
And all these pangs of feeling souls escaped.

Pity! a man so good, so mild, so meek,
At such an age, should have his bread to seek;
And all those rude and fierce attacks to dread,
That are more harrowing than the want of bread.

—Crabbe.

A curate remarks:—

Alas: Sir, I am no Vicar, I,
Bound to a humble curacy
With all my care can scarce contrive
To keep my family alive
While the fat rector can afford
To eat and drink like any Lord.

The curate requests that his pay may be raised by £10 a year, as he has now "children five," and his wife will shortly present him with another. The living is worth £1,000 a year, but the rector curtly refuses the suggestion, adding that "beggars should not dare to marry."

As the nineteenth century advanced, the Church felt the power of the religious awakening, and many philanthropic effects were seen, as in the foundation of missionary societies (Church Missionary Society, 1799, etc.), the establishment of Sunday Schools started by William Raikes (1725-1811), the strong feelings on the abolition of the slave trade and efforts towards the amelioration of the condition of prisoners.

PLATE XXXIII.

The Established Church.   St Mary's, Rotherhithe.
From a drawing by E. Dayes (1795).

"Enthusiasm displayed."   A print showing Whitefield Preaching in the Open Air.
After a painting by J. Griffiths.

PLATE XXXIV.

A View of Bradford in the Early Years of the Nineteenth Century. The Industrial Revolution has worked its transformation.

The germ of the Industrial Revolution. Watt's Workshop, now re-erected in the Science Museum, South Kensington.

CHAPTER IV

TRADES AND INDUSTRIES

So far we have discussed some aspects of Georgian social conditions. It now remains to give an account of the industries of the period, many of which were coming to depend much upon mechanical aid. We have noted in a previous chapter the invention of Hargreave's spinning jenny, Arkwright's water-frame, and Crompton's " Mule." The manufacture of cotton as a result of these inventions was increased to an enormous extent, and in turn gave rise to Cartwright's power loom, which enabled the weavers to cope adequately with the output of cotton. Steam power had been experimented with early in the century, when, for example, Newcomen had devised a steam pump for mining in 1705, but it was not until James Watt produced his beam-engine in 1768 that steam power was used for milling purposes. By the year 1775, in the North and the Midlands, rural England was beginning to respond to the newer forms of industry. The Duke of Bridgewater had concentrated on the canal between Manchester and Worsley, and later he embarked on that between Manchester and Liverpool. In this he was assisted by the inventive genius of the self-taught Brindley. Henceforth, thanks to these artificial waterways, there was an assured means of fairly rapid transport for the fuel necessary for steam power.

We have evidence of the expansion of industry in Wilkinson's ironworks at Bersham and the development of the collieries of Staffordshire, as well as in the foundries of Newcastle and Carron. Soon after this the industry of the collieries and the ironworks was augmented by the output of the textile factories of Lancashire and Yorkshire, until, within the short space of a quarter of a century, machinery was to change the whole aspect of ordinary life in the North and in the Midlands (see Plate xxxiv.).

At the beginning of the century, and up till 1770, the main industry was agriculture; the peasantry worked in the fields and the women worked at home, adding spinning and weaving to their ordinary domestic duties (Plate xxxv.).

Steam power changed all this. The wool-stapling industry of Devonshire and East Anglia now began to drift northwards. Among the workers there was an abrupt end of independence, and the factory system began with all its horrors of child labour, long hours and privation. To our eyes it appears strange that quite young children were working in coal-mines, rope works and textile factories. There was no time for schooling, and the lot of the workers was more wretched than that of the slaves of Maryland and Virginia.

A remarkable contrast is afforded between the England of the reign of Queen Anne, with its population of five and a half millions, and the increase of over nine millions during the reign of George III. Then came into existence those mean towns and houses contiguous to Manchester and Birmingham, and the collieries which are such disfigurements to-day. The tenements of the time were evils in themselves, huddled around diminutive courts and forming the sides of narrow streets in the towns which sprang up close to steam power. The working population of that time, in the main recruited from the countryside, was becoming less dependent on the ruling classes. In fact, beyond the mean surroundings where they lived and worked, they saw and knew little of the larger world.

Handwork in the industrial trades persisted side by side with the products of the machine—in fact, in many cases it was essential to the machine. For example, the wool-comber had to prepare wool ready for the making of worsted, and the methods followed were substantially those pursued from mediæval times. While the machine-driven loom was increasing production in the North, spinning was continued by women and children in the country villages (see Plate xxxv.). In summer-time the work went on out of doors. In Norfolk the distaff and spindle were still in use as late as 1815. The spinners were frequently employed by the master wool-combers, their task being to reduce silk, flax, hemp, wool and hair into thread. Another industry was basket-making (Plate xxxv.), which belonged to the marshy districts where osiers and sallows were plentiful. It was in the neighbourhood of Taunton that baskets, trays and all sorts of bird cages were made.

The Georgian hat-maker was a townsman, his material wool and the hair of the beaver, the rabbit or the camel. In the late eighteenth century both men and women were employed in the manufacture of beaver hats. Bristol was the chief centre, and the industry was carried on in the surrounding villages. Straw hats were made at Luton and Dunstable as well as in every large Bedfordshire village.

PLATE XXXV.

The Basket-maker and Cooper at Work.

Ropemaking.

Cottage Women making Lace and Spinning Flax.

Coppersmiths at work.

All drawn and etched by W. H. Pyne.

PLATE XXXVI.

A Printing House in the Mid-Eighteenth Century.

An Eighteenth-century Iron Forge.
From the mezzotint after Joseph Wright of Derby.

Fig. 16.—A Jeweller's Trade Card.

In the eighteenth century the small jeweller had his place in town life. In every sense of the word he was a working jeweller, as a typical trade card (Fig. 16) shows. Such craftsmen made rings, perfume and match boxes, buckles and the tops of canes, and carried out minor repairs to plate. During the American War, owing to slackness in trade, thousands of jewellers were thrown out of work. But as the volume of trinkets issued from the Birmingham factories increased, individual craftsmanship was checked.

Another trade which was then essential was that of the sawyer, who cut up timber for builders. This was a very laborious task, but it was comparatively lucrative. At the close of the century sawing-machines worked by steam were introduced into the Royal dockyards.

Smithery included the blacksmiths (Plate XXXVI.) and the whitesmiths or brightsmiths. Some smiths were skilful enough to undertake the hanging of church bells as well as the bells for houses, and others specialised in the trade of locksmithery. The Georgian blacksmith, however, did not confine his attention entirely to the shoeing of horses. He was frequently called upon to make hammered work, such as stair-rails, window-bars, torch-extinguishers, lamp-irons and other fitments. Some of the bolts and hinges in country buildings were made by blacksmiths who carried on a very old tradition, and in some parts of the country traditional craftsmanship still survives.[1]

In London a good many fire-grates were made at Brodie's, in Carey Street, by skilled smiths, and some of these stoves were listed at a hundred pounds. Nearly all the large furnishing ironmongers of the second half of the century kept a large stock of fire-grates, which were designed to suit the architectural fashion. The architect merely had to specify and the contractor to provide.

A very important trade was that of mercantile shipbuilding, which was the province of master shipwrights who employed quartermen to carry out the work on the slipway. One of the famous private shipyards was at Bucklers Hard, in Hampshire, and every port from Lymington to London (Deptford and then Blackwall), Harwich, Yarmouth, Hull and Newcastle had extensive shipyards. Shipbuilders of St Mary's in the Isles of Scilly were noted for the sailing qualities of their sloops and brigs. Naval architecture was regarded as an exact science, and its direction came from the Admiralty.

The business of the currier was to prepare hides for the

---

[1] This subject has been dealt with as a separate issue in another section of this work (*vide* p. 120).

SOAP, CANDLES AND DYEING

use of the shoemakers, coachmakers, saddlers and bookbinders. They used special Cirencester knives for the work. The craft was of recognised standing, the Curriers' Company having been incorporated in the reign of James I.

The Georgian apothecary was considered to be a superior sort of tradesman. He was called upon to attend to the sick and to prepare medicines either on his own judgment or to the prescription of a physician. An Act of 1712 exempted apothecaries from serving the offices of constable and other ward and parish duties, and they were further exempted from serving on juries. As the business of an apothecary was considered genteel, it was essential for a boy to have a good knowledge of Latin when he started his apprenticeship of eight years.

Soap-making and candle-making came under the restriction of the Excise Laws. Large fortunes were made by certain Georgian soap-boilers in a big way of business.

The business of the dyer seems to have centred in London. In 1790 there were, for instance, dyers of wool and of silk. Some dyers confined themselves to particular colours, such as scarlets and blues, the former being the most profitable. Yet another trade followed in London was type-founding, which was combined with letter-cutting. The later eighteenth-century printers ordered their founts by the ton, and as the work required skill, the volume of output will be appreciated.

As will have been gathered from other sections of this work, coach-making (Fig. 17) was one of the leading trades. There were both body-builders and carriage-makers. The Georgian carriage called for skilled

Fig. 17.—Georgian Coach-making.

craftsmen of all trades. There were the carpenters and the joiners to fashion the construction, which was chiefly of ash, the leather-workers to prepare the leather for the top, and the whitesmiths to provide the plated fittings. The inside of the coaches were lined with woollen cloth stuffed with horsehair. Private travelling carriages were lined with silk, velvet or dressed leather. In the reign of George III. the coachmakers designed and made chariots, landaus, berlins, gigs, curricles and tandems. One of the leading coach-makers was William Felton, who wrote a "Treatise on Carriages" in 1794. He appears to have specialised in gentlemen's chariots.

As we continue our investigation of the lesser trades we find the hairdressers (Plate xxxvii.) combining combing, shaving and blood-letting, together with hair-cutting and the making of wigs and braids. All through the Georgian period the barber was busy making perukes and wigs for men and women, as the illustration shows. There was a considerable trade in human hair for wigs, but the tax on hair-powder, which came into force in 1795, changed the fashion if it did not entirely abolish the artificial covering of the head. By the year 1820 ridicule was poured upon the fashions of the preceding century.

The Georgian comb-maker was in close touch with the barber, using horn, tortoiseshell and box or holly for his wares. In 1790 a factory was established at Camden Town by a man called Bundy, who obtained a patent for cutting combs by machinery. The Georgian comb was used solely for ornamenting the heads of women of fashion—real tortoiseshell was the most favoured, and the combs were frequently set with diamonds and other precious stones.

Lace-making was an industry reserved for the country, Devonshire, Buckinghamshire and Bedfordshire being the principal counties for its manufacture. This minor art had survived from late Tudor times.

In the cities the business of a milliner (Fig. 18) was a lucrative one. The fashions of London and Paris towards the end of the century were changing very rapidly. The business of the milliner was to make up hats, caps and bonnets, as well as cloaks, muffs and tippets. She was an artist in the treatment of feathers, artificial flowers, muslin, gauze, crapes and velvets. The effect of her handiwork is to be seen in the canvases of Reynolds, Gainsborough, Romney and Downman, so it will be agreed that the milliner played her part in shaping the delicacies of the social picture. The feather-workers (Plate xxxvii.) ranged from those who prepared the feathers

PLATE XXXVII.

"All through the Georgian period the barber was busy making perukes and wigs for men and women."

"The feather workers . . . trimmed ostrich feathers for court head-dresses."

PLATE XXXVIII

Late Eighteenth-century Shop Interiors. (*Above*) Hall's Library at Margate. (*Below*) A Furrier's Shop.

for beds to those who trimmed ostrich feathers for Court head-dresses.

Throughout the Georgian period the making of trunks, chests, portmanteaux and leather buckets gave employment to scores of craftsmen who had served a regular apprenticeship. Trunks suited for private carriages formed the chief output, then came bags for strapping on the backs of horses, strong boxes for the use of boys and girls going to boarding schools, and leather fire-buckets for houses—sometimes it happened that sixty leather buckets were ordered for one house. Leather was not always used for small cases. Some trunk-makers made a speciality of shagreen for what they termed "neat work." The shagreen of Georgian times was a kind of grained leather prepared from fish skin covered with bruised mustard seed, exposed to the weather and afterwards tanned. It was imported from Constantinople and was frequently coloured red, green or black. Its use was reserved for knife cases, instrument cases and the covers of pocket-books.

FIG. 18.—A Milliner's Trade Card of the Early Georgian Period.

In an age when wheeled carriages formed the chief means of transport, the business of the wheelwright was lucrative. In the towns the making of wheels for coaches and private carriages called for highly skilled labour. In the country the wheelwrights made farm-carts, wagons, barrows and sledges.

Brewing was regarded almost as an art. Every country was celebrated for a different kind of ale, and London porter was famous on the Continent. Even in those days inventions were in demand for improving plant, and it is not surprising to find the steam-engine introduced into breweries at the end of the century. Distilling forms a branch separate from brewing. One of the most famous distilleries in 1780 was in Holborn and was burnt by the Gordon rioters.

From these prosperous trades we turn to the makers of cutlery, who, after 1740, centred at Birmingham and Sheffield. London also had its cutlery manufacturers, but the practice gradually crept in of adding the names of the London firms to Birmingham and Sheffield goods.

Brick-making was another paying trade. This was carried on in the vicinity of the large towns, and as the streets were extended, so the brick-fields were moved farther out. Georgian London had its brick-fields at Pentonville, Bagnigge Wells, Paddington, Battersea, Lambeth, Bow, Kingsland and Highbury. The white bricks used by Robert Adam came from Woolpit in Suffolk.

So we pass to the trades of rope-making, sail-making and the weaving of list carpets for ordinary houses. The dressmakers were very numerous, and studied the fashions from France just as is the case to-day. In the fashionable quarters the mantua-maker employed many hands, but the ordinary dressmaker worked at home, and obtained orders through recommendations.

Pin-making was essentially an English industry. There were pin mills in various parts of the country, such as the famous one at Stroud, in Gloucestershire, but the London makers recovered most of the trade. Steel needles were also produced in London, but the finest came from Germany.

The paper-making industry was confined to country districts, the mills being placed near water. There is a late eighteenth-century paper mill at Water End near Hemel Hempstead, and others were at Enfield and Sittingbourne. The mills were always built near a stream to obtain power for the machinery. The end of the century saw the production of Whatman's drawing-paper, rough and hot-pressed, and at this time blotting-paper came into use. Much of the distinction of eighteenth-century printing is due to the fine quality of the paper.

Printing consisted of three kinds, *i.e.*, copper-plate printing for illustrations, from type set up by compositors, and from blocks for printing calicoes and cottons. Printing from type was carried out by hand, two pressmen being required to work each press (Plate xxxvi.). Calico-printing was introduced into London in the year 1676.

Another industry, tin-plate working, began in the late

The BOOK of
Common Prayer,
And Adminiſtration of the
SACRAMENTS,
AND OTHER

RITES and CEREMONIES

OF THE

CHURCH,
According to the Uſe of

The CHURCH of ENGLAND:

TOGETHER WITH THE

PSALTER
OR

PSALMS of DAVID,
Pointed as they are to be ſung or ſaid in Churches.

CAMBRIDGE,
Printed by JOHN BASKERVILLE, Printer to the Univerſity;
by whom they are ſold, and by B. DOD, Bookſeller,
in Ave-Mary Lane, London. M DCC LXI.

(*Price Eight Shillings and Six Pence, unbound.*)

FIG. 19.—This title-page, by John Baskerville, the celebrated printer, of a contemporary prayer-book shows what extraordinary diversity in design the craftsman could achieve by the judicious display of his type.

seventeenth century, but for some obscure reason tinned ware did not flourish, and it was not until 1740 that the trade was revived and brought to perfection. Examples of tinned ware of the Georgian period are not very plentiful even in museums to-day. From 1740 to 1820 the coppersmiths (Plate xxxv.) made kettles, saucepans, canisters, milk-pails, lanterns, candle-boxes and candlesticks. In 1795 the principal manufacturers in London were Jones & Taylor, who had a warehouse in Tottenham Court Road, and Howard's, in Old Street, St Luke's. In addition there were hundreds of smaller tradesmen who combined their trade with lamp-lighting. The large firms employed travellers to carry samples in saddle-bags from town to town, as well as drawings of tinned articles for domestic use, such as jelly-moulds and drinking utensils.

Colonel Magniac, the famous clockmaker of Clerkenwell, used tin for those exquisite figures which form part of his automatic clocks. One such figure in tin represents a clock pedlar carrying two miniature bracket clocks (Plate xx.). The figure is dressed in the costume of 1795, and is as perfect in its way as the most delicate china figures from Chelsea or Derby.

In the eighteenth century, tin-mining was a flourishing industry in Cornwall, the towns of Liskeard, Lostwithiel, Truro, Helston and Penzance being the centres for the coinage of tin. To Cornwall also belongs the credit of Trevithick's steam-engines and the early locomotive "Catch me who can," which was brought to London early in the nineteenth century, and formed the subject of one of Rowlandson's drawings.

The braziers and the coppersmiths were associated with Birmingham, and produced brass candlesticks, copper coal-scuttles, saucepans, lanterns, kettles, pails and fireplace-mounts. The furnishing ironmonger sold brass, tin and copper goods, besides keeping a stock of cutlery, fire-grates, and stoves. He was a retailer and not a manufacturer. Some of the Georgian brass and copper goods were beaten out with a hammer, and united in their several parts by solder. Others were cast, and these especially belong to the category of foundry goods.

Button-making was a British industry, and was protected by Act of Parliament; it was, in fact, unlawful to import buttons from abroad. Birmingham was the chief centre of the button-making industry.

Cabinetmakers ranged from the firms who had large ware-houses in St Paul's Churchyard, to those such as Chippendale, who had their shops in St Martin's Lane, or showrooms in Bond Street. At the end of the eighteenth century there was a famous furniture showroom in Tottenham Court Road.

The trade of a saddler was as important as that of the coachmaker and the wheelwright. The tree-maker furnished the wooden part of the saddle, the saddler's ironmonger furnished the steel stirrups, the bucklers, bits for bridles and the brass furniture for the harness—most of the latter articles were made wholesale at Birmingham. The horse milliner made roses for bridles and other ornaments. He was generally a man of some taste, whose task it was to arrange the "furniture" of a horse.

In addition to saddle-making the saddler made coach and chaise harness, bridles, reins, whips and traces. He employed a whole band of tradesmen, ranging from the leather-cutter, the currier and the embroiderer. He bought broadcloth woollens from the draper, velvet and silk from the mercer, gold and silver lace from the laceman and buckram and thread from the haberdasher. His trade, therefore, was a comprehensive one.

From the Restoration to the days of George IV. clock and watch making was a first-class industry. To the names of Tompion and Quare, the Avenells of Surrey, Colonel Magniac and Vulliamy, must be added thousands of lesser-known men whose productions were at one time world-famous. The industry gradually began to congregate in Clerkenwell and to attract foreigners as well as Englishmen. After the year 1740, clock parts were made at Birmingham, a special branch being dial-making. Cabinetmakers were called upon to provide the clock cases. The smaller town and country clockmakers soon began to give up active participation in the making of works for clocks and watches, their task being to assemble parts obtained elsewhere.

At the present time, when old English clocks are discovered in China, Japan, Turkey and America, some index to the vast export trade of the period is forthcoming.[1]

There can be no doubt that at the close of the century English clocks were the best in the world. The cases were the work of experienced cabinetmakers, the metal clock-faces were exquisitely worked, and the design of clocks, large and small, showed both restraint and dignity. The trade continued to flourish well into the nineteenth century, but it was suffered to decline, and eventually dwindled to a shadow of its old proportions.

[1] The subject of clock-making is almost inexhaustible and is best understood by a study of Britten's authoritative book.

The Architecture of Shops

It was Louis XIV. who first called the English a nation of shopkeepers, and judging by the number of shops in the main streets of London and other cities in the Georgian period, Napoleon had every right to revive the quotation. When we inspect the many examples of old shops which have survived, some for two hundred, and others for a hundred and fifty-odd years, we give little thought to the customs they represented. There are none of the shop fronts built in London soon after the Great Fire in existence to-day, neither can we point to many still extant of a date earlier than 1770, while even those of 1775 are surprisingly few. We are forced, therefore, to a study of old prints for the earlier examples, and to those of Adam's date and later which happily survive for the refined examples.

The shop fronts of London from the time of George I. to the beginning of the reign of George II. were generally closed from the street by a range of three or more sashed windows divided by uprights between each. At the end of the range of windows was the shop door, which was also glazed. The openings were spanned by a breastsummer of wood and one-storey post by the side of the door. Grooves were left in the window-sills for the shutters. The butchers' shops were left open, with the joints of meat exposed on a double row of hooks (Plate XXXIX). Another type had a projecting bulk which served to protect passengers and goods. Yet another example is forthcoming in the design of the Chelsea bun house, with its loggia and rails.

In the reign of George III. a reaction seems to have set in, favouring shop fronts of greater interest, a typical example being the front of Birch's[1] (Plate XXXIX.), the pastrycook's, in Cornhill. Then follow the fronts with double curvatures and central doors, as in those shown on Plate XL., or the famous example of Fribourg and Treyer's in the Haymarket. Lastly, there are such delightful Regency shops as those at Woburn, in Bedfordshire, and at Cheltenham.

In the early part of the century the shop was decorated by the immense signs of which we are reminded in Gay's "Trivia":

> Be sure observe the signs, for signs remain
> Like faithful landmarks to the Walking train.

Every shop, in lieu of a number, had a distinctive sign; some were of copper, others of pewter, and yet others of wood,

---

[1] Now in the Victoria and Albert Museum, Kensington.

PLATE XXXIX.

A particularly graceful Shop-front of the Later Eighteenth Century. "Birch's," in Cornhill (now removed to the Victoria and Albert Museum, London).

A Typical Open-fronted Butcher's Shop.
From a print by Henry Alken.

PLATE XL

Typical Georgian Shop-fronts.

painted and gilded. These signs were carried on wrought-iron brackets. Not only were the shops situated in the principal streets, but they flourished also in courts and passages. In the eighteenth century the city shopkeeper lived over his shop, but the practice crept in for a shopkeeper to imitate his social superiors and to have a small country box at Bow, Kennington or Islington, within sight of St Paul's, to which he could retire from Saturday to Monday.

To name a few varieties of shops, there were booksellers

Fig. 20.—" The Macaroni Print Shop."
A caricature by Mathew Darly.

and publishers (Plate XXXVIII., *above*), printsellers (Fig. 20), brasiers, confectioners, tea-dealers, grocers, carpenters, chemists, chimney-sweepers, china and glass sellers, shoemakers, ready-made clothes shops, artists' colourmen, engine-makers, picture-frame makers, goldsmiths, basket-makers, haberdashers, hat-makers, sedan-chair makers, optical instrument makers, lamp-makers, drapers, silk mercers, perfumers, wig-makers, razor-makers, chandlers, trunk-makers, saddlers, undertakers, etc. From a study of contemporary prints, as well as from those delightful examples of old shops which have survived, it is possible to gather accurate details of the setting in which domestic trading flourished.

CHAPTER V

SPORT, PASTIME AND RECREATION

THE earlier portion of the eighteenth century reveals surprisingly few books devoted to the sport and pastimes of the period, and it is necessary to consult novels, paintings and sporting prints to gather information on the subject. By the end of the century, however, sporting books had become the fashion, and sport had ceased to be solely a privilege of the upper classes. Here the information available is varied and almost unlimited.

In the period under review, hunting and racing formed the chief survivals of the sports of the Middle Ages, the latter in some degree taking the place of the mediæval tournament. Horse-racing as the "sport of kings," with Newmarket as its chief centre, dates from the early seventeenth century. Discontinued during the period of the Civil War and Commonwealth, racing was revived during the reign of Charles II., who liked the sport, and has continued uninterruptedly, increasing in popularity up to the present day.

Among the common people in the early years of the century there were few sporting diversions beyond the ordinary village amusements and local traditional games and dances, trials of strength and feats of pedestrianism. The holding of statute fairs in towns and villages, and the local assizes, were the only events that drew the people together in masses. Sports that were to develop to quite large proportions, such as the cockpit, wrestling and the ring, date from the days of Queen Anne, and doubtless had their origin in local country amusements. Bear and bull baiting were among the more reprehensible forms of sport which attracted the crowd.

Hunting the fox was the prerogative of the landed gentry, while the mediæval severity of the game laws created poachers by the hundred. Fishing (Plate XLIII.) was a sport for quieter, studious men in the tradition of Walton, and fowling (Plate XLI.) was pursued with due regard to economy in powder and shot, and with an eye to the stocking of the larder. The rougher sports, such as football, cricket or cudgel-playing, were not viewed with

PLATE XLI.

"The hunt in its scarlet coats, pushing across stream and forest heath, following the hounds in full cry."

From a print by Sartorius (1795).

Shooting.

From a print by Alken after Howitt (1784).

PLATE XLII

Coursing with Greyhounds.
From a print by Alken after Howitt.

Gamekeepers.
From an engraving after Stubbs.

Fig. 21.—Billiards was a somewhat elegant pastime, as the dresses of the players show in this contemporary engraving.

favour by men of breeding, while the more exquisite regarded even hunting as a trifle arduous. A gentleman of fashion usually found his time fully occupied by the politer accomplishments of dancing, fencing and elegant horsemanship. Lord Chesterfield wrote to his godson : " Eat as much game as you please, but I hope you will never kill any yourself ; and, indeed, I think you are above any of these rustick, illiberal sports of guns, dogs and horses, which characterise our English Bumpkin Country Gentlemen."

The man-about-town in early Georgian times had certainly scant respect for the country gentleman, who, at the same time, was contented enough with his own small world and found plenty to occupy his energies throughout the year. He could amuse himself with racing, hunting, coursing, shooting or fishing as he pleased. Each of these sports was followed in season ; each produced definite codes, special breeds of horses and dogs, and customs peculiar to it. The mediæval sports had almost completely disappeared, though hawking was still carried on early in the century with conservative enthusiasm by Sir John Sebright and the Duke of St Albans, Grand Falconer of England ; while the illustration (Fig. 22) shows duck-hawking being carried on quite late in the century. Archery was practically dormant, and only reintroduced as a graceful pastime for ladies at the close of the century (Plate XLIII.).

Fig. 22.—Duck-hawking. A somewhat prosaic survival of the ancient sport.

Horse-racing attracted larger and larger crowds as the century advanced, the principal meetings being at Newmarket, Epsom, Ascot, Heath and Doncaster. Winter was the season for hunting, coursing and shooting, and the fox-chase remained the principal national sport—a sport that was considered thoroughly worthy of a gentleman. Sir Robert Walpole used to find the chase at Houghton a pleasant interlude from the cares and intrigues of his administration; for here was a sport that not only gave a man pleasure and an appetite, but also demanded skill in horsemanship and skill to outwit the artfulness of the fox. Clergymen would sometimes wear their hunting-boots in the pulpit, ready at a moment's notice to finish off the sermon, doff their cassocks, and leave their congregations behind, to hunt a hare.

For the average man of substance in the country, hunting was indeed often regarded as the principal object in life. And these huntsmen were a hardy breed. Rowlandson and his school have depicted the hunt in its scarlet coats, pushing across stream and forest heath, following the hounds in full cry (Plate XLI.). This later period (1780-1800) was indeed the heyday of fox-hunting, George III., himself a keen huntsman, giving the lead to his subjects. For Londoners, an occasional Cockney hunt,

FIG. 23.—Partridge-netting.

FIG. 24.—Otter-hunting.

such as the famous annual meeting in Epping Forest, had to suffice. There were others at Muswell Hill and Enfield Chase; for in those days there was real country reaching to the extremities of the growing streets of Bloomsbury and Mayfair. We read of the chief porter at the Middle Temple blowing a horn to recall the young gentlemen to their studies from rabbit-coursing on Lambeth Marshes.

Those who preferred shooting had to make the best of flint-lock guns, and a man had to be a dead shot to secure even a respectable bag with such a weapon. Extraordinarily elaborate systems of traps and springs were used to outwit poachers, and sharp justice was dealt to those who were discovered contravening the game laws. Bloody affrays with keepers were commonly followed by hangings or a sentence to the hulks. The world went well in those hard-fisted times for those sportsmen who governed. And as a class they were hardly remarkable for refinement or polished manners. The average squire visited London only if he held a seat in Parliament. His conversation was of agriculture, horses and live stock, with, of course, the eternal topic of hunting. After administering justice to poachers and others in the Hall, he would inspect his stables and kennels, dealing out praise or abuse to his ostlers, grooms and keepers. Groups of the gentry would arrange weekly

FIG. 25.—" The tippling squire."
A caricature by Mathew Darly.

PLATE XLIII.

Bowls.

Quoits.

Skittles.

Angling.

Archery.

All drawn and etched by W. H. Pyne.

PLATE XLIV.

Stag-hunting.
From an engraving by Alken after Howitt.

Breaking-in and Training Horses.

dinners, at which they feasted heavily, drank more than copiously, and discussed the usual topics with a spice of politics (Plate XLV.). For literary recreation there was Daniel's "Rural Sports," but generally, after a hard day in the saddle, a heavy meal and a bottle, a man was content to be strummed to sleep by the ladies of the family with pleasant, simple tunes on an ancient harpsichord or small, flat piano. Barrel-organs were often substituted if there was no competent executant. While every squire possessed a library, the books were seldom consulted beyond their titles, for intellectual recreations were apt to pall before the pleasures of a hard day out of doors and somnolent relaxation before a great wood fire in the evenings.

Contests with pointers and setters between rural parties were a common recreation among neighbouring landowners and their friends, and bets were laid on the result. Betting also often accompanied partridge or game shooting, wagers being laid on the number of winged game which could be killed between sunrise and sunset. Using a flint-lock gun, the marksman had to judge correctly and fire well ahead of rising game, so that the element of chance was very great. It is on record that Coke of Holkham, in 1801, killed as many as 726 partridges in five days.

It is important to comprehend the working of the game laws during the period. The Caroline Statute authorised the keeping of gamekeepers (Plate XLII.), and prohibited all persons under the rank of the heir apparent of an esquire, or not holding lands to the value of £100 per annum or leaseholds to the value of £150 per annum, from keeping dogs and shooting weapons on their premises. Thus a series of statutes, over a period of three hundred and seventeen years, transferred the right to kill game into the privilege of an ill-defined class.

The game itself could not be sold. If a man was not an unqualified freeholder, he was not permitted to kill the game on his own land, neither could anyone else do so without the owner's leave. As a consequence, an uneven quantity of game accumulated in the coverts of woods and plantations which naturally attracted the attention of poachers. Man-traps and steel guns were set to catch them, and affrays between keepers and poachers often enough ended in maiming and death.

The laws urged the destruction of the fox as a pest, but this was not encouraged by the squirearchy, who did its best to preserve the animal for foxhunting. Those with the temerity to snare or kill a fox could claim a reward from the parish, such being paid by the churchwardens. But there were few among the farmers or peasantry who dared to face the wrath of a whole coterie of foxhunting squires.

Another sport much favoured by the country gentry was that of greyhound-coursing (**Plate XLII.**). Hares were employed as the prey in the eighteenth century, though the sport had originated in mediæval times in the coursing of game and deer by dogs, not by scent but by sight. Rules had, in fact, been drawn up for its practice in the reign of Queen Elizabeth by the Duke of Norfolk.

In 1776 Lord Orford founded a coursing club at Swaffham, in Norfolk. The number of its members was limited to the number of letters in the alphabet, and each member's dog was named after the initial letter that he bore in the club. When a member died or retired his place was filled by ballot. This club was superseded by the Ashdown Park Club, and presently other courses were instituted, notably at Amesbury, Stockbridge, Newmarket, and Longton in Cumberland. This was an exceedingly select pastime which must have seemed thrilling enough to its participants, for in 1791 Lord Orford was brought to such a pitch of excitement by the victory of his famous dog Czarian, already the victor of forty-seven races, that he fell from his pony and died.

The rougher and often more disgusting amusements were also popular, such as cockfighting, sparring matches, bull and bear baiting, ratting and so on. There was also plenty of scope for feats of horsemanship, and matches were often arranged between rival parties. We read of amateur sporting events being carried out on the King's highway for substantial stakes, and one such, described in the *Gentleman's Magazine* for 1756, describes a race between a nobleman and a gentleman in the army, which entailed the walking of five geese and five turkeys from Norwich Market to Mile End Turnpike, " that person to win who brings in most cattle alive to the turnpike." This was evidently the match alluded to by Horace Walpole, who wrote : " My Lord Rockingham and my nephew, Lord Orford, have made a match for five hundred pounds between five turkies and five geese to run from Norwich to London. Don't you believe in the transmigration of souls ? And are you not convinced that the race is between Marquis Sardanapalus and Earl Heliogabalus ? "

As the century advanced we find women of the higher grades of society beginning to enter the sporting lists. The caricatures of Sayer and Carrington Bowles form a commentary on the latest sporting tendencies, and those such as " The Sporting Lady " (1776) and " Miss Wicket and Miss Trigger," with its

PLATE XLV.

"Groups of the gentry would arrange weekly dinners at which they feasted heavily and drank more than copiously."

From a print by Rowlandson.

Ascot Races.

From a print by Sartorius.

PLATE XLVI.

Street Football in Barnet.

Playing at Fives in the Tennis Court in Leicester Fields.

Both from contemporary prints.

doggerel couplet : " Miss Trigger you see is an excellent shot, and forty-five notches Miss Wicket's just got," are well known. The drawing by Rowlandson, reproduced on Plate XLVII., also shows a cricket match between " ladies." Another tendency that we find reflected in the caricature of the period is that of speeding (Fig. 26), one of the delights of the macaronies. The machine most favoured was the cabriolet. Horace Walpole, writing to Mann in 1755, says : " All we hear from France is that a new madness reigns there as strong as that of Pantinsious. This is *la fureur des Cabriolets; Anglais,* one-horse chaises, a mode introduced by Mr Child (brother of Lord Tilney) ; they not only universally go in them but wear them ; that is, everything is to be *en cabriolet* ; the men paint them on their waistcoats and have them embroidered for clocks on their stockings ; and the women,

FIG. 26.—" Speeding " at Newmarket.

who have gone all the winter without anything on their heads, are now muffled up in great caps, with round sides, in the form of, and scarce less than, the wheels of chaises." This craze for light, lofty and spidery vehicles seems to have dominated the minds of all who could afford the luxury. Prints of the fashionable London squares of the time nearly always depict one or more of them. Small wonder that Sir Geoffrey Gigg was imitated by the shopmen of Cheapside who spent their savings on hiring similar vehicles to go driving in on Sundays. On these days the roads to Richmond, Windsor, Greenwich and Hampstead were choked with a crowd of gigs, phaetons and curricles ; though it is interesting to remember that the running of stage coaches was prohibited on the Sabbath.

Besides driving into the country, the Londoner could avail himself of the river if he was minded to row a boat ; and contests like that for " Dogget's Coat and Badge " were a popular diversion. Of the rougher sports we are able to gain a good enough idea from Hogarth's engravings executed about halfway through the century. One of the most famous of these, the Cockpit (Plate XLVIII.), published in 1759, shows the scene accurately depicted from life with a rather savage realism, including the penalty of the basket, which was one of the actual rules. Bear and bull baiting and dog-fighting were also carried on, one of the most famous meeting places being Hockley in the Hole, Clerkenwell; here also were held disgusting fights between women, and bruising matches between butchers and porters.

While sports and pastimes in the country proceeded on time-honoured lines, excitement and diversity were demanded by the more exacting population of London. Great national events, State trials, and executions, of course, brought out the people in their masses. The appearance of the celebrated Lunardi in his balloon in 1784 (Fig. 27) was long remembered, and commemorated in innumerable prints. The intrepid aeronaut made his first ascent from the grounds of the Honourable Artillery Company in City Road on 17th September of that year. His balloon measured 30 feet in diameter, and was provided with a car and a parachute. He proposed to direct the course of the balloon by means of paddles, and the services of Dr Fordyce, a famous chemist, were enlisted to direct the filling of the envelope. The recipe for the "rarefied air" included zinc, oil of vitriol, and steel shavings. The event is chiefly interesting for the fact

FIG. 27.—Lunardi's Balloon Ascent in 1784.
A contemporary print.

that the greatest assembly of people ever known to have attended a sporting occasion gathered to watch it. The number is said to have approached nearly two hundred thousand, including a party from Carlton House. It must be conceded, however, that Lunardi's paddle wings were a failure. By good fortune the aeronaut rose to a great height, and landed safely in the fields near Ware. Afterwards his balloon was exhibited under the dome of the Pantheon in Oxford Street.

Horse-racing

This great sport has already been touched upon. In 1640 the first important races took place at Newmarket, although previously James I. had built stables then near his palace. The most reputable races throughout the kingdom were those known as "Bell Courses," from the fact that the winning horses were awarded a bell. The Chester meeting is probably the most ancient of all. There, in 1610, the customary prize of a silver bell was changed into one of three cups, the event being known as "St George's Race."

Horse-racing in this country undoubtedly owes its rise in the national favour to the patronage of the Stuart kings. Charles II. was a devotee of the sport, and deemed it no hardship to ride to Newmarket, where Sir Christopher Wren had built a house for the royal use. When in residence at Windsor he was a familiar figure on Datchett Mead. In those days, of course, the horse was essential for purposes of communication, and the breed had to be continually improved for speed and stamina. By the year 1700 the breeds of English horses were famous throughout Europe. This was partly due to importations of foreign stock and partly to the observance of various old statutes regulating the breeding of horses in general.

From the time of the Stuarts to the coming of the Hanoverians, royal patronage continued to be extended to horse-racing. William of Orange and Queen Anne showed their interest by adding new plates to be competed for, and though it is difficult to imagine Queen Anne keeping a stud of race-horses to be run in her own name, she actually did so from a desire to keep alive a tradition of the Stuarts. Neither of the first two Georges appear to have manifested much interest in the sport, and it was left for Frederick, Prince of Wales, to re-establish royal patronage. Prince George, afterwards George IV., owned his own race-horses as early as 1789. This famous stud had to be sold on account of his debts, but Parliament came to the rescue and increased the Prince's allowance, thereby enabling him to return to the turf.

In the days of Queen Anne, Newmarket races took the prior place in the public estimation. There were also important meetings at Stapleton Leys, in Yorkshire, and at Langton Wolds and Black Hambleton in the same county. Ascot races were inaugurated in 1713 (Plate XLV.), Epsom in 1703, and the Derby stakes in 1780. The famous St Leger sweepstakes were instituted by Colonel St Leger in 1776. Steeplechasing can be traced back to the year 1752, the sport first originating from the feats of dare-devil riders in Ireland. In England it first took the form of matches between groups of the country gentry for more or less nominal stakes, the principal object being to test the prowess of rival horses. Some convenient point on the landscape, such as a church steeple, was taken as the post for a ride across the fields, over ditches, hedges, walls and streams. More than fifty years elapsed before steeplechasing developed into a popular spectacle for watching crowds.

Between the years 1750 and 1758 the Jockey Club came into being. At this time, rules were laid down for racing, the most important being that all riders had to pass the scales when they came in, under pain of disqualification. The season for horse-racing began at the end of March and lasted until the end of November.

With so rapid an increase in the popularity of racing it was natural that large sums should be staked on the results of races. Bookmaking grew increasingly common amongst turf enthusiasts, but it was not until one William Ogden made it a regular business in 1793 that it took its place as a recognised profession. The betting-book at Brooks's, which dates from the founding of the Club in 1775, contains the names of many famous men who were, apparently, ready to make wagers with their friends on almost any pretext.

Ball Games

Bowling.—This is another eighteenth-century pastime of extremely ancient origin. William Fitzstephen mentions it as early as the twelfth century, and in the fifteenth and sixteenth centuries it was much played in the alleys of London. At one time it was thought that its popularity would interfere with the practice of archery, and so it was forbidden for a period. Henry VIII. used to play the game of bowls at Hampton Court, and there is, of course, the well-known story of Sir Francis Drake on Plymouth Hoe.

In the eighteenth century the bowling-green was a favourite resort for men of fashion. The game of skittles, or ninepins, was played indoors. There are few skittle-alleys left in this country, though the author has seen one at Tetbury, in Gloucestershire, but many old bowling-greens still remain. The jack was first thrown to the end of the green, the object being for the players to roll their balls as near as they could to it. This was a quiet sport for steady citizens, who flocked in their leisure time to the bowling-greens or skittle-alleys as the mood or the season took them (Plate XLIII.). In London there has been a bowling-green at Hoxton since the days of Queen Anne.

Football.—Football-playing in the Strand is commented upon by various eighteenth-century authors. Stubbs, for instance, refers to it as a " bloody and murthering practice rather than a fellowy sport or pastime," while foreigners seem to have regarded it as a particularly brutal game. D'Avenant's Frenchman satirises the English habit of always choosing what would seem especially unfavourable localities for playing it (see Plate XLVI.). " I would now make a safe retreat," he is made to say, " but that methinks I am stopped by one of your heroic games, called foot-ball ; which I conceive (under your favour) not very conveniently civil in the streets ; especially in such irregular and narrow roads as Crooked Lane. Yet it argues your courage, much like your military pastime of throwing at Cocks. But your mettle would be more magnified (since you have allowed these two valient exercises in the streets) to draw your archers from Finsbury, and during high market let them shoot at in Cheapside."

Still the game went on. In the early part of the eighteenth century, Gay, in his " Trivia," records :

> The printer quits his shop to join the crew ;
> Increasing crowds the flying game pursue.

Football day was often celebrated in small towns and villages, notably Teddington, Twickenham, Bushey or Hampton Wick. Then all windows overlooking the green were secured from the ground to the roof, some by placing bundles before them and some by nailing laths across the frames. The proceedings opened by a procession with the football carried in front, while the collectors begged money from door to door. There were several parties, each having a ball. The game lasted four hours, during which time the shops were shuttered though the taverns remained open. The game was legally continued till the middle of the nineteenth century, and at Dorking, on Shrove Tuesdays, until quite recent times. Mention must also be made of the river football games of the North Country.

In Scotland, in the parish of Scone, Perth, a game was played every Shrove Tuesday between the married men and bachelors of the town, from two o'clock in the afternoon until sunset. The game was this : he who at any time got the ball into his hands ran with it until overtaken by one of the opposite party ; and then if he could shake himself loose from those on the opposite side who seized him, he ran on ; if not, he threw the ball from him, unless it was wrested from him by the other party, but no person was allowed to kick it. The object of the married men was to " hang " it, that is, to hit it three times into a round hole in the moor, which was the " dool," or limit, on the one hand. That of the bachelors was to " drown " it, or dip it three times in a deep place in the river, the limit on the other. The party able to effect one of these objects won the game, and if neither won, the ball was cut into equal parts at sunset. In the course of the play there was usually some violence between the parties. The local proverb : " All is fair at the ball of Scone," covered all foul play.

At Bury St Edmunds on Shrove Tuesday, Easter Monday and Whitsuntide, a game of trap and ball was played by twelve old women, six a side. The game ended at sunset. In many towns, at Easter and Whitsuntide, the Corporations would go out before the townsmen to play ball. For example, the mayor, aldermen and sheriffs of Newcastle-on-Tyne, with a great number of the burgesses, went yearly to the Forth, or little wall of the town, with the hoop, sword and cap of maintenance carried before them, and patronised the playing at hand-ball, dancing and other amusements of the populace, sometimes joining in at the ball play or joining hands with the women at the dance.

Fives (Plate XLVI.) is an old form of hand-tennis, and, as such, a very ancient game. The most famous player of the late eighteenth century was one John Cavanagh, who frequented the fives courts at Copenhagen House. The four best racket players of whom there is record were Jack Spires, Jem Harding, Armitage and Church. In the Fleet and the King's Bench prisons, fives formed almost the only exercise taken by the debtors. It differed very considerably from the hand-fives now played in special narrow courts.

Cricket is another sport whose origin is lost in history. The Saxons had a game called " Creag " that was played with a bent wooden bat. This game persisted into the Middle Ages. In Phillip's " Mysteries of Love and Eloquence," published in 1695, the game is alluded to, and an old writer in 1640 states that " Maidstone was formerly a very prophane town, inasmuch that before 1640 I have seen morris dancing, cudgel playing, stool-ball, cricket and many other sports openly and publickly on the Lord's Day."

The earliest writers on the game, Nyren, Lambert and Pyecroft, reveal how different the original game was from that in practice to-day. *The Postman* for 24th July 1705 notices that "A Cricket match will be plaid between eleven gentlemen of the west part of Kent and those of Chatham for eleven guineas a man." Six years later Kent played all England. *The Evening Post*, 7th August 1729, states : " On Tuesday was played a cricket match on Kennington Common between the Londoners and the Dartford men for a considerable sum of money, wagers and Betts, and the latter beat the former very much."

In 1735 two teams were brought together by the Prince of Wales and the Earl of Middlesex for a bet of £1000. In 1746 Kent again played all England. This was an exciting match which the county won by a wicket. There are also records that Surrey played all England in 1747, and of a match between Surrey and Kent in 1773 in which the former was victorious by thirty-five runs. From now on county cricket was an established practice.

About 1750 the Hambledon Club was formed, the first of its kind. It had grounds on Broad Halfpenny and Windmill Downs, and here modern cricket was brought into being by such famous players as David Harris and William Beldham. In 1774 definite rules were first laid down for the game and the first written statutes drawn up. In the early days of cricket only two stumps, rather widely spaced, had been used, but towards the close of the century three stumps were introduced. The size of the bat was also limited, the early bats having been of any size to suit the players' convenience, and bowed like a club (see Plate XLVII.). The score was formerly kept by cutting notches in a stick, one for each run.

In 1791 the Hambledon Club was disbanded and its place taken by the Marylebone Club, which had come into existence in 1789, its first ground being in Dorset Square, Marylebone. In 1814 the ground of Thomas Lord in St John's Wood was taken over, and exists to the present day as Lord's Cricket Ground.

Golf.—The royal and ancient game of golf, which in the first place was derived from the Dutch, found ready acceptance in Scotland before the middle of the fifteenth century. James I. is held to have been the first royal person to play it in England,

and the oldest of all golf clubs, the Royal Blackheath, was founded in 1608. Charles I. was a golfer, as was also Charles II., but the game was never generally played in the eighteenth century, and remained to be rediscovered in the nineteenth.

There is, however, an amusing account by Carlyle of Inveresk of a day's sport in Garrick's garden at Twickenham. "Garrick," he writes, "was so friendly to John Horne that he gave a dinner to his friends and companions at his house at Hampton which he did but seldom. He told us to bring golf clubs and balls that we might play at the game on Molesey Hurst. We accordingly set out in good time, six of us in a landau. As we passed through Kensington, the Coldstream regiment was changing guard, and on seeing our clubs they gave us three cheers in honour of a diversion peculiar to Scotland. Garrick met us half way, so impatient he seemed for our company.

". . . Immediately after we arrived, we crossed the river to the golfing ground which was very good. None of the company could play but John Horne and myself, and Parson Black from Aberdeen. . . . Having observed a green mound in the garden opposite the archway, I said to our landlord that while the servants were preparing the collation in the Temple, I would surprise him with a stroke at the golf, as I should drive a ball through his archway into the Thames once in three strokes. I had measured the distance with my eye in walking about the garden, and accordingly, at the second stroke, made the ball alight in the mouth of the gateway and roll down the green slope into the river. This was so dexterous that he was quite surprised and begged the club of me by which such a feat had been performed. We passed an agreeable afternoon, and it is hard to say which were the happier, the landlord and landlady or the guests."

Boxing

Boxing first comes into notice in this country in the early part of the eighteenth century when James Fry, the Oxford Professor, opened the first boxing booth in London in 1719. During the reigns of the Georges it continually increased in popularity.

The gloves were first introduced by Jack Broughton, and were called "mufflers." Broughton also drew up the first set of rules, and the appearance of the first of the great champions, Tom Johnson, did much to swell the increasing public interest. The great matches were generally held in the open country (see Plate XLIX.), spectators coming quite considerable distances to watch the sport. Of course in these matches the mufflers were not used, and the formidable champions would inflict quite

PLATE XLVII.

Cricket with the Old Curved Bat.
From an old painting at Lord's Cricket Ground.

A "Ladies'" Cricket Match.
From an original cartoon by Rowlandson at Lord's Cricket Ground.

PLATE XLVIII.

Bull-running at Stamford.
From a contemporary painting.

The Interior of a Cockpit.
From an engraving by Cook after Hogarth.

The penalty of the "basket" is shown in the shadow of the unfortunate individual so suspended who is offering his watch to anyone who will haul him down.

severe injuries upon each other with their bare fists. The victor would receive a substantial purse.

At the close of the century boxing became an exceedingly popular and fashionable sport in which many of the younger bucks of the Regency were exceedingly proficient. Boxing and hard driving were, indeed, often enough their favourite occupations, and such redoubtable champions as "Gentleman" Jackson, Mendoza the Jew, Jem Belcher, Humphreys, Tom Cribb, Spring and Dutch Sam drew large and fashionable crowds. Gloves for public contests were not introduced till the next century, when the Queensberry Rules were drawn up.

The Barbarous Sports

Many of the popular sporting diversions of the eighteenth century were, to modern eyes, exceedingly brutal. Cock-fighting, to which reference has already been made, is a case in point. Our first knowledge of it dates from the reign of Henry I., when specially bred and trained cocks were pitted against each other to fight to the death. In Tudor times Henry VIII. built the famous Cockpit at Whitehall, while under the Stuarts it continued as a royal diversion. It was, however, opposed by the Puritans and suppressed by Cromwell. By the beginning of the eighteenth century it was an extremely popular amusement in town and country.

The cockpits were usually circular (see Plate XLVIII.), and about 20 feet in diameter. They consisted of a stage covered with matting, and circled by a barrier round which the audience stood. Every town in the kingdom had at least one pit, and the larger cities three or four. In London the best known were in Westminster, Drury Lane, Jewin Street, Birdcage Walk, Pall Mall, the Haymarket and Covent Garden.

The usual form of the combat was that in which an agreed number of pairs of birds fought together, the final result being decided by the majority of victories on the one side or the other. The "battle royal" was the most important and popular display. Here a number of birds were set upon each other, and left to fight till all but one were killed.

A cock was not fought until it had attained two years of age, being trained by diet and exercise for a month previous to the fight. Then it was carefully trimmed, and steel spurs, from 1 to $2\frac{1}{2}$ inches in length, were attached by leather shackles to the heels

Cock-throwing was closely allied to cock-fighting. Here the birds were first placed in a pit, and staves or short sticks were thrown at them with the object of breaking their legs or knocking them out. There is abundant evidence that throwing at cocks took place in all parts of the kingdom on Shrove Tuesday, even children and schoolboys taking a part in this cruel pastime.

Another practice was to put a cock in an earthenware vessel, made for the purpose, in such a manner that only his head and tail were exposed to view. The vessel with the bird in it was then suspended about 12 or 14 feet from the ground to be thrown at by those who cared to try their skill. Twopence was usually charged for five throws, and he who broke the pot and delivered the cock from his confinement kept him as a reward.

Another engaging sport was to place a duck in a pond and loose several dogs on it. This is the origin of the "Dog and Duck" signs to be found on old inns. A ducking-pond was, indeed, the usual adjunct of taverns, especially in the vicinity of London. Persons came with their dogs, paid a small fee for admission, and were considered the chief patrons and supporters of the pond. Spectators paid a double fee.

Dog-fighting and pigeon-shooting were also popular. The fights were between trained bulldogs, and were largely patronised by the nobility and gentry at the close of the century, when enormous sums were paid for prize dogs.

As regards bull and bear baiting the following extracts speak for themselves :—

> The bear and badger are baited with the same barbarity ; and if the rabble can get nothing else, they will divert themselves by worrying cats to death . . .

and at Stamford in 1780 [1] :—

> The butchers of the town, at their own expense, purchased a wild bull ; the bull was stabled for the night in a barn belonging to the aldermen. The next morning proclamation was made by the common bellman of the town that all shop doors and gates be closed. At the same time the townsfolk were warned that as the town was a great thoroughfare to the north, none were to do harm to strangers. A guard was appointed for the passing of all travellers through the same. The rules read : None to have any iron upon their bull clubs or other staff which they pursue the bull with ; which proclamation made, and the gates all shut up, the bull is turned out of the aldermen's barn, and then, hivy skivy, tag rag, men, women and

---

[1] The illustration on Plate XLVIII. is from a contemporary painting of bull-running at Stamford.

children, of all sorts and sizes, with all the dogs in the town, promiscuously running after him with their bull clubs.

This bull-running was considered a jolly sport.

> A ragged troop of boys and girls
> Do pellow him with stones,
> With clubs, with whips and many nibs
> They part his skin from bones.

The disgusting brutality of this is obvious to any normal mind at the present day. At Wokingham the bull-baiting took place yearly on the 21st of December, and the custom survived as late as 1835. The bull was purchased each year in accordance with the will of one George Stavetton who died in 1661.

Rural Amusements and Fairs

The reaping and harvesting of the wheat was attended with many ancient customs. At the close of each day's labour, for instance, a small sheaf was bound up and set upon the top of one of the ridges of the fields. The reapers then retired to a certain distance, and each threw his reap-hook at the sheaf until one struck it down. This achieved, the field would resound with cheers and huzzas, and the party would retire to the farm-house for supper.

Another rural sport was called the "Mazes." A path was drawn on the sward of the village-green and defined on each side by a narrow trench, a few inches in width. The competitors who entered the mazes were required to run through all its intricacies carefully, to avoid stepping across the trench, and to arrive at the central goal in a time specified by the judges.

Dancing was a popular country pastime. Many villages had their maypoles on the green, and here, on May Day, country dances of ancient origin would take place round it. Indoor dances and assemblies also took place from time to time, as shown in the accompanying illustration (Fig. 28).

Newly-married couples were "trashed" or pelted with old shoes on their return from church, while "sowbelling" was an uproarious method of public reproof adopted by the neighbours of a man and wife accustomed to domestic strife. "Riding the Skimmington" (Plate XLIX.) was a representation in a drawn cart of a wife beating her husband with a long basting-handle, enacted before the doors of known husband or wife beaters.

There is little space here to deal with the innumerable traditional sports, pastimes and customs of the English country-

FIG. 28.—" The Village Assembly."
By Mathew Darly.

FIG. 29.—A Country Amusement. Grinning through a horse collar for a flitch of bacon.

PLATE XLIX.

"Riding the Skimmington." The Quarrelsome Husband and Wife are represented by the Couple on the Donkey.

From an illustration to " Syntax " by Rowlandson.

A Milling Match between Cribb and Molyneux; the Knock-out.

From a drawing by Rowlandson.

The Edmonton Statute Fair.
From a drawing by John Nixon in the Victoria and Albert Museum, London.

PLATE L.

side in the eighteenth century. It was, generally speaking, a calm enough life for those contented to stay on the land and not to seek fortune in the towns. The fairs were the great annual events that brought the country men and women together in their thousands, and every district could boast of at least one of these. Their catalogue would be endless, but mention should be made of some of the most famous, such as Brough Hill Cattle Fair, in Westmorland, of which Gray has left us a description, the Sheep Fair at Finden in Sussex, the Goose Fair at Nottingham, and Weyhills Fair in Surrey, noted for its sheep, hops and cheese.

Servants were hired at Michaelmas in each year at what were known as "Statee," or Statute Fairs, also called Mop Fairs.

These were held in the market square or principal street of villages and country towns (see Plate L.). The servants were chosen on the spot, and no testimonials or characters were either given or required. Emblems of calling were worn in the hatbands — for instance, ploughboys would wear a whipcord, shepherds a lock of wool, milkboys a tuft of cow's hair, while auctioneers would carry ink horns. Masters and mistresses inspected and questioned the candidates, and the hiring would conclude at noon when the church bells rang. Such persons as were hired were presented by their employers with a small sum of money which they spent at the booths either in frolics or in purchases of clothes and useful articles. A fortnight later, a second or supplementary fair was held in the same localities for the convenience of masters and servants who had in the interval failed to suit each other and equally desired exchanges.

London Pleasures and Pastimes

London has always been celebrated for its beautiful parks, and in the eighteenth century these were as popular as they are to-day. Swift was fond of taking exercise in them, but was apprehensive of the activities of the Mohochs, or sets of wild young gentlemen who played pranks of a rather extreme kind on innocent pedestrians. This writer records in 1711 : " Delicate walking weather, and the Canal and Rosamund's Pond full of the rabble, sliding and with skaits, if you know what that is." St James's Park was, indeed, a great resort of skaters when the weather ordained this favourite sport. It was also one of the recognised beauty spots of London, as, indeed, it is to-day ; and a contemporary writer speaks of " the irregularity of the trees, the rise of the ground and the venerable Abbey affording great entertainment to the contemplative eye." Rosamund's Pond, incidentally, earned a ghastly reputation for suicides.

Other popular places of semi-rustic entertainment were Belsize House, on the road to Hampstead, a floating coffee-house on the Thames, the Folly House at Blackwall and the White Conduit House. The most interesting of these was, perhaps, Belsize House, a stately seventeenth-century manor, with a large park and handsome gardens. In addition it commanded a magnificent view of London, from which it was separated by undulating meadowlands and scattered dairy farms. An advertisement of 1720 states that " the park, wilderness and gardens have been wonderfully improved and filled with a variety of birds which compose a most melodious and delightsome harmony. Every morning at seven o'clock the music begins to play and continues the whole day through; and any persons inclined to walk and divert themselves in the morning may as cheaply breakfast there, on tea or coffee, as in their own chambers." A regular series of coaches plied between Belsize and Hampstead at a charge of sixpence for each passenger. For the security of the guests, the management provided an escort of twelve stout fellows, fully armed, to prevent attacks by highwaymen or footpads. For a time Belsize was a centre of fashion, and the Prince and Princess of Wales often dined there; but its decline, once started, was rapid. The armed escort had to be increased to thirty, and the innocent amusements of hunting, fishing and dancing gave place to gambling and vice.

Eighteenth-century London was a continuous bustle of business and gaiety. Public spectacles, such as visits of royalty to the City, thanksgiving services in St Paul's Cathedral for victories, such as that on 7th September 1709, when Queen Anne drove in state to St Paul's to give thanks for the victory of Blenheim, drew vast crowds. On 1st May 1707 there was a day of public rejoicing for the Union of England with Scotland, which ended with the pealing of bells, bonfires, illuminations and a good deal of tipsiness. Such gala days were common throughout the period.

The Lord Mayor's Show was, as to-day, a popular spectacle for the masses. The windows above the shops in Cheapside would be literally stuck with faces and, at night, balconies and window-sashes were filled with lighted candles. The show itself included artillerymen, marching two by two, burlesqued in buff and bandoliers, and pageant spectacles following the chariots of the civic dignitaries. The huge crowd was interspersed with pickpockets, prostitutes, thieves and every sort of harpy eager to prey on the crowd, and a mass of excited children and apprentices added to the confusion.

Other popular spectacles were, of course, the fairs at St Bartholomew's (which later became such a source of scandal that an end had to be put to them), Mayfair and Southwark. In the vicinity of the great inns at Smithfield and Southwark were shows for the poorer classes, and here freaks of every sort, dwarfs, fat women, Indian chiefs, and so-called "wild men" were marshalled for the public entertainment. Here also were posture-makers and acrobats, jugglers, quack doctors and gipsy fortune-tellers. The waxwork exhibition became popular in the reign of Queen Anne, and one such show was that kept by a Mrs Salmon, a view of which, showing the sign of the fish indicative of the lady's name, is given in the accompanying illustration (Fig. 30). The waxworks at Westminster Abbey, lifelike representation of the English kings and queens, were also considered a great sight, and those in search of an afternoon's amusement could go to laugh at the lunatics at Bedlam, or visit the Royal Menagerie at the Tower.

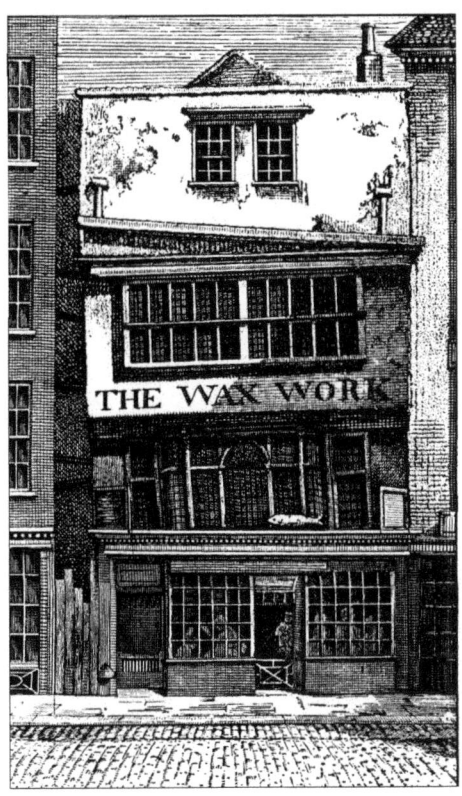

FIG. 30.—Mrs Salmon's Fleet Street Waxwork Show.

From an engraving by J. T. Smith.

London, indeed, though its vicious and squalid aspects were always apparent, was a gay enough city in the eighteenth century, and those who had the time or the money could find a hundred ways of diverting themselves according to their taste. We to-day who have our " amusements " served up to us by mass-production methods and our curfew prescribed by civic vigilance, can have nothing but envy for our ancestors for the good time they undoubtedly had, and some of us at least would sacrifice a good many modern improvements and systems for a measure of this care-free, intimate, individual spirit in the pursuit of pleasure at the present day.

Fig. 31.—Inigo Jones.   *G. H. Birch*, del.

CHAPTER VI

THE ARCHITECTURAL BACKGROUND

The classic phase of English building begins with the introduction of academic forms by Inigo Jones. Jones was brought into contact with contemporary Italian art, particularly the middle phases, during a visit to Italy where he studied the buildings of Rome and Vicenza, became acquainted with Serlio and Maderna, and finally based his style on the academic manner of Palladio and Peruzzi. The completion of the Banqueting Hall at Whitehall from his designs established a style in England more advanced than that in vogue in any other country except Italy. The façade is Palladian, and has classical orders in two storeys, a flat balustraded roof and an entablature broken about the supports. His other academic designs include the church of St Paul's, Covent Garden, with its free standing portico, the portico to old St Paul's, and the Queen's House at Greenwich. The design of the first of the official works at Greenwich, drawn by John Webb, also shows regard for Maderna's work at St Peter's, Rome. Recent inquiry has shown that many buildings long attributed to Jones are not from his hand.

Until the Restoration, the work of Jones remained in a class by itself. The appearance of Sir Christopher Wren, a distinguished mathematician, whose architectural training was partly spontaneous, marks the next development in English building. Wren's interest in architecture began with the study of books and developed during a six-months' visit to Paris, which coincided with Bernini's reception at the Court of Louis XIV. His work represents a compromise between the mediæval, the academic and the baroque. At the time of the Restoration a Dutch influence permeated the whole of the English crafts, and it is now obvious that Wren recoursed to Vingboom and other Dutch authors for ideas relative to the treatment of brick and stone in his lesser works. Particularly in his towers and spires, usually in Portland stone, he shows a happy inclination towards originality and a remarkable gift for variety of treatment.

Wren was also familiar with architectural books published in Italy and France, probably through his friend John Evelyn; and the library at Trinity College, Cambridge, bears in its exterior a striking affinity to Sansovino's at St Mark's, Venice. The design for the monument commemorating the Great Fire was based on the Trajan Column, and the façade of St Paul's was influenced by that of Sta Agnese at Rome. He quickly gained power as a designer, and his most important commission was for the building of St Paul's Cathedral. His first plan, based on an octagonal form, with a great central area, was an idea too advanced for a clergy steeped in conservatism or even mediæval in trend; hence the substitution of the cruciform plan. He retained, however, the theory of a domed structure in his final design, following the two-storeyed scheme then in vogue for Italian churches. Thus the design of St Paul's is both academic and baroque. It is based upon a mediæval plan, and represents more than any other building the spirit of compromise that was typical of the age.

In the work of his contemporary, Vanbrugh, the tendency towards the academic mingled with the baroque is seen in an even greater degree. In his designs for Castle Howard (Plate LI.) and Blenheim Palace, the scale of the rooms and employment of giant orders enhanced the daring originality of the component masses. The skyline of his buildings follows baroque custom, while the composition of the masses is more or less academic.

The Georgian period opened with the supremacy of the Palladian school, and the whole culture of the times favoured academic classicism. The fashion of the " Grand Tour " among the wealthy classes helped to establish a new coterie, the amateurs, who busied themselves forming theories for the direction of architects. The foremost of these was Lord

PLATE LI.

Castle Howard, Yorkshire (1714), by Sir John Vanbrugh.
From the water-colour by J. C. Buckler in the collection of Mrs Mango.

Houghton Hall, Norfolk (1723). Colin Campbell, architect.
(The interior design is attributed to William Kent.)

PLATE LII.

The Central Court at Somerset House   Sir William Chambers, architect.
From the aquatint by Thomas Malton.

The "Four Courts," Dublin, by Gandon.
From the aquatint by James Malton.

Burlington, who purchased Palladio's drawings and assisted the publication of books on classical architecture. The extent of this nobleman's influence can be judged from the careers of the men who were fortunate enough to secure his patronage. All of them, including William Kent, Colin Campbell and Leoni, had profound respect for the theories of Palladio, and made every effort to revive the taste started almost a century earlier by Inigo Jones. As evidence of the reaction from the school of Wren, there is old Burlington House, by Campbell, which was strictly Palladian, Holkham and Houghton (Plate LI.) in Norfolk, by William Kent and Colin Campbell respectively, and Devonshire House in Piccadilly (lately demolished), by Kent. Lord Burlington's predilection for Palladio's designs is shown in his villa at Chiswick. It followed as a natural corollary that, in an age of private palace-building, the free-standing portico, adapted from Palladio, should become a standard feature in design.

The academic simplicity of Palladio's work exactly suited the temperament of the Georgian age. Its exploitation by the early Georgian architects put an end to the free treatment favoured by Vanbrugh and Hawksmoor, and established a purity of surface which would not tolerate the application of such extraneous decoration as trophies and swags. In this restraint and love of pure composition in balanced lines, English architecture of the eighteenth century was ahead of its time, and at a much later period probably had its share of influence in the reaction of French and German architects towards more restrained forms.

But as the century proceeded, this taste changed more and more in the direction of an exact repetition of classical forms and compositions. Architects began to approach the antique directly, instead of through the works of the Italians. The fashion of decorating wall surfaces with orders and pilasters gave way to the introduction of columns which stood free and formed part of the structural system. Masonry became more precise as the passion for surface developed, and such classic forms as the rectangular temple and the circular Pantheon were referred to for a variety of buildings ranging from churches to the halls of banks. This change in favour of academic classicism was a gradual one that began with the adoption of Roman motives and ended with the use of Greek.

In the works of the brothers Adam we see evidence of the renewed stimulus given to architectural design by this frank adaptation of Roman forms. These architects not only introduced free-standing columns, but drew from their notebooks

Fig. 32.—" The Antique Architect."
A caricature by Mathew Darly.

every feature of antiquity that had caught their eye during their Italian tours. Here is explanation of the coffered vaults, niches and low reliefs which occur constantly in their designs, even for the interior of quite small houses. This passion for classicism extended to furniture and ceramics (especially to those of Wedgwood) : it is to be traced in the design of fireplaces and even in sedan-chairs. In Italy, Piranesi had been at work making his imaginative renderings on copper of old Rome, and Stuart and Revett had ventured to Athens, but it was the Adam brothers who brought these various influences together in the style they introduced.

Meanwhile, notwithstanding the influx of Roman and Greek ideas obtained direct from the fount-head, Palladianism, in a modified form, persisted from the time of William Kent to the days when Nash evolved his stuccoed conventions for London street architecture. The strongest bias, however, was always towards Roman detail. Social conditions during the second half of the century were also beginning to affect the design of buildings. It was realised that architecture could not always be in accordance with precedent, although such a policy might apply to detail. Hence a tradition grew up which admitted of a differentiation of character for buildings intended for administrative purposes.

We have briefly reviewed two great phases of Georgian architecture, those of church and of private palace-building. Apart from Wren's official buildings, the only one worthy of note and erected for commercial purposes had been the original Bank of England, built by Sampson. To England belongs the credit for one of the earliest, as well as one of the finest, of modern Government structures. In the design of Somerset House (Plate LII.) Sir William Chambers correlated all the previous tendencies as well as incorporating ideas from contemporary work in France. The interior is rather a rabbit-warren, as shown in H. M. Bateman's amusing series of the man who tried to get a document stamped. He evolved a new type of bureaucratic office which had its counterparts in Dublin in the " Four Courts " (Plate LII.) and the Customs House. This new type gave stimulus to the character of every Government building subsequently erected.

Many other types of buildings were evolved by the consolidation and progress of the age. Architects were learning how to adapt the monumental features of classical art and at the same time to express scholarship without pedantry. For example, Dance the younger, in his design for Newgate Jail (Plate LIII.), attained a remarkably dramatic effect by the massive dignity of blank walls, and a similar treatment was employed in the docks and warehouses then being erected in the Port of London. Sir John Soane, perhaps one of the most original of the late Georgian architects, adopted the same free treatment of masonry combined with columns, when he remodelled the earlier works of Sampson and Sir Robert Taylor at the Bank of England. Again, the late eighteenth-century theatre demanded a new treatment, and this was splendidly met by Henry Holland, who improved on the earlier design of Robert Adam at Drury Lane Theatre. The solution of the problem in the theatre was to erect a rectangular building with a stage and horseshoe galleries, and to reserve the classical features for the vestibules and main staircases. More attention was given to the suitability of plans to the purpose of the building, and here an excellent case in point is the small Town Hall at Bury St Edmunds (Plate LIII.).

But the architects and craftsmen who interpreted such designs knew better than to dispense altogether with a tradition that had become pliant. A reaction had now set in against literal classicism. Architects were beginning to cultivate a more cosmopolitan outlook, and Sir William Chambers was looking towards France, favouring in particular the designs of Gabriel. Henry Holland, also, had come under the French influence, and there ensued, as a result of this change of attitude, a reaction in favour of the more reasonable employment of classical motives.

The full force of the Greek revival was not apparent until the close of the century, and followed on the researches of English archæologists. Greek orders and details were introduced into the composition of designs which were partly the result of the new conditions of planning and partly a blend of the old Palladian style. Soane was the chief exponent of this new method, and such men as Wilkins, Hamilton and Playfair brought it to its fulfilment.

Town Planning

In no other characteristic is eighteenth-century architecture displayed to fuller advantage than in the unified planning of the streets and squares of cities and towns. The tradition was originated in this country by Inigo Jones, who designed Covent Garden as a piazza surrounded by open arcades with a church on the west side. This was followed by the building of Lincoln's Inn Fields, which gave the western extremity of London something of the appearance of a continental town. The plan prepared by Wren for the rebuilding of London after the Great Fire was based on a principle then popular in France, but considered by the citizens of London too radical an encroachment on their ancient rights to be adopted. Wren's ordinances, however, drawn up by the architect for the rebuilding of the individual streets of houses, aided the movement in favour of regularity, and it was due to his influence that the unified streets of Queen Anne's time became a feature of London and other cities.

It was due also to the far-sighted policy of the landed proprietors in London that, at a later period, the Georgian squares and streets, which mark the progress of the city in a westerly direction, were erected on dignified lines. The system of creating ground-rents and leaving the administration of the

PLATE LIII.

Old Newgate Jail, by Dance the younger.

The Town Hall, Bury St Edmunds. Reconstructed by Robert Adam, 1775.

PLATE LIV.

Queen Square, Bloomsbury.

From an old drawing (circ. 1820).

Cavendish Square. Notice the contemporary vehicles.

From an aquatint by Thomas Malton.

estate to a body of stewards also proved highly successful from the financial point of view.

The first growth of regularly planned streets, squares and alleys that appeared in London following the Great Fire includes among others Clifford's Inn, built in 1666; Jermyn Street, 1667; Norfolk Street, 1682; Bloomsbury Square, 1680; Grosvenor Street, 1695; Great Marlborough Street, 1698; Hanover Square, 1718; Queen Anne's Gate, 1705; Red Lion Square, 1698; Craig's Court, 1702; Barton Street and Cowley Street, Westminster, 1722; Golden Square, 1699 (Fig. 33); Great Ormond Street, 1709; Queen Square, Bloomsbury,

FIG. 33.—An Early View of Golden Square (1699).

1704 (Plate LIV.); Soho Square, 1681; St James's Square, 1680; Lincoln's Inn, New Square, 1698. Purely Georgian developments include: George Street and Hanover Square, 1718-19; Cavendish Square, 1717-18 (Plate LIV.); Manchester Square, 1750; Portman Square, 1764; Bedford Square, 1769; Portland Place, 1778; Charlotte Street, 1763-77. Finally we come to Russell Square, 1805, and Regent's Park, Regent Street, and the Metropolitan Improvements of 1820.

During the middle Georgian period the best examples of town-planning are to be seen outside London—for example, at Bath, where the work of John Wood includes streets, squares, terraces and crescents treated with admirable success in the academic manner (see Plate VIII.). Architects and landowners at this period had come thoroughly to realise the value of unification in town-planning, and among the many instances that occur can be mentioned the work of Carr of York, of Leroux at Southampton, and of Robert Mylne in the neighbourhood of London. The desire for order and regularity apparent in the additions to London extended to Bristol, Clifton, Edinburgh, Dublin, Liverpool and Exeter, besides a score of places well outside the metropolitan influence. That the system had become highly developed by the time of the Napoleonic wars is evident in the character of the crescents, paragons and quadrants of the seaside and inland watering-places then becoming popular.

In this movement for the development of towns on ordered and regular lines we encounter further evidence of the revolt against the crowded streets and tenements of the seventeenth century, an attitude that coincides with the rise of the middle classes. The Georgians had learned to delight in the vista. Houses grouped in sequence to give the effect of a large palace, and spacious gardens, replaced the narrow crowded streets of a century earlier, and lent a dignity and elegance to the late Georgian town that, despite the efforts of Victorian eclecticism, in many places survives to the present day.

Country Mansions

House-building of the eighteenth century can be grouped in two distinct categories, those of the great houses and the lesser, in town and country. The reign of George I. inaugurated a period of vast activity in the building of large mansions by the ruling and wealthy classes. Conditions of life in the great houses had changed considerably since the days of Elizabeth, when the mediæval custom of the entire household dining in hall was still maintained. Family life was more exclusive, servants were kept at a distance, and even the family chaplain, when asked to dine, left the table with the serving of the pudding. The classic designing now in vogue relegated the servants to the basement, and sent them to bed in attic dormitories behind pediments or tall parapets.

A vast pile of building became the focal centre of a landscape which was trimmed and disposed like a picture by Claude; and the position of mansion, gardens and park-land can be seen to full advantage in the contemporary engravings of Kip and others. Never since the days of Wolsey had persons of rank dared approach so near to royal state. It was fashionable to emulate the "French state" of the reign of Louis XIV., and, indeed, Ralph, Lord Montague, had his house at Boughton in Northamptonshire built in imitation of the stables at Versailles. When this house was built, comfort and convenience were sacrificed to a splendid and dignified external effect and to spacious state apartments, while the fact that the bedrooms all led one into another was apparently not considered to matter.

Such houses, with their lengthy and draughty corridors, could be occupied in comfort only for a short time every year. The company of servants needed to keep them in order, from the steward to the porter, numbered two score, which accounts for the gradual falling into disuse of many of these vast buildings. But their compensating attractions are impossible to deny. The splendour of their interiors, the large marble chimney-pieces, the panelling of the walls, the moulded plaster-work of the ceilings, the mythological paintings forming an airy canopy above gilt chandeliers, the rich needlework and tapestries bring home to us the magnificence of the rich nobleman's estate at this period. But it is open to doubt whether these great houses were ever fully occupied. Travelling was difficult, and guests could not be obtained at a moment's notice. A little reluctantly we are forced to the conclusion that some of the rooms at least needed occupants.

In the design of Chatsworth in Derbyshire, which Talman built for the first Duke of Devonshire, is to be seen an early example of an order applied to a rectangular block. At Easton Neston in Northamptonshire, by Hawksmoor, the plan of the closed-avenue type recalls the centre part of the entrance front at Versailles. This design, though altered by demolition, has also something in common with the lay-out of Blenheim, whilst the use of the giant order shows how Hawksmoor thought with Vanbrugh. Lord Burlington's villa at Chiswick, both in plan and elevation, closely follows Palladio's villa at Vicenza, though in comparison with the urbane design of the latter it has something of the appearance of a public building. Two enormous piles built by Vanbrugh, Castle Howard in Yorkshire (Plate LI.) and Blenheim Palace—which latter was conceived as a national memorial to Marlborough's triumphant campaigns—were only equalled in magnificence by the river front of Greenwich Hospital. The key to such compositions is to be found in the arrangement of the plan, which was conceived not for convenience, but solely to produce a dignified lay-out of masses.

But with Blenheim the desire for houses built on such a

phenomenal scale began to decline, and Pope's satirical pen may have helped to change opinion. The effect of such houses did not end with the main building, with its curved screen walls, its entrance gate and dependent buildings. The houses were so great that the owners, if they wished to take in the elevations in their entirety, had to retire to pavilions built specially for the purpose. The views from the windows had to be considered, if only to relieve dullness from within, hence the Palladian bridges in the grounds, the obelisks terminating vistas, the gigantic vases in pedestals, and the garden pavilions such as that built by

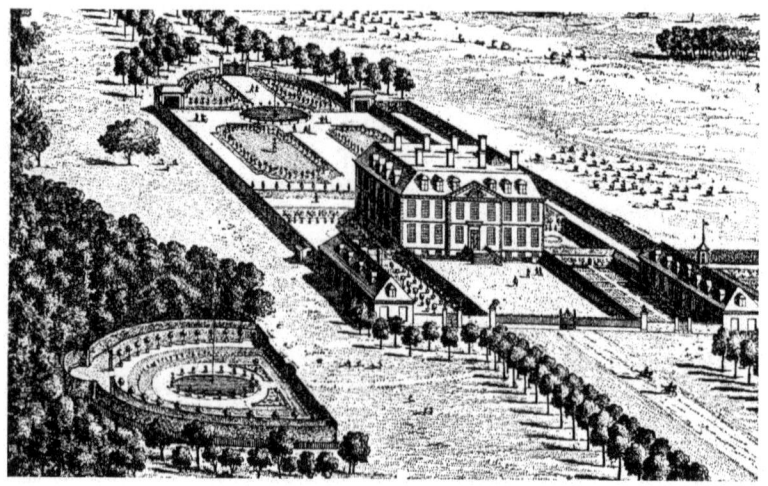

Fig. 34.—Stansted, Sussex. The House and Garden.
After Kip.

Archer at Wrest, large enough to house a family. Such effects are well illustrated in the bird's-eye view, by Kip, of Stansted, Sussex, shown on Fig. 34. The patrons of the first quarter of the eighteenth century certainly provided amazing scope for architectural magnificence, and men like Vanbrugh could indulge their fancy freely at the expense of their clients.

How the lay-out of the grounds contributed to such schemes is exemplified by the gardens and groves at Stowe. Before the days of "Capability" Brown, the lay-outs were always formal, with great walks and vistas over miles of country. The view from the west front at Woburn, for example, seems to extend half across the county. It is difficult, however, to equal in attraction the trim scenery at Stowe, and the accompanying

PLATE LV.

Gorhambury, St Albans. Sir Robert Taylor, architect.

A Small House at Swaffham, Cambridge (*circ.* 1754).

PLATE LVI.

A House, formerly at Denmark Hill, London (*circ.* 1740).
From an original water-colour by J. C. Buckler.

Spencer House, St James's Park, by Vardy.

engraving by Jean Rigaud (Fig. 35) shows but a small section of that elaborately planned estate.

One of the finest of the lesser mansions of the period is Warbrook in Hampshire, built for himself by the architect John James. Here is a design of reasonable size combined with a dignified garden of not more than twenty acres. James introduced a long canal and diagonal vistas into the scheme, and the influence of his predecessors, Vanbrugh and Hawksmoor, can be traced. Such moderate conceptions are of no less

FIG. 35.—View of the Queen's Theatre from the Rotunda at Stowe House.
From the engraving by Rigaud.

interest to us to-day than the more pretentious lay-outs very difficult now to maintain.

As the century proceeded, large houses continued to be built and old ones to be adapted. Anthony in Cornwall and Weston Underwood in Buckinghamshire are two excellent examples by James Gibbs. Other outstanding examples are Wrotham Park, near Barnet, a large mansion built of Portland stone by Isaac Ware ; Prior Park, at Bath, by Wood ; Wardour Castle by Paine ; Gorhambury (Plate LV.) by Sir Robert Taylor ; Kedleston by James Paine and Robert Adam ; and Southill by Henry Holland. All of these, though they can be classified as large houses, are of reasonable scale and conveniently planned.

Town Mansions

At the end of the reign of Queen Anne, London could show a number of mansions that, in point of size, could rival many country seats. Among these were Clarendon House and the first Burlington House, both in Piccadilly, Buckingham House (Fig. 36), at the west end of St James's Park, Montague House in Bloomsbury (Fig. 37), and Leicester House in Leicester Fields. In addition there were Monmouth House in Soho Square, said to have been designed by Wren; Marlborough House, built in 1709 on ground leased to the Duchess of Marlborough by the

Fig. 36.—Buckingham House, St James's Park.
From an engraving by John Harris.

Queen, also designed by Wren, and Newcastle House in Lincoln's Inn Fields. Side by side with these imposing private residences were the older buildings which had survived from the days of Elizabeth and the first of the Stuarts.

With the rise of the powerful Whig families came an increased stimulus to the building of great mansions in town. The taste for classical houses on the Italian model was already apparent, and the revival of interest in the works of Inigo Jones, brought about by the publication of Kent's book and Colin Campbell's " Vitruvius Britannicus," was soon expressed in terms of brick and stone. There is no better evidence of the wealth and power of the nobility of the time than the series of splendid mansions which now began to spring up on the fringes of old London. Among these was Devonshire House, built on the site of old

Berkely House, designed by Hugh May in 1665. The property passed to the Duke of Devonshire, and the house was rebuilt by Kent in 1733. As originally planned, the house was entered by an external staircase which led direct to the hall on the first floor, which was given over entirely to state apartments. The bedrooms were small, and occupied the whole of the second floor, while the basement storey held the offices and rooms for the servants. Although little of the house could be seen from Piccadilly, Kent arranged a scenic composition for the benefit

FIG. 37.—Old Montague House (the site of the British Museum).
From an engraving by James Simon.

of the owner within the severe screen wall. On one side were the stables and on the other the kitchens, both blocks being connected to the main building by quadrant curvatures. In an age accustomed to architectural display the plainness of the elevations caused considerable criticism.

Another town house of interest is Burlington House, as reconstructed for Richard, third Earl of Burlington, by Colin Campbell. The scheme included the casing of the old brick fabric with stone, and the general extent of this is visible in the front facing on the courtyard. Walpole writes of this nobleman : " Never was protection and great wealth more generously and more judiciously diffused than by this great person, who had every quality of a genius and artist except envy." Both Pope and Gay were among the friends of this talented amateur, of whom the former wrote :—

> You show us Rome was generous, not profuse,
> And pompous buildings once were things of use.

While Gay addressed the Earl in an epistle which begins :—

> While you, my Lord, bid stately piles ascend.

Chesterfield House was built in 1749 by Isaac Ware for the Earl of Chesterfield, a concrete instance of that nobleman's desire for elegance. Other examples include Norfolk House in St James's Square, by the elder Brettingham, and the neighbouring Spencer House (Plate LVI.) by Vardy, which faces the Green Park. From such excellent models the architects who succeeded Gibbs, Kent, Ware and Vardy could not widely depart, though Robert Adam, at Lansdowne House, evolved a new type of plan, and James Stuart, at Portman House, introduced detail of Greek origin. But for the remainder of the century the large town house inherited such essential features as a suite of state apartments, an imposing entrance hall and staircase, and a noble, if severe, exterior elevation.

Many provincial towns contain counterparts of smaller size to these London mansions, and it was often the custom of the nobility to spend some weeks in winter in the town nearest their country seats. In such towns as Bath, Truro, Bury St Edmunds, Salisbury, York and Stamford can be seen houses which, while far from unwieldy, have an air of spaciousness out of the ordinary.

SMALLER TOWN HOUSES

Excellent examples of the smaller town architecture remain— to the present day, or at least to recent times—to us in the old streets of London, such as Hatton Garden, Bedford Row, Queen Anne's Gate, Queen Square, Great Ormond Street (Plate LVII.), and Barton Street, Westminster. Prior to the building of Lincoln's Inn Fields, as first designed by Inigo Jones, and the noble Piazza at Covent Garden, town houses of the lesser sort were built side by side. In the second half of the century the practice of building houses in terraces became common. This system, based on Wren's method, had been adopted by the Woods for the Royal Crescent and other parts of Bath, and was continued in Edinburgh by the Adam brothers. It found its ultimate expression in the development of Portland Place and the streets and squares between there and the Edgware Road. This led to the final treatment of Nash and his successors, when

PLATE LVII.

Town Houses of the Early Eighteenth Century. (*Left*) Schomberg House, Pall Mall (*circ.* 1700). (*Right*) A House in Great Ormond Street, now demolished (*circ.* 1720).

PLATE LVIII.

Nelson House, Devonport (1775). An excellent example of a Devonshire slate-hung house.

A Monumental Composition of the Regency Period, faced in Stucco. The entrance to Chester Terrace, Regent's Park, London. John Nash, architect.

was evolved a fresh version of the eighteenth-century manner which for convenience can be termed " Regency."

It will be seen that throughout the century there was a desire always evident for regularity and order in the outward appearance of the streets. Surface differences there might be, but the principle of houses in rectangular blocks, relieved in some cases by applied embellishments, was continued from first to last. Regent's Park is a case in point. Here are immense compositions designed to give the effect of single palaces, and each made up of twenty or more houses (see Plate LVIII.) ; and at convenient points there are large town houses on isolated sites. In the same category can be placed the terraces of Clifton, the vast squares and tall houses of Dublin which, with the buildings of Weymouth and Margate, belong to the close of the Georgian period.

Reverting to the early years of the century, lesser houses erected in London from 1666 to 1720 almost always show traces of Dutch influence, a case in point being Schomberg House, Pall Mall, built about 1700 (Plate LVII.). They are best described by referring to an advertisement of the reign of Queen Anne which runs :—

> To be Let, a New Brick House, Built after the Newest Fashion, the Rooms wainscotted and Painted, Lofty Stories, Marble Foot paces to the Chimneys, Sash Windows, glaised with fine Crown Glass, large half Pace Stairs, that 2 people may go up on a Breast, in a new pleasant Court planted with Vines, Jesamin and other Greens, next door to the Crown near the Sarazen's Head Inn in Carter Lane, near St Paul's Church Yard, London.

Another advertisement of the year 1712 refers to a house and shop. It reads :—

> To be Lett, near Cheapside, a large new-built House that fronts two Streets of Great Trade : The shop is lined with Deal all round, and is about 60 Foot deep one way. There is under the Shop a very good dry Warehouse that is brickt at Bottom. Joyce and boarded over it, the Sides and Top is lined with Deal, it is 9 foot between Floor and Top. There is above Stairs 4 Rooms on a Floor, almost all Wainscotted, and a large Staircase all Wainscotted. All the Flat is covered with very thick Lead, with Rails and Bannisters round the Leads and a Large Cupolo on the Top. Inquire of Mr Richard Wright at the Periwig in Bread Street.

There is a house of practically similar design at Bury St Edmunds in Suffolk, which is complete to the cupola. Defoe stayed in this house, and must have found the panelled interiors very similar to those in his own small house at Stoke Newington. Similar examples, often with ornamental features of Dutch origin, can be seen at Exeter, King's Lynn and Ipswich. It is evident that throughout the country the whole system of proportioning the smaller type of houses was based on the provisions for rebuilding the city embodied in an order made by the Lord Mayor, Aldermen and Common Council of the City of London in May 1667. Here is evidence of Wren's masterly organisation. He it was who advised on and drew up the table for the "first, second and third sort of houses." In a measure, Wren seems to have been anticipating the arrival of the " middling sort of people."

Fig. 38.—The Elevation of a Small House at Stamford, Lincolnshire.

Between the years 1720 and 1760 the character of the elevations of lesser houses began to change, but these changes were slight and mainly connected with the treatment of windows and of the trims of the doors. A representative house of this new type is the one at the corner of Soho Square which Isaac Ware built for Alderman Beckford, now the House of Charity. Prior to the year 1730, the fine old London brick had been used for house-building, with rubbed bricks for the quoins and arches of the windows, and tiles for the roofs. After this date, following the building of Devonshire House by William Kent, stock bricks came into general use.

From 1760 to the end of the century these types of exteriors lost much of the picturesque detail and intimate interest which gave distinction to the earlier examples. Architects were beginning to master the technique of their art, and aimed at greater precision in the treatment of materials, which was not without effect in the gradual refinement of house fronts. In this regard the work of the Adams, of Leverton, and of Henry Holland, who built Sloane Street, is outstanding. More attention was given by architects to the preparation of working drawings, plans, elevations and sections, which, with full-size details, were drawn in thick ink lines. And such instructions were followed with meticulous care and craftsmanship by the builders—another explanation of the elegance and refinement of detail to be found in the buildings of the period. In cities and large towns there were master builders who undertook contracts much in the same way as to-day, men who could command their own bricklayers and carpenters, who took in apprentices and were alive to current architectural opinion. A mass of architectural books dealing with both design and construction was on the market, and the value of these to the country architect or builder must have been considerable, and have had no small effect in standardising the best features of design and detail about the country. But it was the system of apprenticeship that probably had most effect in keeping alive the traditions of good building. Again, in almost every town were builders' merchants ready to supply grates, stoves and chimney-pieces of good design. Locks and door furniture were manufactured at Birmingham, and were on sale at all ironmongers, and special catalogues were issued showing designs for metal fitments in sympathy with the prevalent taste.

THE SMALLER COUNTRY HOUSE

If the larger country houses previously described were often inconveniently planned, this criticism certainly does not apply to those of the " middling " people. These include residences, manor houses, farms and large cottages, and no account of the architecture of the Georgian period would be complete without reference to this important aspect of domestic building. These houses, more directly than the large monumental buildings, interpret the social divisions of the time. Yet it is seldom that there are to be seen two of these houses or cottages alike, even in the older suburban districts of London and other towns. At the same time, all exhibit a harmony of *ensemble* and an air of unconscious dignity in their design. There is, for instance, the broad-fronted house of the days of Queen Anne, with its double tiering of sash windows and accented cornice marking the rise of the steep roof. Many such can be seen in Sussex and Kent, in Hertfordshire, Essex and Suffolk. There the walls are of cheerful red brick, the tiled roofs and dormer windows forming agreeable accents in company with the massive chimney-stacks. In the Cotswolds are many houses of almost similar design built of stone, fine examples of which are to be seen at Bourton-on-the-Water, Chipping Camden and Moreton-in-the-Marsh. At Exeter many of the houses were built of local brick and the roofs furnished with local slate. A contrast to the steep-roofed house is afforded by the box-like house, foursquare and upright, finished by a parapet and covered with two small hipped roofs, in M-fashion, the tiled ridges scarcely exceeding the parapet in height.

The plans of these houses in all parts of the country follow a somewhat similar arrangement. The central doorway opens into the hall, the main staircase is seen beyond, with another door leading into the garden. On either side of the hall are the two main rooms. At Eggington Manor in Bedfordshire the plan is particularly attractive. By a slight adjustment which admits of a window, as well as a door, to the hall, the room to the left is smaller by one bay than that to the right, this allowing the drawing-room, which is on the south-east side, to have four windows.

After 1727 the tradition was further developed on lines of greater formality. There is, for example, Rainham House in Essex, and Warbrook, near Eversley, in Hampshire, already referred to, which is a miniature great house. The rebuilding of the town of Woburn after the fire of 1747 brought several new types into being. At Lavenham in Suffolk there is a small house of the period 1750 which reflects the change in design. The front has three features, comprising two bays and a slightly projecting pedimented busk in the centre. At Saffron Walden there are many other examples of the year 1770 which show further modifications. These are of the same character as the Wick at Richmond, the plan of which is given on Fig. 39, built by Robert Mylne in 1775, and St Paul's, Waldenbury in Hertfordshire, which was designed by Robert Adam. From this date until the end of the Georgian regime the tradition was continued with certain slight changes in the treatment of detail and the introduction of balconies and trellised verandahs.

The reasonableness of these designs is their chief attraction. Nothing very ostentatious was required; the rooms had to face in certain directions, and to be of a size and number determined by the limit of cost. The living-rooms varied from two to three in the average middle-class house, and from four to five in those slightly larger. In addition there were the kitchens, front and back, the pantries and china cupboards, a place for coal, and, in houses built after 1770, two water-closets. Structural considerations determined the placing of the chimney-stacks, and it was not therefore usual to have a fireplace in every room.

In the eighteenth century the more important of these houses, many of which can still be seen in average villages or towns, were the houses of doctors, bankers, lawyers, brewers and merchants. Many have gardens of from two to five acres, and some stabling and coach-houses with accommodation for the coachman. Excellent examples of this type of house are that at Swaffham, Cambridgeshire (Plate LV.), and the house formerly at Denmark Hill, which Buckler drew, with its splendid ironwork entrance screen (Plate LVI.). Most were designed by local architects who often combined their business with that of land-surveying; while others were built by master bricklayers working in conjunction with master carpenters. In certain cases the owners obtained plans from London architects, or incorporated ideas from one of the standard books on building, employing local labour for the building. Thus can be imagined the effect of one good house on a quite large district. The fashion once started by a gentleman would be followed by the prosperous tradesmen, while older buildings, including those of mediæval date, would be refronted in the current fashion, as at Thaxted and Clare, Suffolk. Building in Georgian times amongst all classes almost amounted to a passion. A substantial house, a well-kept garden, a travelling carriage and a gig, with at least four horses in the stables, assured the envy of the less fortunate and no little standing in the neighbourhood.

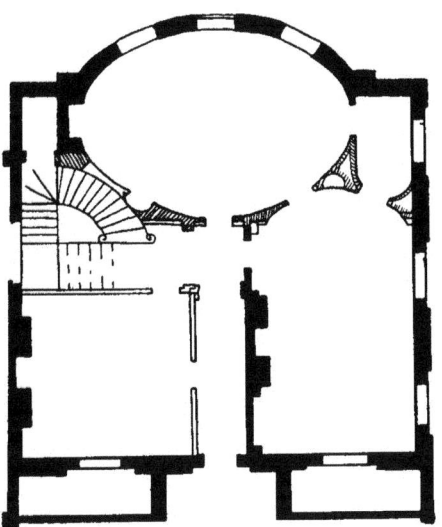

FIG. 39.—A delightfully compact plan for a small house. "The Wick," Richmond, by Robert Mylne (1775).

CHAPTER VII

THE BUILDING CRAFTS

Masonry

MEDIÆVAL methods of building construction may be said to have persisted in England until the early nineteenth century, but during the Tudor age the old guild system was developed into one of apprenticeship. In this lies the secret of the thoroughness that distinguished the Georgian trades, even during the time of building speculation at the close of the century. At the same time, the gap between the professional architect and the master mason or carpenter was never too great to be bridged.

Building during the eighteenth century was prejudiced by considerable difficulties of transport. Heavy materials had to be conveyed by road or water, and thus local materials were always used where possible, which accounts for regional characteristics which new methods of design did not perceptibly change. The masonry of the period perhaps affords the most direct evidence of the close relationship between expression and material, even more so than brickwork or carpentry. Inigo Jones had shown in the Banqueting-house at Whitehall how classical proportions demanded a nicety of shaping and dressing in stone. Wren had learnt this lesson also, and almost always used dressed Portland stone. At St Paul's, economy forced him to follow the mediæval custom of using rubble for the cores of the piers supporting the dome, and it was not until Labeyle built the first bridge at Westminster that solid Portland-stone piers were employed.

During the late seventeenth and early eighteenth centuries, in such different parts of the country as Somerset, the Cotswolds, Westmorland and Yorkshire, local stone dressed to suit the new style was used. In Cornwall the old tradition of dressed granite was employed by Gibbs at Anthony. Local materials thus had their influence on the development of classic design in the country, though the main source of influence was the Metropolis. In districts such as the neighbourhoods of Bath,

Cirencester and Bristol, as well as at Northampton and Kendal, local craftsmen retained throughout the century the inventive gift of being able to devise detail in the materials they used, based on classical prototypes. We turn, therefore, to the smaller houses, farms and cottages, as well as to the house fronts in small towns, for those evidences which constitute regional buildings. This tradition, however, was gradually lost, particularly when stucco came into almost universal use.

From the reign of Queen Anne until the year 1800, worked stone, either Bath or Portland, but preferably the latter, was considered essential to the appearance and lasting quality of buildings of the first rank. Economy, however, often demanded an admixture of brick and stone, and this had been used with effect by Wren in many of the City churches and in lesser buildings, such as the Middle Temple Gatehouse. But from the time when masonry was employed by Vanbrugh in gigantic masses to the period when Soane erected his screen wall to the Bank of England, the craft of the mason was in demand. There had been several innovations during this intervening period, particularly in the dressing of stone by means of tooling and drafting. Reference to such buildings as Stone Buildings, Lincoln's Inn, by Sir Robert Taylor, Trinity House, by Wyatt, or the elevations of Newgate (Plate LIII.) by the younger Dance, demonstrates the regard paid to this important branch of construction, as do the splendid bridges designed by Robert Mylne, Carr of York, and James Paine. The finest example of eighteenth-century masonry, however, is to be seen in Somerset House (Plate LII.), the work of Sir William Chambers.

The Adam brothers did not always forego the use of Portland stone for their favourite Roman cement. Portland stone was employed in Fitzroy Square, the last of their speculative works, as a kind of veneer over brick, the material being used in thin slabs and the surface polished to produce something of the effect of marble. The closer study of classical antiquity placed the rendering of civic architecture somewhat beyond the attainments of the ordinary mason, but did not prevent the skilful interpretation of an architect's drawings, though it meant that the architect had personally to supervise every detail.

The skill and knowledge required of a mason at this time added prestige to one of the oldest crafts in the country. Many local masons could command a wide variety of work ranging from colonnaded porticoes to chimney-pieces and tombstones. In this regard the name of John Wing of Bedford stands prominently, and between the years 1775 and 1814 he carried out nearly all the masonry required in his county. His final work was the design and erection of the splendid bridge across the Ouse at Bedford. This is only a detached instance, and we must not forget that we owe the skilful repair and preservation of scores of old churches about the country to the skill of the masons of the eighteenth century. Thus these men in the country carried on the earlier traditions of the seventeenth century in the face of such opposition as that of Mrs Coade's factory at Lambeth, where, towards the end of the century, stuccoed ornaments and imitation stone capitals were manufactured and supplied ready-made to builders.

Brickwork

In England, brickwork, which was first introduced by the Flemings who settled in East Anglia, has always been accounted as important a building material as stone. Inigo Jones employed it in building the north arcade at Houghton House in Bedfordshire, 1615. Other fine examples of dressed and cut brickwork are to be seen in the front of Cromwell House at Highgate, and the design of the fine brick piers in front of Lindsay House, Lincoln's Inn Fields (Fig. 40). Hatton mentions that in 1708 there were eight of these piers on this side of the square. The use of fine rubbed brickwork on a more extensive scale is a distinctive feature of Wren's manner, and excellent examples include the brick enrichments to the houses in the Temple, particularly the doorways in King's Bench Walk, and the Chapter House in St Paul's Churchyard.

Fig. 40.—Brick Gate Pier at Lindsay House, Lincoln's Inn Fields.
Henry Tanner, del.

Englishmen of the seventeenth century had inherited their fondness for brickwork from the fifteenth century. It satisfied their demand for colour and particularly suited the English atmosphere and landscape. It is not strange, therefore, that in the late seventeenth century vast quantities of rubbed and moulded bricks were shipped from Holland to London, to King's Lynn, to Harwich and to Exeter.

In the rebuilding of London after the Great Fire it had been amply shown that brick surfaces could be made attractive by simple surface treatment and judicious enrichment. While there was a considerable importation of fancy bricks from abroad, brick-making had also become a specialised industry in this country, and there were minute directions governing the general manufacture, the bond and the size of stock sections. No " builders' guide " of the time was considered adequate that did not contain directions for brickmaking.

Despite the popularity of stone buildings in the earlier part of the century, brick continued to be used as one of the chief materials. At Holkham in Norfolk stock brick was used, and at Devonshire House its employment created a new mode. The smaller town houses, built by Isaac Ware, Taylor, Ripley, Chambers and the Adam brothers, are sufficiently numerous to indicate how extensive was the employment of brickwork throughout the century. But after the time of Wren the brick bond was changed from old English to Flemish. The Georgians found that it was not always possible to obtain red clay for brickmaking, and hence were produced such pleasing variations as the Luton greys of Bedfordshire and the purple bricks of Buckinghamshire. These two varieties made excellent vitrified headers for patternings, which to a certain extent continued the traditions of chequering in Tudor brickwork. It was not until the days of the Regency that brickwork was ever entirely covered with stucco.

TILING

The extensive use of tiling belongs to the seventeenth century. In Kent, Sussex, Surrey and parts of Hampshire the fronts of late seventeenth and eighteenth century houses were often hung partly or wholly with red tiles—these tiles are either of the plain rectangular types, or consist of numerous alternations of hall-round, fish-scale, and other shapes which conform into a variety of patterns. After the Great Fire tiles came into general use for roofing. In contemporary views of London the steep-pitched roofs are shown tiled and pierced with dormers. As the century advanced, mansard roofs were introduced, and slating followed as a matter of convenience.

SLATING

Slate appears as early as the reign of Queen Anne for roofings not intended to form a distinctive feature of a design. It was a useful and much cheaper substitute for the covering of a roof with lead.

In Westmorland, Wales, Cornwall and Devon, where an abundance of slate was obtainable, the practice of slate-hanging the fronts of houses was general (Plate LVIII.). At Totnes and Ashburton this craft is to be seen at its best, and at Plymouth and Truro there are many good examples of late eighteenth-century work. This practice of using slate and tiles as a vertical covering for walls was derived from the timber shingling of other days. In the West Country slate is still used to protect timber from the weather, and when this occurs at gable ends it is known as "scripping."

STUCCO FOR EXTERNAL WORK

Modern opinion has restored stucco to the estimation in which it was once held. In Queen Anne's reign it was often applied to large surfaces or treated in imitation of rusticated stonework. Later on in the century it reappears in imitation of dressed stone, and finally in the hands of the later architects it is used quite frankly as a facing in connection with brick, as in the terraces of Regent's Park (Plate LVIII.). The Adam brothers used Liardet's cement, which was formed with oil. Mention must also be made of Coade's Patent Stone, a species of refined terra-cotta which was in general demand, particularly in cases where it was necessary to ensure exact repetition. All the later architects, including Taylor, Chambers, Gandon and Soane, valued the productions of this Lambeth works.

IRONWORK

Not until the reign of James I. did ironwork become an external accessory of architectural utility, and then only to a limited extent. Inigo Jones is credited with the first introduction of iron balconies at Lincoln's Inn Fields and at Kirby Hall, Northamptonshire. The rules for rebuilding after the Great Fire prescribed the nature of the balconies when used on house fronts.

Up to the end of the seventeenth century the old methods of smithcraft had survived, and were employed for gates and screens. It was principally due to a foreign craftsman, Jean Tijou, who worked under Sir Christopher Wren, that grace and variety were introduced into metalcraft design. This artist in iron inspired the English smiths of the early eighteenth century and thus helped to establish the fine Georgian traditions of English ironwork. A large variety of effective and restrained grilles exist about the country, as, for example, the screen to the garden of the Inner Temple, the gate to Gray's Inn Gardens, the overthrows to the gates at Trinity College, Cambridge (Plate LIX.), and many pleasant gates at Richmond and the outer suburbs of London. The drawing of a now demolished house on Denmark Hill (Plate LVI.) shows a fine example of an ironwork screen of its period, though this is only sketched in roughly. Throughout the period iron balustrades were adopted for staircases, and these varied in type from the elaborate example in the Tijou style formerly at No. 35 Lincoln's Inn Fields [1] to the scrolled forms used by Chambers and the Wyatts (see Plate LXXI.). After 1760, design in ironwork began to change, the forms growing more severe and correct, and vase tops replacing the earlier finials. Finally, cast iron replaced wrought, and by 1820 Cottingham's patterns put an end to freedom in design. Other features made in wrought iron included lamp-standards, torch-extinguishers, door-head brackets, and footscrapers. Many of the designs for door-knockers, such as the lion mask and other types, were based upon Italian models of contemporary and earlier date in Rome.

LEADWORK

Leadwork as a craft dates from mediæval times, the term covering a variety of features of ornament and utility, including coverings for roofs of steep pitch, the flats on the tops of buildings and rain-water cess-heads. Under Wren's influence the design of lead cisterns, rain-water heads, vases and architectural finials took on a more fanciful character, and in this connection mention must be made of the lead figures and urns of the gardens of the seventeenth century.

In London, after the Fire, plumbers found prosperity at their doors, and no doubt they availed themselves of ornamental styles from Holland. The leadwork on Wren's buildings is

---

[1] Now in the Victoria and Albert Museum, South Kensington.

refined enough to suggest that the rain-water heads were made to specification. With the accession of William and Mary, a lead yard was established by a Dutchman named John Van Nost, who undertook to " design, cast and supply ornamental leadwork for building " ; and it is reasonable to assume that most of Wren's followers availed themselves of the stock. Van Nost's business in time passed to John Cheese, and after 1711 was continued by him practically to the end of the century. There were at least four lead yards in Piccadilly, besides the yard of a statuary at Hyde Park Corner. Bonnell Thornton has satirised the craze for leaden gods and goddesses in the pages of *The Connoisseur*.

The practice of dating houses by including the year when the building was completed in the design of the rain-water head extended a tradition dating back to Tudor times. Sometimes, and particularly when the brick fronts were exceptionally plain, the whole ornamental interest appears to have been centred on the cess-heads, many of which bore the initials of the owner (see Plate LIX.). Most country towns can show examples of this practice.

The cess-heads of the early eighteenth century in the ordinary way were quite plain with the exception of a lion mask, the moulded portions beginning with a cyma recta and a small moulding below, and terminating with a roll. Below this is a cavetto necking leading to the round or square downpipes. The lead heads used by Vanbrugh for the store-houses at the Gun Wharf, Devonport, are plain, the slight ornament being reserved for the tacks immediately below the head. We find the design of lead heads fairly consistent in character from 1700 to 1760. After this they were elaborated, especially in the case of Government works. The Adam style brought further changes, including the hopper form which was enriched with festoons and fluting. Mention must also be made of the elaborate pump-head designs which continued to be made as late as 1820.

Leadwork as a specialised craft continued to flourish, and found new expression in the fanlights for doorways of the late eighteenth century. Architects were always sure of a varied stock of these at Bottomley's in Cheapside. Neither is it to be supposed that lead glazing went out of fashion abruptly. The sashed window had began to supersede the mullioned-transome type as early as 1680, and by 1700 its use, except for dormer windows, was general. But notwithstanding the new fashion, the rim-iron framed window with leaded lights, both reticulated and rectangular, still found favour for farm buildings, inns and cottages in all parts of the country. A good example of this continuance of a minor tradition is to be seen at the Ostrich Inn on the outskirts of Ipswich, and numerous other examples could be named as late as the reign of George IV. Even in large houses the leaded window was often retained for offices, cellars and outbuildings.

During the whole span of the Georgian period the business of the plumber consisted in casting and working the lead used in buildings. He made lead cisterns, sinks for the kitchens, rain-water heads, drain-pipes, and lead flats for houses. He could cast ornaments in lead, and even country plumbers could model and cast leaden figures. Another branch of the plumber's trade consisted in making lead coffins. After the year 1760, when " patent " water-closets began to be used, the plumber found a new branch to his trade, and his business became frequently combined with that of glazier and painter, the journeyman being usually paid at the rate of 30s. a week.

Glass

The glass used in building-work during the eighteenth century was produced by the igneous fusion of siliceous earth with certain alkaline earths or salts and metallic oxides. It was the practice to blow it in cylinders, and this was called window or table glass. Plate glass was also blown in cylinders, other varieties being cast. It appears that in the first quarter of the eighteenth century the chief glassworks were at Ratcliffe (established at Southwark in 1691), at Lambeth, and at Newcastle (1725), crown glass being produced at all three places. Staffordshire glass at this stage was not used in London, and Bristol glass was rare, although it could be obtained at reasonable prices. The large sheets of cast plate glass used for mirrors were made at the Old Bear Garden, Southwark, and at Vauxhall—hence the term " Vauxhall plate." An Act of Parliament of the time of George II., 1745, names crown, plate, flint or white glass.

In the year 1773 a charter was granted to the Governor and Company of Bristol Plate Glass Makers; this company had a warehouse in Upper Thames Street, near Blackfriars Bridge, the works being at Ravenhead in Lancashire. It specialised in large-sized pier-glasses, and popularised concave and convex mirrors at the close of the period.

It will thus be seen that glass-making had developed into a national industry, and during the Georgian period English makers seriously competed with the foreign sources. As previously mentioned, the business of glazier was frequently combined with that of plumber. From the time of Queen Anne the two divisions of glazing had been known as sash-work and leadwork, referring, of course, to the two types of windows. In the eighteenth century many glaziers undertook the additional task of cleaning windows, and this led to the invention known as the "glazier's horse," which enabled a man to clean the outside of a sash window with safety. It is not generally known that, prior to this, hundreds of servants lost their lives annually during the Georgian period in cleaning the upper windows of houses.

Plasterwork

The comparatively few clearly authenticated examples of design in plasterwork left by Inigo Jones and Webb mark a great advance in the direction of definite late Renaissance character, and undoubtedly influenced the succeeding work of the latter half of the seventeenth century. Unlike Inigo Jones, Wren had neither the time nor the desire to adapt and assimilate the ornament he selected, and the craftsmen who worked for him must have been new to the later Renaissance tradition, so different from the detailed elaboration that had distinguished the work of their predecessors prior to the Civil Wars. In the City churches, nevertheless, plasterwork was liberally employed for vaults, ceilings and cornices, with moulded ribs for the panels, and cupids' heads, palmettes and cartouches for the principal enrichments. It is surprising to find the astonishing virtuosity of Grinling Gibbons' carvings of natural objects and forms influencing workers in plastic materials.

But if the craftsmanship was not so consummate, the design was far more architectonic, and the ably moulded wreaths of fruit and flowers compose well with the architectural settings of their more formal ornament. Nevertheless, the fine native school of high relief plasterwork decoration had, remarkably enough, come to an end by the close of the seventeenth century.

The ceilings in the principal rooms in smaller houses of this early period generally consisted of a large oval panel enriched with fruit and flowers, modelled in high relief (see Plate LX., *above*), with sometimes in the central space a flying cupid, with a hook to carry the chandelier. Early in the century English architects found a new source for elaborate decorative schemes from the publication of Marot's designs, and these had a strong influence in many actually carried out by William Kent. In the first half of the eighteenth century the relief is slighter, and classical motives, such as the guilloche and fret, are repeated continually along the raised bands of ceilings, divided up according to a geometrical scheme, or of walls split up into panels. The detached and filling pieces of ornament are usually of rococo type.

But the average architect was content to make a sketch for a ceiling and to hand it over to a native or Italian worker to be interpreted; for instance, James Gibbs employed two Italians, Artari and Bagutti, for the plasterwork at the Radcliffe Library (Fig. 41). After the year 1730, ornamental motives of French origin were still employed by architects and

FIG. 41.—Modelled Relief Ornament at the Radcliffe Library, Oxford.
James Gibbs, architect. Engraved by Fourdrinier.

plasterworkers, John James and Isaac Ware showing a particular predilection for this style. At Warbrook, James's own house, to which reference has already been made, French ornament is combined with details of the severe Palladian form. For example, while the decoration of the drawing-room ceiling is florid, the walls of the staircase are enriched with panels and blind niches complete with cornices and consoles. The early work of Sir Robert Taylor shows the same tendency, and Sir William Chambers, who was as much influenced by the conjectural restorations of Clérisseau as by the works of Neufforge, Gabriel and Antoine, developed some abstract forms which are spirited and interesting. Besides using frets, guilloches and plaques, he prepared designs for friezes which displayed a considerable interest in the plasterer's craft. In these friezes he employed motives such as dolphins and shells, besides using conventional wreaths and palmettes. The general frame of the ceiling was usually charged with frets or Vitruvian scrolls, with spaces arranged for pictures or *bassi relievi* inspired by antique decoration. The flat portion of the ceiling had a circle of wreaths, and in the centre was often a bust or Medusa head.

With the brothers Adam, the fine traditions of the plasterer's craft were revived and stimulated (see Plate LX.). Robert Adam had brought back Pergolesi from Italy to work for him, and had encouraged Bonomi to set up in London as a designer. Previously both Sir Robert Taylor and James Paine had experimented with plasterwork of slight and delicate design, the former in the fine Court Room of the Bank of England and the latter at Brocket Hall, Hertfordshire. Another distinctive contribution was made by Henry Holland at Brooks's Club in St James's Street. The ceiling of the Subscription Room and the decorative work in the walls is dignified and shows more restraint than much Adam decoration.

About 1750 there were numbers of Italian plasterworkers in England whose names have since passed into obscurity.[1] Owners of buildings often sent to London for a complete scheme of internal decoration and asked for Italians to come down to carry it out. This took place in 1775 at Whiteford in Cornwall, when the whole house was redecorated by Italian craftsmen for Sir William Call.

The last twenty-five years of the eighteenth century witnessed the acceptance of the Adam manner in all parts of the country for the decoration of houses large or small; but we must note that two architects, Holland and Soane, made a stand against their prolific use of plaster ornaments. Holland was in sympathy both with Chambers and the French manner. His best designs for plasterwork were carried out in the state apartments at Woburn Abbey (Fig. 48), and at Southill in Bedfordshire for Samuel Whitbread.

No one who has studied the work of Sir John Soane can fail to be impressed by the originality of design shown in his plaster ceilings and vaults. Soane began by imitating Robert Adam, but soon forsook this style and began to experiment with segmental ceilings, developing the " umbrella " form, of which he was particularly fond (see Fig. 42). Many of his designs were carried out by the famous Joseph Papworth, who had previously worked for Sir William Chambers. At this

---

[1] Miss Jourdain has traced many of the names of these craftsmen in her " English Decorative Plasterwork," 1926.

PLATE LIX.

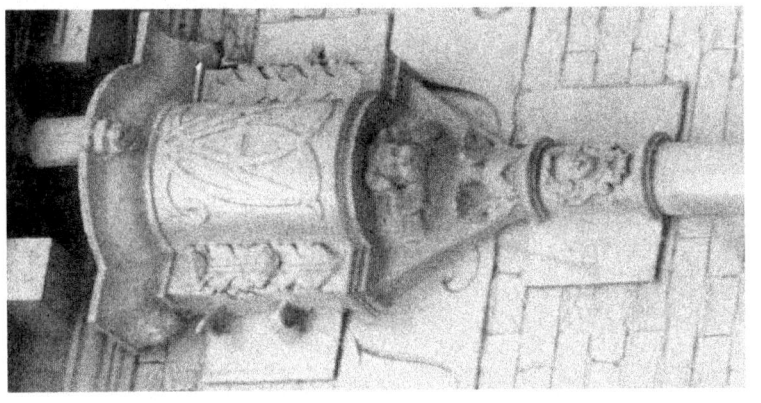

An Ornamental Lead Rain-water Head of the Late Seventeenth Century at Shrewsbury.

Ornamental Lead Urn at Hampton Court.

Gateway; Grille in Ornamental Ironwork at Trinity College, Cambridge; Early Eighteenth Century.

PLATE LX.

Typical Palladian Ceiling at Holkham Hall, Norfolk. Designed by William Kent.

A Typical London Ceiling in the Adam Style. The delicate plaster mouldings are alternated with painted medallions.

Fig. 42.—Fan-shaped Ceiling by Sir John Soane in the National Debt and Redemption Office.
From the architect's " Designs for Public and Private Buildings."

juncture plasterwork, far from being a lost art, had merely changed in character. The architects who followed Soane, such as Foulston, Goodridge of Bath, and John Papworth, employed Greek frets and honeysuckle for the flat members of the ceilings and large foliated centres for the chandeliers and oil lamps. From 1810 to 1825 coffered ceilings were also in vogue.

The differences in style noticeable throughout the Georgian period in architecture are reflected very clearly in this important craft. The richness of plasterwork and ornamentation varied with each decade of architectural achievement, passing from native hands to foreign and back again. Like the art of woodcarving it began to lose its spontaneity directly it came under the control of architects whose chief interest was in the preparation of designs, for the plasterworkers gradually gave up the initiative and the work grew mechanical. When architects finally began to copy and reproduce antique and mediæval forms in their designs, without the slightest attempt at adaptation or modification, the fine traditions of the plasterers' craft became degraded and finally extinguished.

Woodwork

As with the other crafts, carpentry at the beginning of the eighteenth century still followed traditional practice, and this is exemplified particularly in the treatment of roof trusses, in

Fig. 43.—Eighteenth-century Carpenters.

the heavy character of some of the open newel and dog-legged staircases, and the method of framing with wooden pins. The change from mediæval custom first occurred under Inigo Jones, who may be said to have set the standard for doors, panelling and staircases. Then, after the Restoration, carpenters and joiners began to abandon those traditional details which generations of workers had followed instinctively. There follows a period of transition in which local taste wavered between mullioned and transomed windows in wood and the double-hung sash. The change was slow, and the ingenuity of carpenters and joiners was allowed plenty of play in the designs of balusters, newels and curtails for staircases. From the great works in progress in London after the Fire, a taste was spread for ornamental construction in wood which was continued with modifications throughout the century. For example, the panelling of rooms demanded treatment in accordance with the broad handling of the whole design. Hence from 1700 to 1760 a high standard was maintained; but the use of stucco for the treatment of wall surfaces in large mansions when an internal scenic effect was attempted in turn reacted on the finish of smaller apartments. Wallpapers and plain painted surfaces were more and more employed as a background for pictures, but the traditions of wainscotting were not entirely forgotten, and after 1760 it is found in the form of a dado in most rooms. In this respect its use was in sympathy with the dado panelling to staircases, which did not finally disappear until the Regency.

Experience and economy, combined with a more thorough appreciation of classical detail, led carpenters to produce work exactly in sympathy with the architecture. The crafts could not remain stationary and each decade brought forth a slightly changed point of view. The most noticeable changes apparent are in the treatment of sash windows which, beginning with small quarries and thick bars, ended with larger glazing surfaces and delicately moulded bars. The introduction of geometrical staircases in stone, with an iron hand-railing, as employed by Sir William Chambers and the brothers Adam, was imitated by joiners who could show equal skill in a rendering in wood. Such staircases, with their perfectly plain balusters, were eventually considered all that was necessary.

CHAPTER VIII

INTERIOR DESIGN

THE classic innovations of Inigo Jones and Webb had their effect in transforming the interior as well as the exterior design of houses. Jones was the first English architect who charged himself with the design of the interiors and interior features of the houses he built, the previous custom having been for the owner to summon craftsmen and furnishers whose manner pleased him to house him according to his taste. At Wilton, which Jones built about 1650, French influence is very noticeable in the introduction of classical effects where before only random classical motives had been employed. Rich marbles and carving, elaborate frieze and bow cornices combined to produce the monumental type of interior which Jones desired, and these features established a new method in design which was soon introduced not only in large mansions but in the smaller town houses then being built in London after the Fire.

This classical conception of interior design was elaborated much further by Vanbrugh in the state apartments of Blenheim and Castle Howard, which were on a scale of magnificence never before attempted in English building. Their gigantic galleries and suites reflect the architect's conviction that buildings " intended for elegance and magnificence must have the parts great." The effects he achieved are stupendous, if somewhat theatrical, and the scale of his conceptions was startling even to the aristocratic taste of the times. The magnificent ostentation of Blenheim may well have caused something of a reversion in favour of more habitable interiors.

Wren's work at Hampton Court represents a more reasonable conception of the state interior, and his influence, which probably owed something to contemporary Dutch productions, largely determined the design of rooms from the Restoration to the death of Queen Anne, particularly in houses of medium or smaller size. He encouraged more sober effects combined with impeccable craftsmanship. Decorative wood-

PLATE LXI.

A Rich Interior by William Kent (see also Plate XII.). The Marble Parlour at Houghton Hall, Norfolk (1723).

PLATE LXII.

Typical Palladian Plaster Decoration at Moor Park, Hertfordshire, by Leoni.

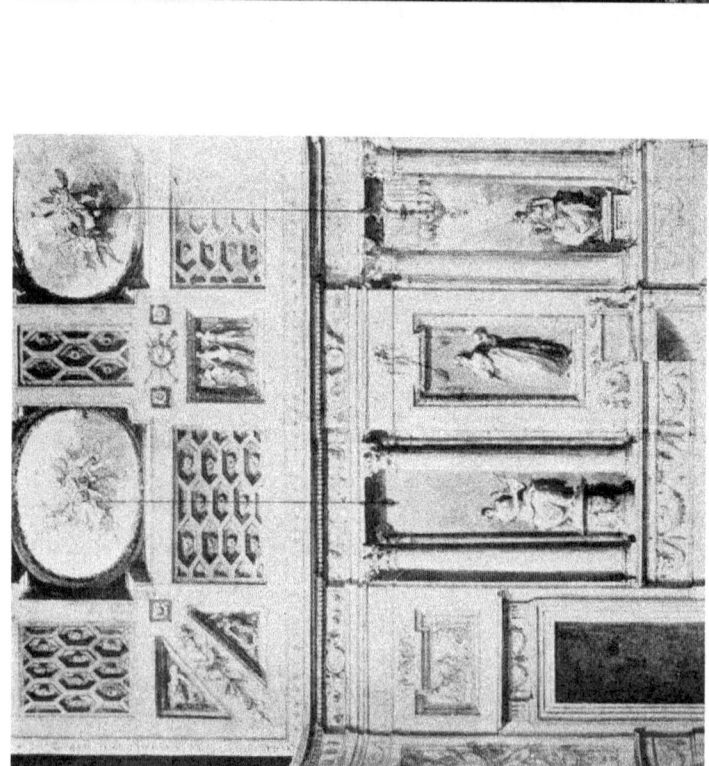

A Design for a Side of a Room and Ceiling by Sir William Chambers.

carving was largely employed in this type of interior, sometimes in the free naturalistic manner of Grinling Gibbons, that included flowers, corn-sheaves, fruit and birds, at other times in a more conventional style and architectural spirit. The plasterwork of ceilings and friezes, moulded in high relief, was executed in a distinct but not dissimilar manner by a separate school of able and active craftsmen. Panelling at this time was in a large, threefold division, with bold bolection mouldings sometimes carved, and occasionally a decorative use of pilasters. Cornices were bold, and in the design of chimney-pieces Wren and his school usually followed Dutch examples, with heavy, simply moulded, marble surrounds to the actual fireplace. The overmantel had often festoons of Gibbons-type fruit and flower carving in the highest relief, or, as alternatives, a mirror, a picture in a richly moulded frame, or stepped mantelshelves to display a China collection. Staircases were broad and spacious, usually constructed of wood, with a heavy rail and large characteristic balusters, as at Marble Hill, Twickenham, and Belton House, but examples with Tijou-type ironwork also occur ; and the elaborately carved wooden staircases with continuous scrolls must also be mentioned.

The publication of Marot's designs in Amsterdam in 1712 brought a Franco-Dutch taste into popularity, though this was a style only properly adapted to more sumptuous interiors. The painted ceilings and staircase walls of Verrio and Laguerre are seen in representative type in Marot's book ; but unfortunately Sir James Thornhill's most complete production at Stoke Edith has recently been entirely gutted by fire. The publication of Kent's " Designs of Inigo Jones " acted as a more local stimulus to a movement which brought in the Palladian style that continued in vogue for forty years, till replaced by the stricter classic phase. Kent was allowed full play to his methods in two great Norfolk houses that have been referred to in a previous chapter, namely, Houghton and Holkham ; and these represent his most typical achievements in interior design (see Plates XII., LXI., LXIII., *left*). The style was florid and lavish in comparison with the reasonable simplicity of Wren's work. Marbles were used in profusion, and the carving of the gigantic chimney-pieces is massive and often over-heavy. The ceilings dispense entirely with the naturalistic high relief of the late seventeenth century and figure with repetitive profusion a number of classical motives. Often wandering foreigners were turned loose to work rococo writhings, occasionally overflowing on to the wall panels, as at Stoneleigh Abbey, Warwickshire. Ceilings entirely painted also occur, as at Kensington Palace, and sometimes Roman coffering was introduced, as at Holkham Great Hall Saloon (Plate LXI.) and Chapel. Figures, putti and medallions, with trophies, swags and other enrichments, crowded the friezes and panels, as in the detail from Moor Park on Plate LXII., and large busts were often set in niches (see Plate XII.), or between broken pediments over doors and chimney-pieces. Large painted panels, generally of somewhat indifferent execution, were frequently introduced, as in the hall of Moor Park, by Leoni, where the scale and vigour of the decoration, with its paintings by Ameconi, might seem over-emphatic, giving an effect of somewhat exaggerated lavishness in the ensemble without sufficient attention to the quality or co-ordination of the detail (Plate LXII., *right*). It must be mentioned, however, that Kent's work at Raynham in Norfolk shows him adopting a simpler, and to many tastes more effective, decorative style.

As the century proceeded, so a refining process began to operate in the design of interiors, though no radical change is observable from the Palladian manner till Robert Adam introduced his innovations and the taste inclined to the employment of late Roman and Pompeian, rather than of Renaissance motives. A tendency towards more reticence, however, becomes noticeable both in design and detail. Chimney-pieces grew more sober and strictly classical in design, and the elaborate overmantel of the "continued" examples was not rarely dispensed with.

The middle of the century saw the inception of several new tastes; Horace Walpole, at Strawberry Hill, evolved a sort of Gothic of his own, which was, however, little adopted by designers, who were making sporadic ventures into the rococo and *chinoiserie* then fashionable in France. The change from the massive grandeur of the Louis XIV. style to the restless delicacy of that of Louis XV. found indeed some slight echo in this country.

The Adam style that followed brought this refining process a step further, and introduced mixed Roman, Pompeian and individual motives into interior decoration. The use of circular and oval ends to rooms was a feature of their methods, with characteristic lighter doorways without orders, and deep-toned doors with their own type of metal furniture. They evolved a delicate type of ceiling with shallow-moulded husk ornament, or radiating or fan-shaped ribs, often studded with medallions of geometrical form containing little paintings by Zucchi, Cipriani or Angelica Kauffmann (see Plate LX., *below*), an arrangement which evoked the scorn of Sir William

PLATE LXIII.

Detail of Chimney-piece in the Billiard-room, Houghton Hall, Norfolk. Attributed to William Kent.

Staircase at "The Vyne," near Basingstoke, Hampshire.

PLATE LXIV.

A Panelled Room (*circ.* 1750-60), from 5 Great George Street, Westminster, now in the Victoria and Albert Museum, London.

An Interior in the Adam Manner at 4 Grafton Street, London.

Chambers. In their usual type of chimney-piece the shelf is composed of architrave, frieze and cornice, the frieze often bearing a small sculptured panel in the centre ; and this was carried on columns or consoles, the whole often executed in coloured marbles (see Plate LXV., *below*). Curved staircases were usual with a balustrade of wrought iron in delicate scrollwork. The Adam style depends for much of its effect on the work of such artists as Cipriani, Angelica Kauffmann and Flaxman whom the brothers employed, while they themselves often designed the entire furnishings for their rooms, even down to such details as the fire-irons (see Plate LXVIII.).

Other architects working in a similar manner included James Wyatt, Dance the younger and Thomas Leverton, the architect of Bedford Square, and it was not until Stuart and Revett published their discoveries at Athens that the full force of the Roman revival began to flag. The adoption of Greek forms that followed with increasing literalness in what is sometimes called the " Regency " style brought reticence in interior decoration to its culminating pitch. Ceilings were now almost bare of ornament, and practically the only relief to the severity of chimney-pieces was the contour of the mouldings or simple friezes in which the Greek fret or " anthemion " motive occurs. Cornices had a minute running Greek pattern, and interiors had probably never before been decorated on such austere lines as at this period, though Henry Holland conceived a variant of the French " Directoire " mode for the decoration of Carlton House. In this, however, he had few followers, and the Regency style, though persisting in a lifeless form well into the fourth decade of the nineteenth century, ultimately gave way to the various eclecticisms of the Romantic movement which in turn forestalled nineteenth-century Gothic.

CHAPTER IX

THE DECORATIVE ARTS

Furniture

EVERY cycle in the history of art owes something to the influence of the patron. A demand has always arisen for social expression, and the artist and craftsman has emerged to fill it. In the seventeenth century the appreciation of art was becoming increasingly general, due to a large extent to the patronage of Charles I., and later of Charles II. and William III. The Parliamentarians, after their successes in the Civil Wars, exercised an iconoclastic prejudice against art as a whole, dispersing the collections made by the King and selling priceless objects of art for next to nothing. The Restoration brought about a change which affected the whole social fabric of Georgian England, and art was restored to something of the prestige it had enjoyed during the reign of Charles I. The Revolution of 1688 not only placed William III. on the throne, but also gave a power to the ruling families who had brought it about which lasted until the end of the eighteenth century. Georgian art enjoyed a patronage from these leaders throughout the period, and if the exteriors of mansions and houses were grave and stately, luxury reigned within, and there was tremendous scope for the craftsman in the embellishment of their beautiful interiors.

No account of the decorative arts in the eighteenth century can begin without an acknowledgment of the earlier tradition which, at the beginning of the period, had become merged with ideas from Holland and France. Mention has already been made of the world-wide influence of the Court art of Louis XIV. during the *Grand Siècle*. Marot's designs, which reflected nearly all the current French tendencies (Fig. 44), were published in England during the reign of William and Mary. The influence of these is, as has been pointed out, very evident in the decorative work of William Kent. During the reigns of Charles II. and James II. the main influence on free design had been derived from Dutch sources, and the

FIG. 44.—A Design for a State Bed.
By Daniel Marot.

resemblance between the furniture of the two countries had grown very pronounced. But in the reign of William and Mary a decided change takes place.

Daniel Marot was a Frenchman who entered the service of William III. The publication of his designs laid the way open for a host of locksmiths, joiners, cabinetmakers, silversmiths and upholsterers who embarked readily on the new style. After the year 1700 the wealthy were still eager to emulate to a certain extent in the interiors of their houses the splendours of Versailles, and this was largely responsible for the use of gilt gesso in the furnishings of rooms. But at the same time plain walnut and walnut-veneered furniture, such as the two chairs shown on Plate LXVI., continued to be made. This furniture was distinguished by the curved construction of the framing to the supports of chairs and tables, and little carving was introduced. The claw and ball foot, derived from a Chinese source, is often to be found in specimens of walnut furniture of this period. This detail became traditional, and was continued throughout the age of mahogany.

In the designs for interiors and furniture by William Kent is to be seen a departure from the Queen Anne style. Not only did Kent profit by Marot's designs but he also introduced motives suggested from the palaces of Venice. These large pieces of boldly carved and gilded furniture are only suitable for very large apartments, and the articles in the design of which his style continued to be felt were chiefly side tables with marble tops and carved frames, such as that shown in the upper example on Plate LXVI., stools, large seats and pedestals for busts.

During the reign of George II. we find a greater originality evident in furniture design, despite certain influences from France introduced by immigrant craftsmen and gentlemen amateurs returning from the Grand Tour. A counter-attack against such influence was launched in the founding of the "Antigallican Society," the object of which was "to promote the British manufactures, to extend the commerce of England and discourage the introduction of French modes and oppose the transportation of French commodities."

In Chippendale's work the French influence, in which "Gothic" and "Chinese" conceits were often incorporated, as in the two upper examples on Plate LXVII., is apparent in the designs for chairs, commodes and couches. We have already seen how the French spirit infected the interior designs produced by Isaac Ware, but the free designs of Meissonnier, Oppenordt, and the silversmiths such as Paul Lamérie, who came over as immigrants, helped the fashion for some years.

PLATE LXV.

A Mid-eighteenth Century Chimney-piece at Wentworth Woodhouse, Yorkshire, by Flitcroft.

A Chimney-piece in the Adam Style at Clonmel House, Dublin.

PLATE LXVI.

A Side-table in the Style of William Kent (circ. 1740).

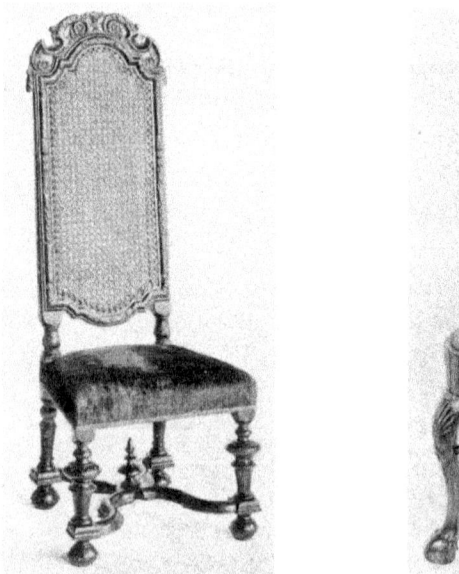

(*Left*) A High-backed "William and Mary" Chair of the Marot Type. (*Right*) A Walnut Queen Anne Chair with Cabriole Legs and Claw-and-ball Feet.

PLATE LXVII.

Two Simple Chairs of Chippendale Type, the one showing Chinese and the other Gothic Influence.

 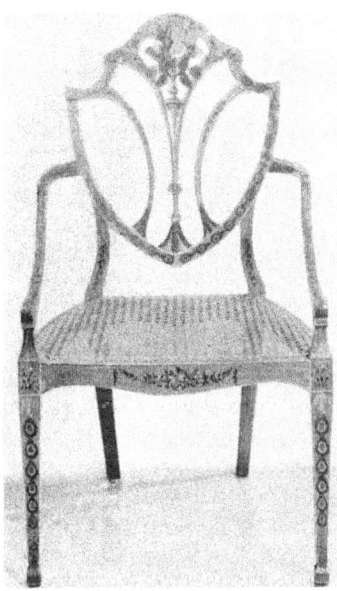

(*Left*) A Hepplewhite Chair with the Prince of Wales's Feathers as a Decoration in the Back. (*Right*) A Sheraton Type Chair in Painted Beechwood.

PLATE LXVIII.

The Saloon at Harewood House, Yorkshire, showing Furniture designed for it by Robert Adam, and executed by Chippendale.

After the year 1760 a change took place in the design of movables, the way having been prepared by the trend of architectural taste towards a more meticulous classicism. The dominant influence then felt was the predilection of archæologists for the authentic models of Greece and Rome. At the same time, French art was entering upon a more classical phase. After the peace of 1763, many Englishmen journeyed to Paris and did not fail to observe the tendencies then acting in opposition to the rococo. It is significant that Madame de Pompadour was at that time about to employ Gabriel and Soufflot. In England, however, the trend of fashion in furniture henceforth was to be directed by Robert Adam, who for over thirty years, with the assistance of his brothers and some Italian draughtsmen, was prepared to furnish designs for every sort of article. In many ways Robert Adam was the true successor to William Kent. He was versatile and adventurous, and from his original sketches and drawings in the Soane Museum, London, can be gained some idea of the volume of work he undertook between the years 1757 and 1790. The large houses which he designed needed furniture to suit them. He designed some of the furniture for Kedleston, and in these early pieces followed the style of Kent, but with greater elegance. As he gained experience he adapted the graceful curves of French chairs and sofas, as in the furniture at Harewood, illustrated on Plate LXVIII., and referred to the same source for his treatment of classical motives, such as sphinxes, scrolls and other ornaments. Adam in his most fanciful moods evolved a series of new forms for wall mirrors, girandoles and light panels, which accord most perfectly with the delicate details of his interior designs (see left-hand subject on Plate LXXII.). Then in a gifted way, after 1775, he began to transpose from the contemporary Louis Seize furniture, and even rivalled the French in painting and gilding his pieces. It was Adam who introduced the painted medallion as part of furniture design and gave employment to Angelica Kauffmann, Cipriani and Pergolesi.

With such architectural guidance, the professional furniture-makers who designed and made for the general public were at liberty to emulate the architects without losing their freedom. Chippendale made furniture to Adam's designs, but the lesser men, who relied for business on the issue of catalogues, built up their trade on the less wealthy patrons whom chance sent their way. So we find the traditions of mahogany continued side by side with veneers such as satinwood, sycamore, and chestnut, polished their natural colours. Furniture was also made of beech and then painted or japanned, as in the Sheraton example on Plate LXVII. This was the period of inlays which consisted of fan bandings, keys, flutings and running scrolls. If reference is made to the designs of Manwaring, Shearer, Hepplewhite and Sheraton, the large demand for glass-fronted bookcases, wardrobes, tallboys, bureaus, commodes, chairs and settees becomes evident. People living in town houses were also beginning to ask for pieces of furniture which would serve a dual purpose. A tallboy, for example, had to serve as a writing-desk, a dressing-table had to be made a writing-table, a fire-screen a writing-desk. Even beds were sometimes disguised as cupboards by day.

In the simpler types of chairs and tables, the shaped leg had given place to tapered supports finished with a tapered block. Hepplewhite used to flute the legs of his chairs with a broad moulding (Plate LXVII.), and other designs introduced three flutings. Carving was very sparingly introduced to the splats and the upper part of the legs. Hepplewhite published his "Cabinet Maker's and Upholsterer's Guide" in 1788, and here is to be seen the later French influence. The upholstered chairs and settees are shaped with curved backs slightly carved in the French manner, the covering showing the same influence as the textiles made at Lyons. Hepplewhite ranks high as a designer, and he contrived to blend some of Chippendale's mannerisms in his bar-back settees and open-back chairs. He it was who worked on the Adam style, with shield and oval back types. His favourite motives were the wheat ear and the Prince of Wales's feathers (see Plate LXVII.). Many of Hepplewhite's designs were emulated by the Gillows of Lancaster.

The next great designer who carried on the eighteenth-century tradition of beautiful furniture was Thomas Sheraton, who published the "Cabinet Makers' London Book of Prices" in 1788, and the "Cabinet Makers' and Upholsterers' Drawing Book" in 1791-94. This book marks the last effort of the old traditions to maintain a high standard. The designs continued some of the fashionable forms, but in the main they show regard for late Louis Seize and Directoire motives, and to some extent reflect the tendencies of the Empire style. After this English furniture became heavy, especially during the Regency, when taste varied between fantastic designs, such as the "Trafalgar" models, and the gilt furniture made for Alderman Fish. Then followed attempts to imitate the designs of Percier and Fontaine, and the series of notable designs for movables prepared by Thomas Hope of Deepdene (Fig. 45). Mahogany inlaid with brass, beech painted black and gilded,

PLATE LXIX.

English Lacquer Cabinet (end of seventeenth century) on Gilt Stand of Later Date.

Secretaire-bookcase of Satinwood, Painted and Inlaid (*circ.* 1780).

Clock in Marquetry Case (*circ.* 1690).

PLATE LXX.

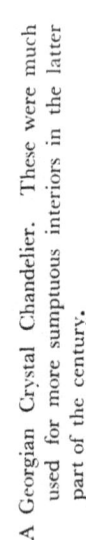

(*Above*) An Engraved Brass Lock Case by Philip Harris (*circ.* 1700).
(*Below*) A Brass Candelabrum dated 1707. Croscombe Church, Somerset.

A Georgian Crystal Chandelier. These were much used for more sumptuous interiors in the latter part of the century.

Fig. 45.—Furniture in the revived Greek Style.
Designed by Thomas Hope of Deepdene.

rosewood inlaid with ivory, and gilt chairs and settees, heralded the end of the tradition and the beginning of a fashion which closed with the Exhibition of 1851.

The various methods employed during this century to enrich plain woods are also of considerable interest. The first is the use of lacquered decoration, an influence imported from the East. In the seventeenth century the Dutch East India Company was instrumental in importing specimens of lacquer-work into Europe. Then came the rival English East India Company, and an increased demand in England for oriental art. It is not surprising that imitations of oriental lacquer provided work for English craftsmen (see Plate LXIX.). English lacquer differs from the authentic eastern variety, which was both smooth and brilliant. It was formed by a paste made of gum, bole ammoniac and whiting ; this mixture was dropped from a brush or a stick on to a design previously traced on the article of furniture, *i.e.*, the door of a cabinet or the long case of a clock. The masses of the design in relief were then carved, trimmed and gilt, and the lesser ornament painted with a brush.

Other varieties of lacquer - work include the Chinese

"Incised" and its imitations called "Bantam" work, a fashion that lasted through the century. Raised lacquer-work was popular until the end of Queen Anne's reign. It appears later in rococo twirls and in the *chinoiseries* of the furniture of the reign of the first two Georges, and no doubt it flourished long after the publication of the famous pattern-book on Oriental Ornament by Edwards and Darly which appeared in 1754. Adam did not view with favour this method of decorating chairs and movables, but he had recourse to it for some of the furniture at Osterley and Nostell in 1770. After 1780 painted furniture became popular and lacquer was regarded as old-fashioned.

Inlaying furniture with different woods began in the sixteenth century, and the practice was continued through the Elizabethan, Jacobean and early Stuart periods to the Restoration. Marquetry was introduced by the Dutch craftsmen who worked in England during the first half of the seventeenth century, and reached its finest expression in the reigns of Charles II., William and Mary, and Queen Anne. This was largely due to Garrett Johnson, a Dutch cabinetmaker who worked under royal patronage. Though the Dutch craftsmen were skilled in marquetry, English work of the late seventeenth century is finer in many respects, being distinguished by the accurate placing of separate pieces of wood cut by the saw. The best examples of marquetry are to be seen in cabinets, chests of drawers, tables, and long-case clocks (see Plate LXIX.) made during the reigns of William and Mary and Queen Anne.

Evelyn mentions that the inlayers of his day used "Fustic, locust or acacia, prince or rosewood, for yellows and reds," besides other imported woods. The process of shading leaves and flowers was by dipping the pieces into sand "heated in some very thin Brasse Pan."

Marquetry in a simplified form was continued through the reigns of the first and second of the Georges until in the succeeding reign it imitated contemporary French work.

The furniture designed by Robert Adam shows characteristic classic details combined with trophies, musical instruments and other forms. Thus in certain of the designs of Adam, Chippendale and Thomas Sheraton are to be seen the last survivals of the influence of the *marqueteurs* of the late seventeenth century. Gilt furniture first became fashionable during the reign of William and Mary, and it continued to be made for the first half of the eighteenth century. It is frequently found enriched with gesso ornament. We have already noted the gilded furniture designed by William Kent. Gesso is a term used for the process by which wood is covered with successive coats of a composition made of whiting and size, forming a ground which could be carved and the surface gilt.

So far it has only been possible to touch upon the main essentials which determined English furniture design. It must not be forgotten that the furniture of the time varied with the purchasing capacity of the customer and that the various stages of society had furniture to suit their needs. The leading craftsmen who made to order had imitators who manufactured for the general purchaser and these had innumerable competitors in town and country who produced first-rate plain work. Eighteenth-century furniture, therefore, can be said to vary both in degree and quality, but although it shows divergences of finish and ornamentation, it never at any period loses the attribute of style.

Before treating of the minor accessories of furnishing, methods of lighting must be touched upon, and first and foremost the chandelier. In general use in the late seventeenth century, this was modelled upon the large globe and S-branched types common in Holland, such as were noticed by Evelyn at the Hague, " with eight sockets from the middle stem, like those we use in churches, having tapers in them." There are several such at Hampton Court, and a fine specimen is shown on Plate LXX. These are often dated and bear the name of the donors.

In addition to brass, gold, silver, tin, copper, iron, wood, faience and crystal were used for chandeliers. In the reign of Charles II. silver ones were popular, and Marot's designs show several in the style of Louis Quatorze. There are, for example, two at Hampton Court which indicate this style. Glass chandeliers or lustres came into use in England after 1764 (Plate LXX.). In the reigns of George I. and George II. the chandeliers were generally of wood, carved and gilt, such as the one shown by Hogarth in " Marriage à la Mode." Chippendale writes, " If neatly done in wood, and gilt with burnished gold [they] would look better and come much cheaper than those of brass and glass."

Although in fact the treatment of the fireplace belongs to the subject of interiors, it may be most conveniently introduced here. In the reign of Charles II. the open fireplace with its fire-back and richly wrought andirons was in general use. The first fire-grate came in with the reign of Queen Anne, when a basket was combined with the andirons and fire-backs. Then followed different types of basket-grates until, by 1727, a regular basket-grate was evolved. There is a notable example of this type at Warbrook in Hampshire, which was the residence of John James. Finally we come to the splendid series of basket-grates and mantel-registers made for the Adam brothers, as well as the series of hob grates manufactured at Carron from 1780 to 1830. The fire implements included a poker, tongs, shovel and hearth-brush, as well as a coal-scuttle of iron, brass or copper.

DOOR FURNITURE AND IRONMONGERY

English locksmiths have long enjoyed a reputation for sound work of a high standard. The change from mediæval practice was slow, and it was not until the Restoration that a great advance was made. In the late seventeenth century locks were made at Birmingham, Wolverhampton and London, two of the early makers being Richard Bickford of London and John Wilkes of Birmingham. Some specimens of their work are to be seen in the Victoria and Albert Museum.

The best locks of William and Mary's time are those which Joshua Key made for the state apartments at Hampton Court. Another fine example of a brass case, dating from about 1700, is in the Victoria and Albert Museum. In this specimen, by Philip Harris, the case is engraved with cupids among foliated scrolls, relieved against a matted ground, and ornamented with applied steel ornaments (Plate LXX.). After the reign of Queen Anne, chasing seems to have been favoured in place of the piercing, which was a survival of mediæval smithery. Plain brass locks were in general use in the reign of the first two Georges. At Warbrook, John James used a plain case with a double-scrolled handle, but Isaac Ware, for Beckford's house in Soho Square, introduced applied filigree. From these examples we go on to the mortice locks of the second half of the eighteenth century. There is the more elaborate type of example originating with Robert Adam to include cast-brass escutcheon plates of scrollwork, which took the key, door handle and snub bolt in one line. This pattern was varied with others of pierced design. In the eighteenth century fine brasswork was hand-polished with a steel burnisher and porter as a liquid. In the late seventeenth century the design of keys was considered almost as important as the design of box locks, but gradually economy ruled a plain handle. There is, however, much ingenuity shown in the baluster forms of eighteenth-century keys, some of which were provided with stops to keep out the dust.

Reference to the catalogues issued by the Birmingham locksmiths shows how closely the architectural and ornamental

PLATE LXXI.

(*Above*) From Somerset House (later eighteenth century); and (*centre right*) Ormolu Door Furniture from Brocket Hall. (*Centre left*) Metal Balusters at Bourdon House, London; and (*below*) Ornamental Basket-grate at the Bank of England (mid-eighteenth century).

PLATE LXXII.

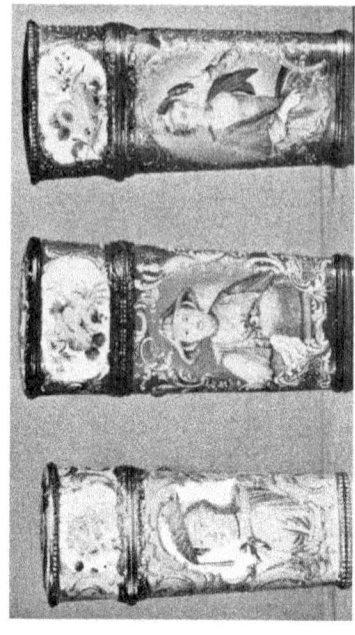

(*Above*) A Plaque in Staffordshire Enamel.
(*Below*) Staffordshire Enamel *étuis* (late eighteenth century).

Mirror and Wall Sconces in the Adam Style.

fashions of the times were followed in the handles of doors and furniture. Almost every change of fashion, French and English, is recorded in these minor details. The "Cupid's bow" drop-handle came in about 1765 and was continued until 1800. Those who have made a study of the subject have remarked on the care given by architects to the selection of locks and door furniture; indeed no detail was too small to escape supervision. In the large towns the retail ironmongers kept a stock of Birmingham locks and other articles, such as picture nails, mirror supports, cup-hooks and curtain-holders, to meet the demand of local builders. In this we have an explanation of the reason why every house of the period, in all parts of the kingdom, can show good examples. The plainer ironmongery was made locally by blacksmiths, and to some extent mediæval traditions were preserved. Hence we have a variety of design in L and H hinges, in Norfolk latches, strap hinges for stable doors and long-tailed bolts. The locks themselves were made with the precision of clockwork. Ivory, bone, china and cut-glass door furniture came in with the period of the Regency.

Enamel-work

Georgian enamel succeeded the productions of the Stuart period after an interval of over seventy years. For this special craft the famous factory established in 1750 at York House, Battersea, was the centre. Here worked Theodore Janssen for six years until his failure, but good work continued to be done until 1780. This beautiful enamel was both coloured and plain. It was used for snuff-boxes, candlesticks, bottle-tickets, knife handles, urns, knife-cases, watch-cases, buttons and other small objects. It is recorded that Horace Walpole sent a friend "a trifling snuff-box" of this material in 1755. The designs show a strong French influence, for Ravenet was employed to engrave the plates, and he adapted from the engravings of Boucher, Watteau and Lancret. In fact the whole manufacture represented an attempt to compete with French work. Hancock, an English engraver, also worked for the Battersea factory.

The ornament in Battersea enamels is executed on a ground of opaque tin-enamel laid on copper, and left white or painted in enamel colours. The plaques and the lids of snuff and toilet boxes are often brilliantly coloured, and so are the stems and sconces of the candlesticks. In some examples pieces are decorated with copperplate engravings.

Enamel-work was carried on at Bilston and Wednesbury in

Staffordshire until the end of the eighteenth century. Some fine examples of this work are shown on Plate LXXII.

ORMOLU

Among the minor crafts must be considered the production of ormolu, which flourished through the genius of Matthew Boulton. Boulton was born in 1728, and at the age of seventeen he had helped in his father's business of toy-making by introducing improvements in the manufacture of buttons, watch-chains and other trinkets. In 1762 he built a new factory at Soho, near Birmingham, his aim being to obtain a large export trade. He set out not only to obtain business but to improve the standard of the objects in which he traded. Thus we find him enjoying the patronage of fashionable clientele and numbering Robert Adam among his friends and supporters. His manufactures included plated ware, and ornaments suitable for enriching stone, bronze and porcelain. Boulton sought inspiration from among the rare works of antiquity in the old British Museum, Montague House. He based some of his designs on antique vases, and sent agents to Italy for rare specimens of metalwork which he could incorporate in his own designs. Writing to his agent, Wendler, he said that he would "be glad to work for all Europe in all things that they have occasion for—gold, silver, copper, plated, gilt, pinchbeck, steel, platino, tortoiseshell, or anything else that may become an artist of general demand."

Not only did Boulton possess taste but he employed the best foreign craftsmen he could command, and later on engaged the services of Flaxman. The metalwork produced at Soho included mounts for clocks, dials, mathematical instruments, sconces for candelabra, and metal enrichments for bases and Wedgwood ornaments. He it was who supplied the mounts for the famous "Blue John" ornaments made of the purple Derbyshire fluorspar. His activities were well known on the Continent and his wares were in great demand. After 1770 the artistic interest of the business entered upon its final phase, for Boulton associated with Watt in furthering the design of the steam-engine and putting it on the market as a power machine. Little did he realise to what degree he was helping to change the artistic history of the crafts in England.

ORNAMENTAL GLASS

This subject has been partially dealt with in connection with window glass and mirrors, but it is necessary to overlap

PLATE LXXIII.

A Tapestry Woven in Coloured Silks in the Fashionable Chinese Taste, and attributed to John Vandrebanc (early eighteenth century).

Glass Drinking Goblets of the Mid-eighteenth Century. The second from the left incorporates a Portrait of the Young Pretender.

PLATE LXXIV.

A Linen Coverlet Quilted and Embroidered with Coloured Silks (early eighteenth century).

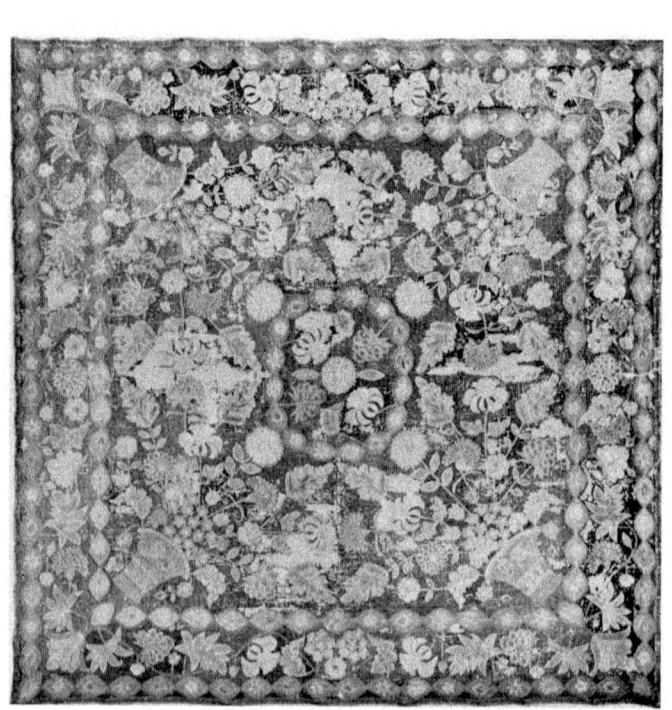

A Carpet Embroidered with Coloured Wools on Linen (early eighteenth century).

this section to some extent and to restate the details of its manufacture in this country. As in the case of many of the lesser crafts, glass-making owes its furtherance to foreigners who came to England for sanctuary. The improvement of the craft began in 1680, and sixteen years later the export trade to the East and West Indies, as well as to the Continent, was considerable.

Late seventeenth-century glasses have the same character as those of Venetian make, but the material has greater brilliancy although the design is not so graceful. The stems of the larger glasses are hollow, and sometimes enclose a coin. In the eighteenth century, drinking glasses became a speciality of the English makers. There are four types : (1) Moulded glasses; (2) glasses with air twists in the stems; (3) glasses with opaque white or coloured twists; (4) cut glasses.

We must pass on to review the fine cut-glass chandeliers which were made at Stonebridge, at Bristol and at other centres. The first glass chandelier was made in 1760. Perry and Parkes made glass chandeliers from 1780 onwards. There are very few eighteenth-century chandeliers in their original condition, although there are many of early nineteenth-century date, of deeply cut facetted ware, which were made in English and Irish centres. Waterford glass was in no way superior to English glass, and the Irish workers only *claimed* that it was " Equal to any in England." As a matter of fact, some glass was exported to Ireland from Bristol. Irish lead-glass was made from sand procured in the Isle of Wight, and a good number of English glass-workers found employment in the glass houses of Dublin, Waterford, Cork and Belfast. There is an erroneous idea that every piece of eighteenth-century glass made in Ireland came from Waterford, and that this particular glass can be detected by its bluish tint. This imperfection, which has been magnified into a charm, was brought about by impure oxide of lead being used in the manufacture, and this might have come about in any of the Irish or English factories.

The first glass house in Waterford was opened in 1729, and another was started in 1783 by George and William Penrose; this factory was closed in 1851. Other Irish glass houses include those in Dublin, the house at Belfast, set up in 1766 by Benjamin Edwards, and the factory at Cork opened in 1782. London long remained the first glass-making centre. Bristol ornamented glass had its decorations painted in enamel colours and burnt on. There were other varieties including translucent glass of peculiar texture and blue glass. From Mr Owen's book, " Two Centuries of Ceramic Art in Bristol," can be obtained the information that a certain M. Edkins was chiefly employed in ornamenting Bristol glass. There are several fine specimens in the Bristol Museum.

Cut glass became a speciality of the makers established in Birmingham, Bristol, Newcastle, Stonebridge and Whittington. The best examples date from 1780 to 1810. Later on it was degraded by a desire for prismatic brilliance rather than translucent softness. At the height of the industry English glass was without a rival in Europe, and most of the French, Austrian and German chandeliers of the late eighteenth century were embellished with English cut glass.

Tapestries, Carpets and Needlework

So far we have seen how foreign arts and craftsmen helped to raise the insular arts to a higher standard. Once started, Englishmen needed no further incentive to rival their teachers. Turning to the textiles of the period we find a similar influence at work. The love of needlework and tapestry was fostered by the importation of tapestries from the Netherlands in the late fifteenth and sixteenth centuries, though there are records of native-made hangings before that date, such as those evolved at Barcheston. We have to turn, however, to the factory at Mortlake, founded in 1619 by James I., for the first important departure. Here were employed Flemish and English weavers, the works continuing to flourish from their inception until the reign of Queen Anne. After this other factories were opened. In Lambeth there was one founded in 1670, and John Vandrebanc had a studio in Great Queen Street until 1728, one of the productions of which is shown on Plate LXXIII. There was also Joshua Morris, who entered into litigation with Hogarth in 1727 for payment of a tapestry designed by the latter but not approved by Morris. Pierre Parisot founded a tapestry factory at Fulham in the reign of George II., the main output being carpets, chair coverings and screens. In the middle of the century a tapestry factory was founded in Dublin. The last tapestry weaver was Paul Saunders of Soho. The fashions for stucco decoration or for beautiful painted wall-papers, generally copied from Chinese models, gradually took the place of tapestry for wall coverings, and by the third quarter of the eighteenth century it was considered démodé. Fig. 46 shows a beautifully engraved advertisement for the wares of one of the new wall-paper makers, with a glimpse of his shop.

The weaving of carpets is almost analogous to the making of tapestry, and the tradition in this country prior to the eighteenth century was slight. It became customary to import

TAPESTRIES, CARPETS, NEEDLEWORK

Fig. 46.—A Wall-paper Manufacturer's Trade Card.

carpets from the East and from the Gobelins and Savonnerie factories of Paris, and it was not until two French workmen came to London in 1750 and set up business with Pierre Parisot that anything was done in this country. This factory was closed in 1755. The successor to the business was another Frenchman named Passavant, who, being unsuccessful in London, moved to Exeter, where he was assisted by French weavers. One of the designs attributed to this maker is a carpet having a ground of powder-blue and a design consisting of scrolls with parrots, garlands, and baskets of flowers.

As a result of premiums offered by the Society of Arts for carpets made in England, " in imitation of those made in Turkey and Persia," the industry gained some increase. Among the winners of the premiums were Thomas Moore of Chiswell Street, who made the famous carpet for the throne-room at Carlton House,[1] and Thomas Whitty of Axminster. Later on Passavant was awarded a prize. After 1760 several fine carpets were made to the design of Robert Adam by Thomas Moore. Such is the red drawing-room carpet at Syon House, and some of the carpets at Osterley. The Adam designs are of geometrical patterns such as figure in the treatment of ceilings, but the details are broader. The Axminster industry was founded by Thomas Whitty, a clothier, who " having seen in London a Turkey carpet ornamented with large figures and without a seam," conceived the idea of rivalling it. The Axminster carpets of the late eighteenth century were brilliant in colour and full in design; the patterning represented fruits, flowers and baskets. The carpets for the Pavilion at Brighton and at Buckingham House were made at Axminster in the third year of George IV.'s reign.

Wilton carpets ante-date those made at Axminster by a few years, their manufacture having been started by the ninth Earl of Pembroke in 1745. These carpets resembled the oriental rugs then imported, and according to Pocoke were about three-quarters of a yard wide. In the late eighteenth and early nineteenth centuries, carpets for large houses were imported from France, but there grew up a fashion for woven carpets with slight patternings of squares and circles which are distinctive and suit the Georgian environment. Many plain-coloured carpets, greens, blues and greys, were made, woven hearth-rugs of floral design giving the touch of enrichment by the fireside.

From carpets we proceed to the story of needlework, which had a long tradition of excellent craftsmanship behind it. After the Restoration, ladies worked designs in cross-stitch and petit-point for covering furniture, the Court ladies of William and Mary's reign being particularly adept at this type of work. The practice of needlework of high quality formed part of a gentlewoman's education, especially the working of floral

[1] Now in the possession of the Author.

patterns. In the days of Queen Anne, the tambour frame was in daily use by ladies for the making of needlework for the tall padded-back armchairs and settees of the time, and the loose cushions. Then in time this homely craft gave way to tapestries, velvets and damasks, and finally leather, silk, brocade and French tapestry stopped all such enterprise.

Needlework, however, continued to survive as a serious pastime for ladies. They could still find employment in working silk pictures, designs of baskets of flowers for pole screens and framing, and drawing on silk of birds, castles, ships and houses. At boarding schools the making of samplers, in the form of abecedaria, maps and texts, sustained the art of needlework until the fashion changed to pictures in wool. Dressmaking and millinery formed the occupation of professional workers, and for this the productions of Spitalfields and of France were in demand. It must not be forgotten that stuff curtains and other furnishings at the end of the century had become the monopoly of the upholders and furniture-men, but the making of patchwork quilts was still deemed worthy of the leisure of a gentlewoman.

Silver-work

As with the other crafts, we have to study the products of the late seventeenth century for the beginnings of the movement which resulted in Georgian silver and plate attaining to such excellence in design and workmanship. After the Restoration, the influence of the Dutch on ornamental design was paramount. When Paris became the recognised art centre of Europe, it was inevitable that English craftsmen should begin to imitate the articles of luxury which had been brought to perfection in a land so near to their own. The churches built by Wren required new plate, the city companies needed silver objects and numerous mayoralities desired maces and other civic symbols. In this connection mention can be made of the maces at St Bride's, Fleet Street, and at the Guild Hall, Guildford. Other fine examples include the plate at the Mansion House and in the royal palaces. So much plate had been melted down during the Commonwealth (and still more had been destroyed by the Great Fire) as to cause the silversmiths of London to work at high pressure and employ Dutch craftsmen to meet the demand.

Silver plate of this period is thinner than are the earlier examples ; it was embossed rather elaborately and the designs are full. The ornamentation consists of acanthus and tulip forms as well as fruit, and the figure-work is exceptionally well-modelled and fanciful. The employment of silver in thin sheets led to the making of silver tables, mirrors, chandeliers and wall sconces in large numbers. To this period belongs the fashion of engraving decorations upon silver tankards, porringers, boxes and mirrors. The pewter of the period carries the same detail and decoration as the silver objects, but of a simplified design.

When the "Britannia standard" was set up in 1696 owing to the shortage of silver for the coinage, the design of silver articles was modified. Then followed the period of gadrooning and of concave and convex fluting, combined with a return to plain surfaces. Thus was brought about the simplified design of silver which led to the austere forms associated with the reign of George I. After the Revocation of the Edict of Nantes many French silversmiths were among those who sought sanctuary in England. These include Pierre Harache, Daniel Garnier, David Guilliaume, Pierre Gillois and Pierre Platel. From this time to 1730 nearly all the leading silversmiths were of French extraction. The records at the Goldsmiths' Hall give the names of Coutauld, Paul Lamérie, Abraham Buteaux, Simon Jouet, Louis Laroche, Aymé Videau and others. To this influx of Huguenot craftsmen can be assigned the second French influence which introduced such motives as scrolls, straps and cast ornament, and at a later period the twirls and scrollwork of the *Régence*. The influence of Oppenordt and Meissonier thus lasted until the year 1760 (see Plate LXXVI., *below*).

Then came a reaction in favour of forms of classical origin. As in the case of furniture and interior decoration of the second half of the eighteenth century, the influence of Robert Adam was predominant. He designed plate for the wealthiest of his patrons and induced silversmiths to attain a delicacy of treatment hitherto unknown (see Plate LXXVI., *above*). The architectural character of these designs, which were based on the orders, classical foliation, and other well-known ornamental details, had all the attributes essential to the technique of silver, but they would have done equally well for bronze. Thus the way was prepared for imitating the heavier types of silver plate by rolling thin sheets of silver on to prepared copper, and producing Sheffield and Soho plate in vast quantities for the middling people. The design, however, of the articles sold as "Patent Plate" did not lose the highly finished character of the contemporary silver plate (see Plate LXXV., *below*). Sometimes Sheffield plate carried cast-silver enrichments, but during

PLATE LXXV.

Pierced Silver Sweetmeat Baskets of the Mid-eighteenth Century.

Silver Candlesticks of Adam type (the middle one silver gilt) bearing the Sheffield Hallmark (*circ.* 1780).

PLATE LXXVI.

Two Covered Vases and a Cream Jug in Silver Gilt, the centre example attributed to Robert Adam. The body of the right-hand piece is a coco-nut enriched with Wedgwood cameos.

Silver Coffee-pot, Teapot, and Candlestick of the Mid-eighteenth Century, showing the prevailing French Influence.

the later phases of the craft, lead was substituted. Pierced silver in ornamental patterns was produced at all periods from the Restoration to the Regency. The ornate type of bread and fruit baskets, showing imitation of wicker-work combined with French scrollwork, date from the reign of George II. (Plate LXXV., *above*). Pierced silver-work of the second half of the century includes *épergnes*, wine-coasters and trays. Wirework baskets and sugar-bowls were made of silver and Sheffield plate, as were countless other articles of everyday table use familiar in Georgian life. We can trace French influences in the designs combined with slight classical details such as the Adams favoured, and, later, the more severe forms of the French Empire. It is interesting to note the altering shapes of teapots, vases, urns, chafing dishes and cream-jugs, and the differences between Irish and English silver, the objects changing in form and substance with the reign of each king.

In all but the very poorest houses some articles of silver or plate were counted a necessity, and every care was given to the arrangement of the dinner-table and the display of silver on the sideboard. This led to the introduction of the table-fender in the time of the Adam brothers, which at first consisted of an elaborate design rather similar to a drawing of a ceiling or the pattern of a carpet, to the plain mirrored types which came into use at the end of the century. Dinner was the principal meal of the day and was observed with every ceremony. The table was arranged in formal state and was lit by candelabra; there was an *épergne* in the centre and glass vases for sweetmeats. This arrangement of silver and glass, with steel knives and forks of silver with felspar handles, needed the closest supervision of the butler and added to the labours of the staff. It is significant that this tradition lasted through the Victorian age and to-day in some houses remains practically unaltered.

Porcelain

To please the noble dame, the courtly Squire
Produced a Tea Pot made in Staffordshire.
So Venus looked, and with such longing eyes,
When Paris first produced the golden prize.
" Such works as this," she cries, " can England do ?
It equals Dresden, and excels St Cloud,"
All modern china now shall hide its head,
And e'en Chantilly must give o'er her trade ;
For lace let Flanders bear away the bell ;
In finest linen let the Dutch excel ;

> For prettiest stuffs let Ireland first be named ;
> And for best fancied silks let France be famed ;
> Do thou, thrice happy England, still prepare
> Thy clay, and build thy fame on Earthen ware.

At the present time when so many people desire to possess some rare specimen of English porcelain, we begin to understand the attitude of our Georgian forbears towards this rare commodity.

The following lines suggest that even slum-dwellers were not without some little scraps of ceramic ware :—

> Above the fire, the mantel-shelf contains
> Of china-ware some poor unmatch'd remains ;
> There many a tea-cup's gaudy fragment stands,
> All placed by vanity's unwearied hands.

At the beginning of the eighteenth century china was indeed rare. There were, it is true, examples of Delft from Holland and specimens of oriental art brought back by the ships of the East India Company. The first record of an English potter attempting to produce a translucent ware dates from 1671. This was John Dwight, who was then making experiments in his stoneware manufactory at Lambeth. Dwight, however, only succeeded in producing fine stoneware. In the same category can be ranged the products of Place, an amateur of York, which, in so far as the specimen at the Victoria and Albert Museum goes, is similar to the marbled stoneware of John Dwight. As the century advanced to its first quarter oriental china was no longer a rarity, for the East India Company had seen that a considerable trade awaited the importation of useful and ornamental articles. From the factories established in the Treaty Ports was exported crate after crate of porcelain for the English markets. The shapes of tea and dinner ware were adapted by native craftsmen to Western uses and painted decorations, coats of arms, crests and monograms were copied from designs sent over from England. We have little idea now of the vastness of this trade.

In France the manufacture of artificial porcelain was steadily rising to perfection, thanks to royal and noble patronage. The English makers had all the odds against them, and herein lies the explanation of why English pottery was late in entering the market. Many of the early undertakings were short-lived owing to lack of support. Bow, Chelsea and other works went the same way, but unfortunate as the enterprises were, they marked the beginnings of what in time grew to be a national industry. Works were opened at Plymouth and Bristol in 1768, but the former lasted only three years. It was then that William Cookworthy made his first attempt to utilise the china clay of Cornwall.

Cookworthy succeeded at Plymouth in producing real porcelain, the same as that made in China and Germany, but although his ware was good he suffered from lack of support, and in 1771 the factory was transferred to Bristol. Here Cookworthy was joined by Richard Champion. After ten years of struggle the Bristol factory was closed in 1781. While these attempts were being made, the factories of Worcester and Derby were continuing to turn out soft china. At the close of the eighteenth century Josiah Spode invented a peculiar substance, or china body, of which bone ash and felspar formed the constituents. This in fact is a species of hard porcelain. When covered with a highly fusible glaze it presents the outward appearance of soft china, and it can be painted in the same colours.

The approximate dates of the founding of the various factories are as follows :—

1745. Bow and Chelsea.
1751. Worcester and Derby.
1752. Longton Hall.
1756. Liverpool.
1768. Plymouth.
1769. Wedgwood (Etruria).
1771. Bristol.
1772. Caughley.
1781. New Hall.
1795. Pinxton and Church Gresley.
1797. Spode (Stoke-on-Trent).
1798. Minton (Stoke-on-Trent).
1798. Coalport.
1800. Davenport (Longport).
1803. Torksey.
1811. Nantgarw.
1814. Swansea.
1820. Rockingham.

The painting on English china rarely shows to advantage by comparison with Continental examples. More often than not the English maker was content to reproduce foreign ideas, and never succeeded in making them his own. But notwithstanding this tendency, English craftsmen occasionally touched on originality and showed a feeling for decorative effects of a high order. We have to refer to the early works of Bow, Chelsea, Longton Hall and Worcester to find the best examples. These placed side by side with the finest productions of Sèvres, Meissen or Dresden more than hold their own.

It is not generally appreciated that paste possesses an intrinsic beauty apart from its coloured decoration. The fine productions of the early periods were not made in considerable quantities, so that they are rarely met with save in museums and select private collections.

Bow china (Plate LXXVII.) first claims attention, the tradition being that these London works were established in 1730. Apart from jugs and articles of utility we have to consider the beautiful specimens of modelling which brought the art of the sculptor into the house. Up to 1750 the Bow works were carried on as a joint company. The works at that date gave employment to three hundred persons. Ninety of them were painters, "all working under one roof." The factory stood on the Essex side of the River Lea, close to Bow Bridge. After the year 1776 it was closed and the industry terminated.

The various examples of Bow include white china embossed with the Mayflower pattern, painted china with a blue decoration roughly painted on the biscuit in a pseudo-Chinese style, plain jugs, cups, plates, baskets and knife-hafts.

Figures and fancy objects, white and painted, were made at Bow, but the speciality was richly decorated domestic ware. The figures are generally small and exceptionally well-modelled. They include gentlemen and ladies, boys and girls, fiddlers and tambourines, shepherds and shepherdesses, Dutch dancers, Harlequins and Columbines, as well as toys and animals. In those days the largest figures were sold at nine shillings each.

London at this date took the lead in the production of English porcelain. In addition to Bow and Chelsea there were two other factories at Stepney and Greenwich. Royalty and the aristocracy favoured Chelsea, both for busts and figures as well as for services of fine porcelain. The works stood near Cheyne Walk and were prosperous in 1754. The entire stock of porcelain toys was annually offered for sale, and after a lapse these annual sales were resumed in 1759. The business continued to prosper until 1783, when the owner of the works, Duesbury, decided to remove all the appliances and models to his Derby manufactory. With the closing of the Chelsea works the trade passed from London. Chelsea made a speciality of

PLATE LXXVII.

Groups in Derby Porcelain, modelled by J. J. Spengler after a painting by Angelica Kauffmann (1795).

Two Groups of Coloured Figures in Bow Porcelain (about 1750-60).

PLATE LXXVIII.

Chelsea Ware (*circ.* 1765).

Jug and Teapot in Bow Porcelain (*circ.* 1755).

A Plate in Longton Hall Porcelain
(*circ.* 1755).

A Plate in Derby Porcelain
(*circ.* 1790).

toys and knick-knacks which include trinkets, buttons, bottle-stoppers, ladies' thimbles, stick knobs, snuff and patch boxes, and charming smelling-bottles in the shape of figures and heads. With these can be classed timepieces, sconces and candelabra. One chandelier made for the Duke of Cumberland is said to have cost £600. The fine Chelsea vases, now mostly in collections, date from the last years of the manufactory.

The specimens that are classed as Longton Hall (Plate LXXVIII.) follow very closely the productions of Chelsea. The business began about the middle of the eighteenth century and lasted for eight years. The story of the connection between Derby and Chelsea goes back to a period long before Duesbury effected the amalgamation. After 1760 some of the productions began to take on the character of the severe classic forms which were beginning to appear in other branches of art and decoration. In addition " services for dessert " and a great variety of useful and ornamental porcelain after the finest Dresden models were made.

At this time most of the Derby modellers were foreigners. Pierre Stephan, a Frenchman, was engaged in 1770. Rossi, whose speciality was vases, was an Italian. J. J. Spengler, a Swiss, modelled groups, and two of these, based on paintings by Angelica Kauffmann, are shown on Plate LXXVII. This craftsman, having worked for Duesbury in London, came to Derby in 1790.

It is not surprising, especially as classic taste was in the ascendant, to find tripods, urns, altars and figures borrowed from mythology and ancient history among the productions, and from now on the shepherds and shepherdesses of old Chelsea ceased to multiply. Space alone precludes more than a brief mention of the factories at Pinxton and Torksey, Swansea, Worcester, Coalport, Caughley, Plymouth and Bristol, other than to say that the traditions of Chelsea and Derby were maintained with certain innovations. Finally we come to Etruria, the new factory opened by Wedgwood in 1769. In 1766 Wedgwood produced his celebrated basalts or black Egyptian ware. It will be interesting to architects to hear that Weber, a modeller of uncommon ability, was recommended to Wedgwood by Sir William Chambers. When Flaxman went to Italy in 1787 he arranged to execute occasionally, when his other engagements permitted, some models for Wedgwood, but he undertook principally to suggest, overlook, and give finishing touches to the works of such artists as were employed expressly in copying from the antique under the direction of Angelo Dalmazzoni.

Bookbinding

From the time of Caxton to the late seventeenth century English bookbinding owed much to foreigners. Private libraries in the sixteenth century were few and the bindings of books were the work of Flemings. Among the private collections of Robert Dudley, Earl of Leicester, Lord Burghley and the Earl of Arundel, were books bound in brown leather with heavy corner-pieces and centre stamps. These, with books from the collection of James I., show the French influence.

We have to look to the period after the Restoration for the development of the industry. The work produced from this time to the reign of William and Mary is beyond question the best of its class. Much of the fine gilt binding has been ascribed to Samuel Mearne, who died in 1685, or to his son, Charles Mearne ; this, however, has been disproved, because although Samuel Mearne was appointed Royal Bookbinder to Charles II. he did not actually bind books.

In the opening years of the eighteenth century minute tooling was continued. Robert Harley, first Earl of Oxford, who collected an important library, gave his name in 1720 to a style which consisted of a broad-tooled border with centre panels, on which a pineapple design figures prominently. The Earl's binders were Eliot and Chapman, who did trade bindings in morocco of a high standard. To these two craftsmen belongs the invention of the " Harleian style." In 1750 Thomas Hollis, the Republican, employed Matthewson the binder to bind his books in red morocco with gold - tooled emblems of Liberty, Owl, Sword, wand of *Æsculapius*, *Mercury*, *Cap of Liberty*, and other small stamps. It is said that Thomas Pingo, the medallist, cut a number of the tools used for this work. London, Edinburgh and Dublin had coteries of craftsmen with distinctive styles. Edinburgh work shows a preference for French and Italian tooling of the seventeenth century, and Dublin had a style almost as delicate. By 1770 the full tide of classical ornamentation was felt as much in the bookbinding industry as in any other section of applied art.

The most famous craftsman of this period was Roger Payne, who began work in London about the middle of the century. He combined ability for design with wonderful delicacy in gold tooling, and has a place in the first rank of decorative binders. He put ornamental linings, or doublures, inside many of his bindings, and sewed his books with silk, often inserting MS. notes in the work he undertook with his own hands. Payne used morocco, russia leather and pigskin. He it was who discovered the possibility of "graining" morocco, but he only used what is now called "straight grain," the further process of "pinhead" grain being perfected later. Payne was assisted by Richard Wier. After his death in 1797 several of his books were left unfinished, but they were admirably completed by Charles Hering, who used Payne's stamps. In 1780, while Payne was entering upon his sphere of fullest activity, James Edwards of Halifax hit upon a way of making vellum transparent, and patented it in 1785. This craftsman covered his bindings with fine white paper and painted decorative designs on it in water-colours. He then covered the work all over with transparent vellum, with edges of thin gold tooling. Edwards' borders are very graceful and his style, known as Etruscan, was much admired and imitated in France during the reign of Louis Seize.

A follower of Edwards was John Whitaker, who bound his books in calf, on which he put painted and stamped work done in very strong soda, making a rich brown stain. The stained calf, a development of which is "Tree" calf, does not last well, as the strong alkali tends to destroy it. At the close of the eighteenth century bookbinding as a fine art entered upon its decline, for although mechanical skill improved, design languished.

CHAPTER X

PAINTING, FROM LELY TO CONSTABLE

From the decline of mediævalism up to the first quarter of the eighteenth century, the course of English painting, such as it was, was largely determined by foreign influences. From the time of Henry VII. it had been customary for patrons to import foreign artists and craftsmen where such work was needed, and the quota of these is august enough, including such names as Holbein, Lely, Rubens and Van Dyck, besides numerous lesser men. There were, of course, several English painters of talent, including the miniaturists Nicholas Hilliard and Peter and Isaac Oliver in the reign of Elizabeth, Samuel Cooper in the mid-seventeenth century, the topographical draughtsman, Loggan, in late Stuart times, and Sir James Thornhill, who did much monumental decorative work for Kent and other architects under the prevailing Baroque influence. But foreign artists were the fashion, and native talent was considered only in the light of an inefficient substitute, as, indeed, to a great extent, it was.

A Dutchman, Sir Peter Lely, was Court Painter to Charles II. and executed a mass of portraits of the beautiful women of the time; and another foreigner, Sir Godfrey Kneller, carried on his work well into the first quarter of the eighteenth century. Up to the time of Hogarth, who came into his maturity at about this period, little important work was done; in fact this early period is one of the most lethargic in the history of the graphic arts in England, a fact that is particularly surprising in the light of the fine work then being accomplished in architecture and decorative design.

The developments that follow Hogarth are so exciting and diverse that it is perhaps more useful to summarise them at once before proceeding to examine them more scrupulously. Hogarth, exquisitely gifted as a draughtsman and painter, was above all else a moralist; and not only that, but an *illustrator* of morals. His work may be said to form the basis of the great tradition of illustration that has continually persisted in English art, and which was so meretriciously exaggerated by

PLATE LXXIX.

A Typical Scene, by Thomas Rowlandson.

"An Election Entertainment," by William Hogarth.

PLATE LXXX.

"At the Door of the Dolphin," by George Morland.

An Allegorical Painting by William Blake,
(National Gallery, London,)

the school of narrative and *genre* painters of the late nineteenth century. It will be seen how this tradition continued to operate during the latter portion of the century.

Another aspect of Georgian art is that it produced a number of strikingly individual painters whose work can never altogether be attributed to any particular school of influence. Here we notice William Blake, George Morland, Thomas Rowlandson, and innovators such as Constable and Crome, whose influence was sufficient to alter the whole trend of landscape painting in succeeding years.

Two further aspects remain to be examined. The great English school of portraitists founded (as might be said) by Sir Joshua Reynolds and including Gainsborough, Romney, Hoppner, Ramsay, Raeburn, Zoffany, Lawrence, Opie and others, definitely placed English art on a footing of some consideration in the eyes of Europe. The portraits of this school have a freshness of colour and a psychological approach to their subject that is quite disarming. The technical virtuosity is considerable ; and each of these artists has a personal idiom —what has been described as a " handwriting "—which distinguishes his work. The quality of charm is almost always subtly evident in English portraiture of the later eighteenth century.

Secondly, the impulse towards a purely pictorial expression that superseded the " classical landscape " practised since the time of Claude Lorrain is a movement of vast significance that marks the close of the century. Though Constable, Cotman, Crome and Girtin belong, properly speaking, to the succeeding age, yet at the same time they mark the culmination of Georgian art. The old horn spectacles of classicism are finally stowed away, and the world is viewed with a new and clear creative vision. In no small degree a result of the great development of water-colour as a medium at this time, the new painting, in form, pattern, texture and composition, defined the lines on which the art of landscape has developed to the present day. This movement is something more than a mere response to Romanticism or a sentimental " return to nature." In the work of these men there is something of the sterling vision and design of the old masters, and their names are linked with the most virile of the periods of English painting.

Hogarth, then, is the first considerable figure in English painting in the eighteenth century. The son of a struggling schoolmaster, he was apprenticed young to a silver-plate engraver, Ellis Gamble of Cranbourne Street. On leaving this employment he supported himself by designing plates for booksellers and tradesmen, but the work of Sir James Thornhill at St Paul's and Greenwich had so impressed itself upon his mind that he determined to embark on the career of a painter. In the meantime he had made a runaway marriage with Thornhill's daughter, and a few years later he began his series of paintings of " The Harlot's Progress," " The Rake's Progress " and " Marriage à la Mode." He was profoundly interested in the morality of the times, which he illustrated in its curious blend of exquisiteness and brutality, lashing it sometimes with a moralist's fury, sometimes with bitter satire, as in " The March of the Guards to Finchley," " The Election Entertainment " (Plate LXXIX.) and " Gin Lane." At the same time he executed some masterly portraits.

The sarcasm and grim humour of his scenes of daily life were readily understood by a public which, if it was often vicious, could also be candid. Fielding said : " He who would call the ingenious Hogarth a burlesque painter would, in my opinion, do him very little honour, for sure it is much easier, much less the subject of admiration, to paint a man with a nose, or any other feature, of a preposterous size, or to expose him in some absurd or monstrous attitude, than to express the affections of man on canvas. It hath been thought a vast commendation of a painter to say his figures seem to breathe, but surely it is a much greater and nobler applause that they appear to think." There is, indeed, a psychological preoccupation in Hogarth's work, a quality indispensable to a great illustrator, that underlies the sarcasm, the humour, and the brutality of the exposure.

Richard Wilson, roughly a contemporary of Hogarth's, was a painter of serene classical landscapes under the Claudian influence (Plate LXXXIV.). His career was an unsuccessful one, for the demands of the age were principally for portraiture. At the age of thirty-six he was enabled to go to Italy, and became so obsessed by the genius of Claude that he ceased entirely to paint the portraits on which, up till then, he had been able to subsist. But the public preferred the pictures of Barret and Smith of Chichester, and the attitude of Sir Joshua Reynolds was one of open hostility. Wilson was careless in dress and manners, and Reynolds did not hesitate to deal with his supposed shortcomings as a painter in the " Discourses." Wilson entered upon the lowest ebb of his fortunes, lodging in a small room and selling sketches for half a crown apiece. Later, a reconciliation was effected with the President, and his fortunes rose when he inherited a small estate where he retired and died in 1782.

Sir Joshua Reynolds had risen to be a very august person indeed. The son of a Devonshire schoolmaster, he was born at Plympton in 1723, and during early youth showed no leanings towards schooling. His father thought him sufficiently equipped for the profession of an apothecary, but wiser counsels prevailed, and in 1741 he was sent to London to study painting under Hudson. Reynolds spent two years with Hudson, and then, until 1746, worked at Plympton. His career as an artist dates from the year 1749, when he was invited by Captain, afterwards Admiral Keppel to make a voyage with him in the Mediterranean in the " Centurion." After touching at many ports, including Lisbon, Gibraltar, Algiers and Leghorn, Reynolds left the ship and travelled to Florence and Rome. He remained in Italy for two years studying the works of the great Italian masters, returning overland in 1752.

He was now fully equipped to set up as a portrait painter, and as such became almost immediately popular and fashionable. Eighteen years of portrait painting followed, during which time he painted most of the celebrated persons of the age (see Plate LXXXI.). He was specially favoured by the Whig party, was elected a member of Brooks's Club, became the intimate of politicians, aristocrats and wits, and was a leading light of the coterie surrounding the pontifical Johnson. He was, in fact, not only a fashionable portrait painter but a man of fashion as well. His figures were thirty-five guineas for painting a head, double that amount for a three-quarter-length portrait, and a hundred and fifty if full-length. A four-and-a-half hours' sitting was required to get the likeness; afterwards the sitter's attendance could be dispensed with.

He was elected first president of the newly formed Royal Academy. In 1761 he bought a house on the west side of Leicester Square and furnished it on a scale that was only equalled by Sir William Chambers at Whitton. He designed his own carriage, which had carved and gilt wheels and painted panels representing the seasons. He dressed his footmen in silver liveries and sent his sister driving through the finest thoroughfares to show his state. When she complained that the carriage was, perhaps, too ostentatious, " What ! " said the painter, " would you have one like an apothecary's carriage ? "

Reynolds commissioned his friend Chambers to build him a villa on Richmond Hill, which still stands next to the " Wick " built by Robert Mylne for Lady St Aubyn. His last appearance at the Academy was in 1790, and his death followed two years later at the age of sixty-nine.

Though his work was probably rather over-estimated at the time, it had solid and sterling qualities which it is impossible to ignore to-day. It is in his allegories and religious pictures that his limitations are most apparent. His portraits, always sound in painting and composition, are often of remarkable quality, whilst some of his slighter studies, as, for instance, those of children, are superb. He was an admirable technician, and, to perfect his media, devoted much study to the pigments used by the famous Italians. His influence was great and lasting, and he did much to stabilise and popularise the painter's art in England. He was an amiable and cultured man, who could assert himself effectively in case of need, and was not without an eye to the main chance. On being appointed the King's Principal Painter he remarked that the salary of £38 a year, reduced from £200, was less than that of the King's Ratcatcher.

In Reynolds' contemporary, Gainsborough, we find a painter of different quality. His art was more individual, his gifts more profound, his imagination more brilliant. He revelled in experiment and technical daring, and devoted the major part of his gifts to portraiture, in which sphere his utterly original technique found him a fashionable following at once. But brilliant as are his portraits (Plate LXXXI.), in landscape, his early love, he would probably have risen to even greater heights if the exigencies of the time had allowed it. In his landscape work he reveals himself as one of the greatest practitioners of this essentially English art, and his influence is very evident in the great revival in landscape painting that marks the beginning of the next century.

Thomas Gainsborough was born at Sudbury in Suffolk in 1727, the youngest of nine children. His father was a milliner, clothier and shroud-maker. At the age of ten he began to show skill with the pencil, and by the time he left school had developed a rare talent for landscape drawing. When he was fourteen his father apprenticed him to Dupont, a silversmith in Wardour Street, who in turn sent him to Gravelot, the engraver and painter. Then followed a course of study in the famous St Martin's Lane Academy, and by the time he was seventeen he was working for dealers and executing landscapes and portraits at an average price of from three to four guineas apiece.

At the age of nineteen he married, and in 1745 set himself up in Ipswich, where he found many clients. From thence he moved to Bath, where he spent fifteen prosperous years painting the fashionable world, during which time his talents came into

PLATE LXXXI.

"Mrs Carnac," by Sir Joshua Reynolds. (Wallace Collection.)

"The Duke and Duchess of Cumberland," by Thomas Gainsborough (Windsor Castle).
By gracious permission of His Majesty The King.

PLATE LXXXII.

Elizabeth, Countess of Derby, by George Romney.

An Eighteenth-century "Life" Class. Mr Pether's pupils sketching a model.
From the mezzotint by Joseph Wright of Derby.

their full maturity. When the Royal Academy was founded in 1768, Gainsborough's reputation was such that he was immediately enrolled a member.

In 1774 he moved to London, where he took the western wing of Schomberg House in Pall Mall (Plate LVII.) at a yearly rental of £300. Here Reynolds called on him, but the call was not returned; for though both artists professed the highest admiration of the other's talents, there was something incompatible in their natures that precluded intimacy. The climax of his career as a portrait painter was a summons to paint the Royal Family at St James's Palace.

Like Reynolds, he was particularly fond of Richmond, and here he spent his summers painting landscapes. Towards the

FIG. 47.—An Eighteenth-century Painter's Studio.

end of his life the breach between himself and Reynolds was healed, and Reynolds was a pall-bearer at his funeral at Kew in 1788.

George Romney, another popular and fashionable portrait painter, though he had not the shining gifts of Gainsborough, yet executed some noteworthy works. The son of a carpenter, he was first apprenticed to an itinerant painter named Christopher Steele, and in 1757 set up a studio at Kendal, where he began to copy the works of Lely and Rigaud at Sizergh Castle, also painting portraits of the local gentry.

A man of great personal charm, he soon migrated to London, and later, in 1769, managed to spend six months in Paris. Nine years later he travelled to Rome, where he became a student once more, and he was over forty when he returned to London, now fully qualified to practise as a portrait painter.

He set up a studio in Cavendish Square, where he became extremely popular, and had soon painted most of the fashionable and celebrated people of his time (see Plate LXXXII.), including the famous Emma Hart, afterwards Lady Hamilton. In 1796 he bought a small property at Flask Walk, Hampstead, but his success was overshadowed by melancholia and madness. He retired to Dalton-in-Furness, where he died in 1802.

Other painters who can only be mentioned briefly in these pages include Allan Ramsay, the Edinburgh portrait painter who at the close of his life was appointed Painter-in-Ordinary to George III.; Francis Cotes, a charming pastellist and portrait painter; Gavin Hamilton, an ardent classicist; John Astley; and Robert Edge Pine, who painted historical subjects. Another excellent painter was George Stubbs, who was keenly interested in anatomy and published several works on this subject which gained him an international reputation. Peter Vandyke, a Dutchman who settled at Bristol, is also worthy of mention.

Another foreigner who settled in England in 1758 and became an important figure in English eighteenth-century art was Johann Zoffany, a native of Ratisbon. He achieved considerable success as a portrait painter, his colour being peculiarly rich, and specialised in conversation groups (Plate XCII.). No summary of the painting of the period would be complete without an account of Joseph Wright of Derby, who began his career, like Reynolds, with Hudson. He first painted historical pictures but later developed a considerable talent for *genre* and conversation subjects, including his celebrated groups by fire and candle light (see Plates XXXVI., *below*, LXXXII.). In the National Gallery can be seen his "Experiment with the Air Pump," and his portraits of Arkwright and Erasmus Darwin.

Benjamin West, a Quaker born in America, studied in Rome and settled in London in 1763. His large historical canvases, with such titles as "Agrippina landing with the Ashes of Germanicus" and "The Death of Wolfe," enjoyed a considerable reputation at the time, though to modern eyes they may often seem rather dull and lifeless. However, after the death of Reynolds in 1792, he was elected President of the Royal Academy.

A fellow-countryman of West's, John Singleton Copley, also executed large historical paintings, including the well-known "Death of Chatham," which are of a somewhat higher quality than those of West. Another Englishman by adoption, the Swiss, Henry Fuseli, began by doing illustrations for

PLATE LXXXIII

The Exhibition at the Royal Academy, 1771.
From a contemporary print after Earlom.

"The Wandering Artist." A joke by Rowlandson at the expense of the new school of landscape painters of the close of the eighteenth century.

PLATE LXXXIV.

A Norfolk Landscape, by John Crome.
(National Gallery, London.)

An Italian Landscape, by Richard Wilson.
(National Gallery, London.)

Boydell's edition of Shakespeare. He produced a large quantity of drawings and paintings, generally somewhat fantastic in conception. Barry, an Irishman, who painted the historical scenes that decorate the great room at the Royal Society of Arts, must be classed among the heroic failures of the century. Decorative paintings for rooms were now again in vogue, and such artists as Cipriani and Angelica Kauffmann found considerable employment in this style of work with architects and patrons.

As the majority of the public could obviously not afford original works by the great painters of the time, there came to be a considerable demand for coloured prints, and this art was developed enormously in the latter part of the century. Mezzotints of celebrated portraits had long been popular, but Francis Wheatley, a charming and capable painter, created a new manner in his coloured prints of subjects of everyday life, of which the most famous are his well-known series of " The Cries of London." A host of other artists who specialised in aquatints, mezzotints and coloured engravings also helped to fill the demand, including Faber, George Vertue, Earlom (Plate LXXXIII.), and those fine architectural artists, James and Thomas Malton (see Plates LII., LIV.). Towards the end of the century, colour-plate books, especially on architectural and topographical subjects, became increasingly numerous.

A large group of talented artists began to specialise in topographical water-colour drawings, including Paul Sandby, Thomas Hearne, Edward Dayes and Henry Edridge. The work of Thomas Rowlandson, however, belongs to a sphere of its own. Though his satirical wit is sometimes reminiscent of Hogarth, yet the slighter and elegant qualities of his style more exactly express the period at which he worked (see Plates VII., XXIII., XLV. and LXXIX.). Rowlandson, after studying in Paris, gave himself up to the making of drawings, working most often in reed pen and colour wash. His vision, though often brutal and harsh, is a vivid expression of the life of the time. He was a natural-born draughtsman with a brilliant energy in his technique which was exactly suited to express the comedy of English life. Another caricaturist, James Gillray, had a marked gift for satire which, mainly used for political ends, is often enough vulgar and gross. Other caricaturists are Henry Bunbury (1750-1811) and Robert Dighton, who comes at the end of the period (see *frontispiece*).

Among minor artists mention may perhaps be made of Julius Cæsar Ibbetson, who did much animal painting. His work is represented at the Victoria and Albert Museum; he also experimented with decorative mural painting, as may be seen at Kenwood, Hampstead. Then there is Matthew William Peters, the parson painter, chaplain to the Royal Academy, whose picture of a girl in bed, afterwards called "Lydia" and recently resold at a considerable figure, caused, soon after its exhibition in 1777, a violent "decency campaign" against the Academy !

After the year 1770 a number of miniature painters sprang into popularity, including John Smart, Cosway and Downman. Of these, Cosway was, perhaps, the most highly talented, and the rage for miniature provided him with a wide range of sitters from among the most celebrated people of the time.

Returning to the great portrait painters of the latter part of the century, Henry Raeburn must first be noticed. Born in 1756, he left school at the age of fifteen and was apprenticed to a goldsmith. As an artist he was almost entirely self-taught, and at the age of twenty-nine he determined to visit Italy, on his way calling on Sir Joshua Reynolds for advice. In 1787 he returned to Edinburgh and set up a studio as a portrait painter, where his crisp, robust style soon made him famous. He was appointed "His Majesty's Limner in Scotland" by George IV. towards the end of his life.

John Hoppner was born in Whitechapel in 1759 of German parents. Though he painted a large number of portraits, including that of the celebrated Mrs Robinson ("Perdita"), and though the Prince of Wales interested himself in his career, he was never very successful as a painter. He was created an Academician in 1795.

John Opie was born in 1761, the son of a carpenter. As a boy he was encouraged by Dr Wolcot—"Peter Pindar"— who found him some commissions. Through the instrumentality of the same patron he was presented to Sir Joshua Reynolds, who also interested himself in him, and he enjoyed a considerable success in London, alternating between fashionable portraiture and historical painting, in which latter his best talent probably lay.

Sir Thomas Lawrence was the most considerable portrait painter of the Regency period. The son of an innkeeper, his rise to fame was meteoric, and he was appointed an A.R.A. in 1791, before he was twenty-one, at the instigation of the King. The aged President was now blind, Raeburn was working in Edinburgh, and Hoppner was the only serious rival in the field ; hence the way was open to a clear success. He was a brilliant if sometimes over-facile painter, and his career was almost unprecedented as regards the number and rank of his sitters. He was popular, elegant and extremely fashionable. But excellent as much of his work is, it cannot compare for solid quality with the works of the great painters of the preceding generation.

Two curiously individual figures stand out among the artists of this period : George Morland and William Blake. The life of Morland is well known, and has often been recounted in detail. The son of a painter, he served his early apprenticeship copying the works of other artists at his father's instigation, and afterwards studied at the Academy Schools. Romney offered to take him as a pupil, but Morland refused, preferring a roving life of freedom in taverns, pot-houses and stables, which even his marriage with William Ward's daughter failed to check. But this round of suburban and countryside taverns meant an intimate acquaintance with the roads, and Morland's wanderings helped him in no small way to depict the life of the countryside with that freedom of technique and clear vision that marks his best work (see Plate LXXX.). At one period his work became extremely popular, but his attachment to low life, to the chance acquaintanceship of the road and the vagabondage he loved, would never allow him altogether to seize his opportunity. His country scenes and pictures of rural life belong to no school of influence and yet they are among the most striking achievements in art of the century. Always in debt and generally tipsy, his life ended in squalor and misery.

Much has been written of William Blake since his works were revived from the obscurity which surrounded them in his lifetime. Blake was almost entirely unrecognised while he lived, and indeed this is not surprising, for he was born completely out of his time. He was a visionary and mystic, a poet and painter at once, and his drawings, paintings and engravings are more allied to the visionary art of the Middle Ages than to the solid background of Georgian England against which they were produced (Plate LXXX.). His striking technique evolved mystical and allegorical subjects which were often used to illustrate his poems, and his colour is strange and disquieting, entirely out of key with the spirit of the age. Blake lived humbly and quietly, publishing his own works from time to time, and ignored by a public which could neither understand nor care for his work. He died in 1827.

In reviewing the course of Georgian painting as it has so far been examined, we notice first and foremost that the art of portrait painting reached its zenith with Reynolds, Gainsborough and Zoffany, and passed on to a new set of men, including Lawrence, Hoppner and Raeburn, who, if they were not of quite the same quality as their predecessors, still were fully competent to maintain a very high standard. The school of illustrative and *genre* painting that begins with Hogarth constantly reappears throughout the century in the work of such men as Wright of Derby, Wheatley and Rowlandson. We have noticed the great and independent figures of Morland and Blake, and now come to the group of innovators whose work marks the turning point of the century, and who brought the art of English landscape to its finest achievement: Constable, Crome, Cotman, David Cox, Girtin and Turner.

We have already examined the landscape work of Richard Wilson and Gainsborough. Such other landscape painters as John and Alexander Cozens, and Wilson's pupils, Farington and Barret, had maintained an excellent level of work in this sphere, whilst the topographical draughtsmen had encouraged the use of the new medium of water-colour, which from now on we find employed frequently by all the principal painters in addition to oil-colour, while its fluidity had a considerable effect on the technique of the art.

John Crome was born at Norwich in 1768. Apprenticed in his youth to a coachmaker for seven years, he was drawing hard all this time, and was later lucky in finding several patrons, one of whom, a Mr Harvey, had a collection of Dutch pictures, including a Hobbema, which profoundly influenced the young artist, as did also the landscape work of Wilson and Gainsborough. Crome always had to struggle hard for a living, but gained a meagre pittance by teaching drawing. Thus his best works were made in almost every case for his own pleasure, and seldom found a buyer. The "Norwich Society of Artists" which he founded in 1810 with Cotman as its first president, included his two sons, Robert Ladbrooke and James Stark among its members. Crome was one of the greatest of English painters of landscape. His style, founded on his personal observation of Nature, was always direct and unassuming, and his pictures, which are almost entirely of the Norfolk flats where he lived and worked (Plate LXXXIV.), have that rare quality that distinguishes the real master.

John Sell Cotman, who also worked as an architectural and topographical draughtsman, was a painter of rare talent whose work envisaged all the highest qualities of the Norwich school (Plate LXXXV.). Girtin, who was born in 1775, died at the early age of twenty-seven, but had already displayed powers that must have placed him, had he lived, in the first rank of English painters. He exercised a considerable influence on

PLATE LXXXV

An Ink and Wash Sketch, "Stoke-by-Nayland, Suffolk," by John Constable.
(Victoria and Albert Museum, London.)

A Water-colour Sketch, "The Lake," by J. S. Cotman.
(Victoria and Albert Museum, London.)

Turner, with whom he studied at Dr Monro's Academy. As for Turner, his achievement belongs rather to the nineteenth century, but it is interesting to note that he was elected A.R.A. in the last year of the eighteenth, though his work had not then developed to the heights of imagination and technical accomplishment which mark its later phases. Peter de Wint and David Cox were two more excellent painters of landscape in both oil and water colour, the latter, also, often depicting scenes of country life.

At this period we find pure landscape, as opposed to the classical landscape of the earlier part of the century, with its ruins and mythological " properties," coming firmly into its own. The new school of English landscape painting was to spread its influence throughout the whole of the nineteenth century to our own day, not only in England but in France as well. It would therefore seem fitting that this chapter should end with the greatest of this school—and perhaps the greatest painter England has ever known—Constable, though the larger part of his work belongs to the early years of the next century.

John Constable was born at East Bergholt in Suffolk in 1776. The son of a miller, his father at first refused to allow the boy to become an artist till he found a patron in Sir George Beaumont, who finally persuaded his parents to allow him to study at the Royal Academy School in 1799. He began to exhibit at the Academy in 1802, spending his summers in the country painting and sketching. He was married in 1816, elected A.R.A. in 1819, and, in 1829, a full Academician.

Constable, as Mr Roger Fry has said of him, was " one of those rare natures which are able to make fruitful discoveries not only in design but in the possibilities of vision." Through the medium of a somewhat revolutionary technique (Plate LXXXV.), he managed to co-ordinate in his pictures the balance of tone, texture and colour that we observe in the works of the old masters. His landscapes have a singular quality of movement and rhythm that marked a revolution in the art, and he perfected a method which has been looked back to by countless painters in succeeding years.

CHAPTER XI

SCULPTURE, FROM GRINLING GIBBONS TO FLAXMAN

ENGLISH Renaissance sculpture, as distinct from carving and embellishment, begins with the Restoration. In the reign of Charles II. the sole English-born sculptor of merit was Grinling Gibbons, but his works belong more to the province of architectural decoration. His contemporary, Caius Gabriel Cibber, ranks as the first real sculptor. This artist carried out the bas-reliefs on the Monument for Sir Christopher Wren, and produced the two figures of Madness and Melancholia, which were suggested by two of the inmates of Bedlam. During the reign of James II., William and Mary, Anne and George I., English sculpture does not figure very highly. Some interesting busts were produced by Le Marchand, and Francis Bird executed some figures for St Paul's Cathedral.

Passing to the reign of George I., we find three foreigners securing the chief commissions for monumental sculpture. These were Rysbrack, Scheemakers and Roubilliac, all of whom worked for architects. Rysbrack soon developed an independent line and produced figures of Newton (Plate LXXXVII.), Lord Stanhope, the poet Prior (Plate LXXXVI.), Sir Godfrey Kneller and other prominent personages. Scheemakers seems to have secured the monopoly for monumental tombs in which the figures are clothed in the costume of the period. The most talented of the trio was Roubilliac, some of whose figures were copied by the Chelsea and Derby potters. Roubilliac had studied in the school of Bernini, but he later forsook to some extent the prevalent Baroque tendencies. He preferred careful detail and excelled in drapery. At the outset of his career in England he had worked in London for Carter & Cheere, a firm of stonemasons and statuaries, but through a fortunate introduction to Sir Edward Walpole he was enabled to set up business on his own account. Roubilliac's work is dignified and free, owing little to classic convention.

PLATE LXXXVI.

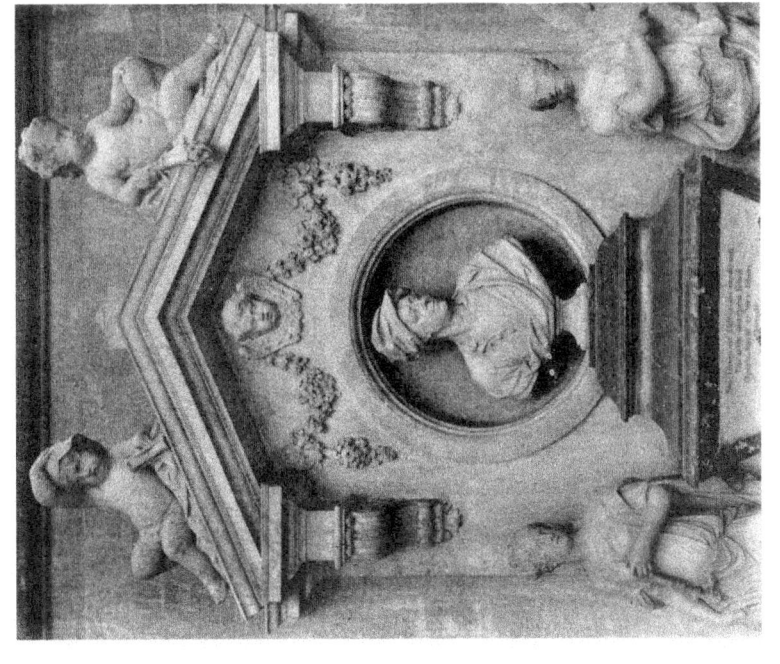

A Monumental Group, by Bacon, at Somerset House. "Navigation and the Thames."

The Memorial to Matthew Prior in Westminster Abbey. Designed by Gibbs with sculpture by Rysbrack.

PLATE LXXXVII.

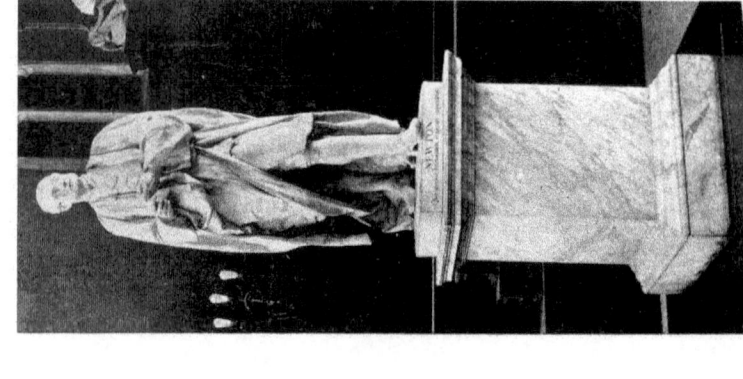

Statue of Newton, by Rysbrack. Trinity College Chapel, Cambridge.

Flaxman's Memorial to Princess Charlotte in St George's Chapel, Windsor.

While these foreigners became English only by adoption, many native statuaries were producing creditable work. Among these men was Robert Taylor, to whom the elder Dance entrusted the design of the sculptured group in the pediment of the Mansion House. Wilton was the first English sculptor of the later period to study the antique in Italy and to make copies of antique statues and busts for the English market. While still a young man he was appointed director of the sculpture gallery formed in Spring Gardens by the Duke of Richmond, and afterwards became "State-coach Carver to the King." Among his most important works were the monument to General Wolfe in Westminster Abbey, and those to Admiral Holmes and the Earl and Countess of Monteith. In the middle of the century a curious tendency became apparent to scheme sculptured subjects in pyramidal formation; or sometimes a pyramid or an obelisk was used to form a background. Wilton was a staunch adherent of this method.

During the reign of George III., sculpture began to be recognised increasingly as a serious art, and the next exponent, Banks, was a sculptor of superior skill and some originality.

In his work is to be seen the next stage towards the improved style of Flaxman. Banks was practically self-taught, but he eventually studied in Rome, and on his return sculptured a group of Caractacus and his family in the presence of Claudius. One of his finest works was a figure of Love catching a butterfly. His works, in conception, were ahead of their time, but patrons still preferred the antiquities of Rome. As it happened, Nollekens and Bacon caught the public taste and obtained wider patronage than the industrious Banks.

Nollekens, while he fell short of the artistry of Banks, was a finer sculptor of busts, and his marble portraiture was in demand almost as much as were the canvases of Reynolds, Gainsborough and Romney. Bacon began his career as a modeller of Chelsea figures and eventually became principal modeller in Coade's factory. In time he started on his own, and for the rest of his life secured a full quota of commissions for monuments, busts and statues.

It is significant that Wilton, Nollekens, Banks and Bacon were all influenced by the monumental school of painting. They aimed at broad and picturesque compositions, which were imitated in miniature in Chelsea and Bow models. The finest work produced by Bacon is perhaps the bronze group in the courtyard of Somerset House (Plate LXXXVI.).

Perhaps the greatest sculptor of the later Georgian period was John Flaxman. At the age of fifteen he was a student at the Royal Academy, and began by modelling wax and making drawings of classical subjects. As he developed, he came under the spell of Greek sculpture, and was fortunate enough to secure work from Wedgwood. Here is one of the first indications of a patron arising from among the new manufacturing class. Flaxman's genius was apparent, and from the first he gave grace and classical simplicity to articles of everyday use and ornament.

At the age of thirty he made his way to Rome, where he divided his time between study and the production of designs for Wedgwood. It was at this time that he produced the magnificent series of designs inspired by the writings of Homer, Æschylus and Dante. On his return to England, Flaxman found Banks, Bacon and Nollekens in full possession of the field, and it was not until after 1797, when he became a full Academician, that he began to receive the reward of his early labours. To this period belong the statues of Lord Howe, Sir Joshua Reynolds, William Pitt, Lord Cornwallis and Warren Hastings. His splendid group erected in St George's Chapel, Windsor, as a memorial to Princess Charlotte, the daughter of George IV., is shown on Plate LXXXVII.

Mention must here be made of two famous sculptors who did a considerable amount of work for architects. The first is Carlini, who worked under Sir William Chambers, and the second is the Irishman Edward Smith, who carried out the trophies and sculptural features at the Customs House, Dublin, for Gandon. Both artists favoured the contemporary French manner, and in the case of Edward Smith a real and unaffected genius is evident. The period closes with the work of Chantrey and Westmacott, which more properly belongs to the next century.

We have seen how the art of sculpture gradually developed from the works of three foreigners domiciled in England to the native genius of Flaxman. We have seen, too, how, as the other arts, it varied in accordance with the fashion for antiquity, first Roman and then Greek, and finally adopted a freer manner with the advent of Romanticism. In the reign of the first three Georges the halls of the largest houses were filled with copies of antique sculpture, vases and busts. At the end of the century a nobleman's mansion was considered incomplete if it did not contain a sculpture gallery. There is, for example, the fine gallery at Woburn, which was designed by Henry Holland for the Duke of Bedford, and is shown in Fig. 48 from a view in Robinson's "Vitruvius Britannicus." Sculpture was also much used in gardens, and at Southill in Bedford-

Fig. 48.—The Sculpture Gallery at Woburn.
Henry Holland, architect.

shire, a house built by the same architect, lead figures were painted to resemble stone.

It cannot be said that Georgian sculpture reached that level of achievement that has been noted in the other arts of the century. Much work of solid talent was executed, but when all is said and done, it is only the figure of Flaxman that stands out pre-eminently as an artist whose works will continue to be considered important.

CHAPTER XII

PLAYS AND PLAYERS, FROM CONGREVE TO SHERIDAN

THE magnificent traditions of Elizabethan drama had passed unscathed through the prescribing period of the Commonwealth and found new life in the brilliant school of the Restoration. The play was, indeed, one of the most popular of English diversions, and the English school of drama, as represented in the works of Congreve, Vanbrugh, Farquhar and others, unrivalled throughout Europe. But with the passing of this finer talent, the theatre, at the beginning of the century, was often debased into an exhibition of bawdiness without wit, or rhetoric without poetry. A faction had entered into severe opposition against the licence of what remained of Restoration comedy, and the result had met with success, inasmuch that at the beginning of the century there were rarely to be found more than two theatres open at once in London. In the first years of the century Italian opera became the rage. The new Queen's Theatre in the Haymarket, designed by Vanbrugh, was opened in 1705 by Vanbrugh and Congreve with an opera translated from the Italian called " The Triumph of Love."

During the first quarter of the century the English theatre sank to as low a level as it has perhaps ever reached. The audience was disorderly and often violent if the play met with its disapprobation. The actors, with the exception of Betterton, who was by then an old man, lacked *finesse* or genius, and comedy had to rely on disgusting plots and vulgar allusions for its success. Wren's Drury Lane was the principal London house. It contained two tiers of galleries, a pit filled with benches, with an amphitheatre behind. If a play or an actor was unpopular, the noise was deafening, and sometimes even the stage was rushed by the young gentlemen in the pit. With its poor plays, weak acting, guttering candles and lack of ventilation, to say nothing of a noisy and dissatisfied audience,

The Interior of Covent Garden Theatre : a Crowded Night.

From a water-colour by E. Dayes.

PLATE LXXXIX.

Provincial Theatres of the Later Eighteenth Century. (*Above*) Theatre Royal, Newcastle. (*Below*) The Theatre at Tunbridge Wells.
From contemporary aquatints.

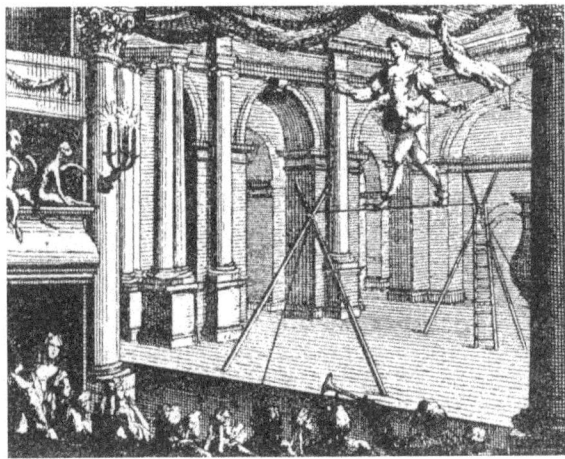

Fig. 49.—The Interior of a Theatre showing a Tight-rope Act. The drawing has especial interest as being from the hand of the architect, William Kent. The people in the box are caricatured in the fashionable *singerie* of the period.

the playhouse can hardly have been an attractive place at this time.

In 1728 Gay's "Beggar's Opera" was produced (Plate XC.) and took the town by storm. Utterly original in its treatment, it mocked the vogue for Italian opera with its homely and charming native airs, and produced one of the greatest and most sensational successes in the history of the English theatre. This period also saw a revival of Shakespeare's plays, though these were often travestied and even burlesqued. George Lillo's "History of George Barnwell," a play with a stern moral message intended for the apprentice, was an enormous success with the masses, and continued to be acted throughout the century.

It was David Garrick who was chiefly concerned in restoring the fallen dignity of the English theatre. Garrick was of a quite different stature to the players who had preceded him. A great actor, a man of culture, an intimate friend of Johnson and his circle, and a patron of the arts, he was well served by the writers of talent of his day, notably by Goldsmith, most of whose comedies he produced. Goldsmith and Garrick let a breath of fresh air into the mephitic stuffiness of the theatre of their time. Once again, real wit and poetry were demanded and supplied, and from thence onwards the standard of production maintained an even level, which, if it could not, perhaps, vie with the brilliance of Restoration drama at its best, did not disgrace the period which produced it.

Though previous to Garrick the century had seen some notable actors, such as Leigh, Estcourt, the Irishman Doggett (who founded the memorable race for the Coat and Badge), Colley Cibber, James Quin and Charles Macklin, none of these had impressed themselves so deeply on the public taste as did Garrick. Not only was he an actor of the first rank, equally at home in Shakespearean tragedy as in the delicate comedy of Goldsmith, but also a competent and successful manager, and one who did much to introduce long necessary improvements in lighting, costumes and *mise-en-scène*. Of the famous actresses of the early century, Mrs Bracegirdle, Vanbrugh's old flame, is perhaps the best remembered, though we also hear of Mrs Oldfield and Elizabeth Barry. Peg Woffington was the prime favourite of Garrick's era, for the culmination of Mrs Siddons' success was not till later. Her first appearance on the London stage was not a particular success, but the *furore* she created at Bath led her to appear again in London, where at Drury Lane, in 1782, she leapt immediately to a fame as great and almost as prolonged as that of Garrick. Her interpretations of the tragic figures of Shakespearean drama were deemed an original departure from precedent, and Reynolds has left us her portrait majestic in the robes of Lady Macbeth.

Though the glory had departed from tragic writing and the taste for it had to be satisfied by revivals of the works of Shakespeare and others, the school of comedy was still alive and was to find fresh inspiration in the plays of Richard Brinsley Sheridan. His first piece, " The Rivals," was not received well when first staged, but, revived in 1777, it met with considerable success. In the same year appeared " A Trip to Scarborough " and " The School for Scandal," both triumphant successes. " The Critic " was staged in 1779.

Sheridan, an impulsive and popular Irishman of considerable charm, was a man of wit, an intimate of the Prince Regent and of all the notable leaders of the Whig party who had from time to time to help him through the chaotic financial troubles in which he was generally immersed. He was for some time general manager of Drury Lane Theatre, and the house was, indeed, rebuilt for him by Henry Holland, having been remodelled at the time of Mrs Siddons' successes by Robert Adam.

The play was an important feature of London life at the

PLATE XC.

A Scene from "The Beggar's Opera." Notice the most fashionable members of the audience in boxes actually on the stage.
From the engraving by Cook after Hogarth.

"The Manager and the Spouter." The declamatory powers of the actor seem to have the worst possible effect on the manager waiting for his breakfast.
A cartoon by Wigstead.

PLATE XCI.

A Concert at Vauxhall Gardens. The diva accompanied by a considerable orchestra.

From a drawing by Rowlandson.

close of the century, and the illustration of the interior of Covent Garden Theatre on Plate LXXXVIII., its vast tiers filled with a fashionable crowd, certainly affords a considerable contrast to the small, badly lit, makeshift houses in which the finest plays of the Restoration period were performed. In the provinces, where any roomy building or barn had been thought suitable for the staging of a play, a crop of theatres arose, some of which, as the illustrations on Plate LXXXIX. will show, were of excellent design. These generally housed a permanent troupe ; the bands of nomadic players and crude " barn stormers," limned by Hogarth, who wandered about the country were housed in village assembly-rooms, barns, or in the booths of fairs.

CHAPTER XIII

MUSIC AND MUSICAL INSTRUMENTS

ENGLISH music may be said to culminate with Henry Purcell, who lived at the time of the Restoration. He had witnessed the banning of the ballad during the Puritan regime, and was ready to interpret the joyous care-free spirit which accompanied the Court life of the Stuarts. His works for the Church gradually displaced the madrigals of Weelkes and the psalms set to metre by Sternhold and Hopkins. His Church music is both voluminous and superb, and his compositions written for the stage included melodies which passed into popular street songs.

He wrote chiefly for the organ, harpsichord and strings, and it is of interest to remember that the notation for *Lillibulero* came from a harpsichord exercise composed by Purcell. His music expresses in melody the sum of the emotions of a period that produced Wren, Newton and Marlborough, but we have to remember the limitations of the instruments then in use. Among the other composers of Church music of the period was Dean Aldrich, who was equally distinguished as an amateur architect. But Purcell died in 1695 at the early age of thirty-seven. He was a lone star, and no one of his magnitude appeared in the firmament of English music for over a century.

The eighteenth century saw the passing of the old tradition in music and the adoption of classical forms since generally followed by composers. There is no space here to discuss forms in music or to touch on the continuing influence of the Reformation in Germany, but at least for the first half of the century, till the death of Bach and Handel at about its middle, the whole basis of music was contrapuntal. The piece was composed in so many " voices " or lines of melody—each went its independent way and joined or clashed. This is admirably shown in the fugue, which in the hands of a master was capable of great flexibility, endless fine effects, and even remarkable harmonies. Later it was replaced by the more modern conception of a fundamental melody supported by chords and developed and changed. In addition to the fugue, the most characteristic early orchestral piece was the suite, consisting of the overture—in the more developed forms having a long and elaborately developed lively air, between a grave beginning and ending—followed by a group of varied dance pieces, grave or gay. Among these were the allemand, courante, bourrée, gigue, minuet and sarabande. Purcell composed a number of suites, now being revived, and Handel's suites are frequently played.

In the latter half of the century the sonata for the piano or accompanied violin or other instruments was devised—K. P. E. Bach had much to do with originating the form; it consisted usually of three movements, and the four-movement symphony took the place, which it has since held, as the chief orchestral composition.

The genius of Handel lifted the whole volume of Georgian music to mighty and exalted realms never reached before. His followers and successors in England were legion, but never at any time during the reigns of the Georges did this country produce a native composer equal to the prolific German. The works of other foreigners, such as Bach and Haydn, were also popular, as was the dramatic oratorio, the Italian opera, and the old melodies of Church music.

We have, however, to return to the theatre in order thoroughly to understand the type of music appreciated by the Georgians. In this regard the most popular was the music of the ballad opera, which from 1727 was the chief means of introducing music to the public at large. Here it was possible to gather up all the popular tunes and to recast them, for they rarely represent original compositions. Among the musicians who assisted in this sort of work were Shield, Thomas Dibdin and Stephen Storace, violinist and personal friend of Mozart. The simplicity of the songs of the eighteenth century is their chief attraction; tremulous and gentle as they are, they are exactly suited to the time. One of these, by Arne, is given on Fig. 50.

There is no finer summary of the ballad music of the eighteenth century than that afforded by the sixty-nine songs of the " Beggar's Opera." Dr Pepusch has long had the credit for the tunes, but it is doubtful if he did more than write the overture and orchestrate the melodies, many of them earlier and traditional. Pepusch could not have had an extensive knowledge of old English music; a scholarly musician who came to London from Berlin, his taste was severe and his

Fig. 50.—A Song by Arne from "Clio and Euterpe, a British Harmony."
A contemporary song-book.

learning gained him the appointment of Doctor of Music at Oxford. He was an enthusiast for the formation of an Academy of Music ; and did his best to foster musical taste in this country. Dr Arne later rearranged the opera and gave the songs accompaniments ; but the melodies were current long before the work was staged. Gay himself may have had the rhythm of the music in his mind when he wrote the book. Contemporary opinion seems to have regarded Pepusch as a " dry-as-dust humdrum " composer. He became a friend of Handel, perhaps through his own connection with the Duke of Chandos.

Handel, on account of his continental reputation, was engaged to come to England as a composer ; and he it was who undertook to write the music for the Italian operas then occupying the London stage. But their lack of success involved the composer in long struggles, from which he only emerged through the popularity of his production of the oratorios, including those he named " didactic oratorios " and others he defined as " sacred drama." His first English oratorio was " Esther," and then followed the cantata " Acis and Galatea," composed for the Duke of Chandos in 1720-21. Handel was assured of success from the time these oratorios were produced in public in 1732. While writing for the Italian opera, he found time to engage a theatre in which to give concerts. In 1741 we find the great musician visiting Dublin with his masterpiece, " The Messiah." Handel's music is thoroughly in accord with the classicism of the time. He wrote for wide effect and produced his tremendous impressions on the thousands of his audiences with the same degree of certitude.

Among other native composers was the popular Dr Arne, whose works exactly suited the temperament of the middle Georgian period. His works are numerous and include a setting for Addison's " Rosamond," " The Opera of Operas," and a number of oratorios and settings for operas in the Italian fashion. He is, perhaps, now best remembered by " Rule Britannia " and the setting of Shakespeare's lyrics. Arne was born in 1710 and died in 1778.

The great musical historian of the time was Dr Charles Burney, the father of Madame d'Arblay. As a fashionable teacher of music and an organist of ability it was natural that he should compile a history of music as well as endeavour to raise taste by writing on and criticising contemporary European music. Another organist, William Croft, flourished from the time of Queen Anne to the period of Handel's supremacy. He was responsible for many hymn tunes which replaced the psalms set to metre by Sternhold and Hopkins. Maurice Green, William Boyce and Thomas Attwood were well-known composers of anthems.

ABSOLUTE The hymn and other Church compositions of Charles Wesley and his two sons, Charles and Samuel, have already been referred to in the section dealing with the Church.

Samuel Arnold and William Jackson contributed song-plays, of which a dozen were also composed by Thomas Linley (1735-1795), the father-in-law of Sheridan, who with his son Thomas composed the music for Sheridan's one opera, "The Duenna," the tuneful lyrics of which have recently been revived. The younger Linley was drowned when pleasure-boating off Lincolnshire, at the age of twenty-two. The music of "The Duenna" was typical of many song-plays of the time; some were composed by foreigners in England, such as Mr Defesch. The Linleys were a remarkable musical family. The elder Thomas had also as sons, William, an author and operatic composer, and Osias Thurston, an organist, while of his daughters, Maria sang in oratorio and at Bath, and Mary was also a singer. In addition there were Francis Linley (1774-1800), also a composer, who was organist at St James's, Pentonville, and was blind from birth, and George Linley (1798-1865), a composer. One of the sons of Linley was a personal friend of Mozart. William Shield, Thomas Carter and Michael Kelly were also with others among the company who composed vocal music. Henry Carey was also a writer of ballad operas and caricatured ably the pomposity of a strain of Italian opera; he has been sometimes held responsible for "God Save the King."

In the eighteenth century the glee replaced the earlier madrigal of the seventeenth century, the foremost writers of this form of music being Samuel Webbe, Stevens, Callurt and Horsley. Gradually the Handel influence gave place to that of Bach, Haydn and Mozart, and it was left to Charles Dibdin to revive the national sources of inspiration in the patriotic songs and lyrics of the "seventeen nineties." Dibdin's inspiring sea-songs included "The Token," "Tom Bowling," etc., the latter-named, of course, well known to-day. It was said at the time that Dibdin's songs were worth ten thousand men to the English navy.

Wilhelm Friedmann Bach, the eldest son of Johann Sebastian, a dissolute erratic genius, visited London, but his youngest son, Johann Christian Bach, really became Handel's successor in London, where he came from Italy at the age of twenty-eight, in 1763. Bach actually did much to popularise good music among the aristocracy by organising series of concerts, among which were those provided by Mrs Cornelys in 1765. In the two following years fifteen concerts were given, and contemporary announcements bear testimony to their crowded popularity. The concerts were transferred to larger halls and continued to Bach's death in 1782. These were the first subscription concerts in England; the receipts from them were extremely large, but Bach died deeply in debt. His compositions, coming in the transition between the earlier eighteenth-century school and the work of Haydn and Mozart, never took high rank, and one of his less worthy efforts was an imitative little tone composition called "The Battle of Rossbach," with many representations of the noises of battle, including the groans of the wounded, which was rendered in the programme by a printer's error "Les l'Amendations des Blesses." Johann Christian Bach had met Mozart when as a boy prodigy the latter visited London, and the two played duets.

It should be remembered that Salomon, the English manager, persuaded Haydn to visit London, where he was received with great acclamation and performed six symphonies specially composed for England. In 1794 he also brought six more symphonies to London. It was his contact with Handel's oratorios that determined him to write "The Creation," and "God Save the King" induced him to write the broad and noble Austrian national hymn.

From music and composers we naturally turn to the musical instruments. First and foremost was the harpsichord, the successor to the spinet and the precursor of the pianoforte. String instruments ranged from the kit, or pocket violin, used by dancing-masters, to the violo, violin, viol da gamba, 'cello, double bass and basso profundo. Among the wind instruments were the following: organs, bassoons, oboes (oboe d'amore, oboe di caccia, and the more modern type), serpents, trombones, horns, flutes and trumpets; later clarionets.

The piano, in its eighteenth-century form, had descended from the harp, the lyre, dulcimer and virginal. Finger-keys had been known as early as the eighth century A.D., but it was not until the

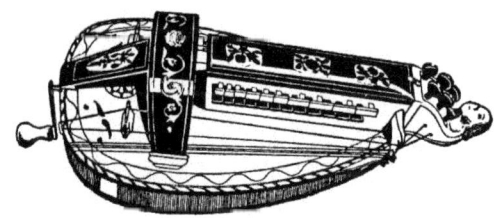

FIG. 51.—The Hurdy-gurdy.

invention of the Clavitherium, about the year 1300, by the Italians, that a keyboard instrument came into use.

The next advance was the clavichord, which also takes its name from the key (*clavis*). The strings were of wire and were set in motion by pressing the keys. It is worthy of note that the great Sebastian Bach preferred this sort of instrument, which he considered best for study, and in general for private

Fig. 52.—A Church Barrel-organ.　　Fig. 53.—A Chamber Organ.

musical entertainment. The revived instruments by Dolmetsch are modelled on the clavichord.

After the clavichord came the virginal of late Tudor times, an improvement on the clavichord. The brass wires were now plucked with raven or crow quills. When the key was pressed down the jack moved upwards, forcing the quill past the string, which it thus set in vibration. The touch of the virginal was extremely sensitive. The tone has been well described by Dr Burney as "a scratch with a sound at the end of it."

The English spinet belongs to the early seventeenth century.

Note.—The illustrations on Figs. 51, 52 and 53 are from drawings of instruments in the permanent collection of Messrs Rushworth & Dreaper Ltd., of Liverpool, by whose kind permission they are here reproduced.

Like the virginal it had but one string to each note, which was set in vibration by means of the jack, with the raven or crow quill attached. The only difference between the spinet and the harpsichord of the late seventeenth century is that the latter has a second string to each note to render the instrument more powerful and capable of some slight degree of expression.

In time harpsichords were made with double keyboards, until by 1720 this instrument was an intricate piece of mechanism. The harpsichords used by Handel had three or four strings to each note, indeed one of them had four strings, two tuned in unison, the third an octave above, and a fourth tuned an octave below the two unison strings, and the two octaves below the highest. This was calculated to produce tonal effects in the great composer's music. Handel's performance on this instrument was considered very fine, for even when his loss of sight compelled him to trust to his inventive powers in playing, the attention of the audience was frequently diverted from the singing to the accompaniment. Handel's favourite instrument was made by Hans Ruckers. The best English makers were the Haywards and John Hitchcock; after them came Keen, Slade, John Harris and Rutgerus Plenius, who invented the lyrichord in 1741.

Improvements now followed in rapid succession. Tabel was responsible for some, but the greater reputation was acquired by one of his foremen, Burckhardt Tschudi. The harpsichord continued in use in various forms, until in 1780 the principal improvements were made by Merlin, who specialised in small instruments. Joseph Kirkman also became a celebrated manufacturer. Throughout the eighteenth century the harpsichord was still known by the name "spinet."

The development of the pianoforte was slow. In England the invention is claimed for Father Wood, an English monk at Rome, who manufactured a pianoforte in 1711. It was, however, defective in its action and impossible for rapid playing. The real credit, however, belongs to an Italian, Bartolommeo Cristofali of Padua, the main improvement being that the jacks which produced sound by quills were replaced by hammers that struck the strings from below. The result was to make the piano and forte heard, as well as degrees of tone as in the 'cello.

In the year 1751 John Broadwood, a young Scottish carpenter and joiner, arrived in London and obtained a situation with Tschudi. Like the industrious apprentice, he found favour with his master and married the daughter of the house. John Broadwood eventually became a partner in the business, and, assisted by Becker and Robert Stodart, succeeded in 1781 in producing a combined grand harpsichord pianoforte which became popular. Here was a pattern for all the makers to copy.

At the close of the eighteenth century the principal pianoforte makers were Broadwood, Stodart, Erard and Pleyel. The English piano had developed from the harpsichord to an instrument powerful in tone and firm of touch. These pianos were far superior to the continental instruments. It was Broadwood who perfected the square type of small upright piano, erroneously named spinets to-day, which were designed for the drawing-rooms of the average house. The design of the cases of harpsichords and pianos reflects the tendencies of the furniture. For example, the harp-shaped grands made between 1700 and 1730 had turned baluster supports to the frame; then followed supports of the cabriole type, and later, classical designs such as that prepared by Robert Adam for the Empress Catherine. Finally is encountered the period of the Regency, when turned legs, ormolu, and brass inlays mark the change of taste in furniture and the acceptance of the French Empire style as a standard.

Chamber music was for long almost the universal diversion of the English upper and middle classes (see Plate XCII.). Scarcely a book of songs of the time exists that does not include illustrations of musical parties and instruments such as pianos, harps, flutes and violins, and these are to be found again in great profusion in the work of such caricaturists as Rowlandson and Gillray.

The violin was first introduced into England at the beginning of the seventeenth century. The viol held its own with the "upstart" violin down to about 1650. The influence of Charles II. with his twenty-four fiddlers gave royal approval and impetus to the English makers. These include the "old school" makers of the eighteenth century, such as Banks, Foster, Duke, Parker, Hill, Warmsley and Betts.

Fiddle-making seems to have flourished in few places outside London during the eighteenth century. There are three notable exceptions, however, of local fiddle-makers—namely, Benjamin Banks of Salisbury, Thomas Perry of Dublin, and James Hardie and his descendants in Edinburgh.

The position of the fiddler in the social scale during the eighteenth century was always associated with the common people, and to be able to play the instrument was looked upon with contempt, which is expressed in such terms we know to-day as "fiddle-sticks," "drunk as a fiddler," "fiddling with it," "to play second fiddle," "face as long as a fiddle." The fiddle, however, was not only the life of the village fairs, but figured largely in services of the Church, with the bassoon, serpent, flute and vamping-horn.

CHAPTER XIV

LITERATURE, FROM THE RESTORATION TO ROMANTICISM

It is not within the scope of the present work to offer more than a summary of the principal tendencies and a sketch of the chief figures in Georgian literature, which, roughly speaking, may be said to form a long road between the twin peaks of Elizabethan adventure and Victorian eclecticism. It is an age of studied verse and polished prose,—as in the case of architecture profoundly occupied with the influences of classicism which, towards the close of the century, were superseded by those of the Romantic movement. At the beginning of the period a tradition had been handed on by the great writers of the Restoration—Dryden, Congreve, Wycherley and Vanbrugh. Their blending of rich human comedy with a powerful idiom of tragic writing derived from classical themes seems to forestall some of the various aspects of Georgian literature. In fact, at the beginning of the century, the influence of Dryden was supreme, though as Pope's fame increased he came to be regarded more and more as the arbiter of literary taste in the country, with a prestige that has seldom been equalled in the case of a living writer, and a crowd of imitators.

Such writers as Pope, Daniel Defoe and Jonathan Swift are among the chief who helped to determine the structure of English literature in the earlier part of the eighteenth century. Others, such as Addison, Steele, Johnson, Richardson, Fielding, Smollett, Sterne and Goldsmith, added in diverse ways to this structure. Pope was a consummate versifier, a writer of vast erudition and culture with a biting satirical wit. Such a work as " The Rape of the Lock," a masterpiece of the most delicate brilliance in a vein that has never been equalled in English literature, is naturally more appreciated at the present day than his lengthy translation of Homer, which, despite a certain monotony of rhythm and quasi-classical diction, as though intended as an adaptation from the antique, is yet

THE
WORKS
OF
Mr. *ALEXANDER POPE.*

CICERO pro ARCH.

Hæc studia adolescentiam alunt, senectutem oblectant; secundas res ornant, adversis perfugium & solatium præbent; delectant domi, non impediunt foris; pernoctant nobiscum, peregrinantur, rusticantur.

LONDON:
Printed by W. BOWYER, for BERNARD LINTOT between the *Temple-Gates.* 1717.

FIG. 54.—A Typical Title-page of the Early Georgian Period, that of Lintot's edition of the Works of Pope.

replete with fine and virile poetry. It is interesting to note that this vast work brought its author a fortune sufficient for the rest of his life. As a witty and often cruel commentator on the faults of the period, though without the moral lash of Hogarth, Pope stands supreme. He was a flawless and audacious technician, and invented an idiom which was eagerly absorbed and copied by countless minor men, often with good enough effect, till the whole temper of poetry was changed by the advent of the Romantic movement.

Daniel Defoe might be described as the first literary journalist of the eighteenth century. He was an omnivorous worker and turned his pen to the most varied subjects—as, for example, the Great Plague, Agriculture, and a Journey to the West of England. He was approaching sixty when he wrote " Robinson Crusoe," and this was followed by other " romances " of which the most famous is perhaps " Moll Flanders," a work in which the baser aspects of the period are presented candidly and unequivocally. His books are models of precise statement, and his gift of narration is masterly. " Robinson Crusoe," the earliest novel of adventure in the English language, is still one of the most popular.

Dean Swift was above all else a moralist, and an angry moralist at that. An Irishman of splendid intellect, his writing brims with an irony and satirical wit that is unsurpassed in English literature. " Gulliver's Travels," a biting satire on the times, is now often vulgarised into a children's reader that would not offend the most prurient-minded—a fact that the Dean would seem hardly likely to appreciate among the immortals.

The periodical essay in prose, innovated by Defoe, was becoming increasingly popular, and continued to develop throughout the eighteenth century and down to the time of Charles Lamb. This was practised by both Addison and Steele in their celebrated *Tatler* and *Spectator*. Credit for the idea of such a form of publication belongs to Steele, but it was the pen of Addison which brought this style of writing to its fullest popularity. Thackeray has given us, in " Henry Esmond," a graphic portrait of Steele, warm-hearted, restless and generally dissolute. Addison was of a totally different type. He lacked the fire of his collaborator but had more of discrimination and grace. Dr Johnson's comment, that " he thinks greatly but he thinks faintly " seems adequately to sum up his character. Both men were admirable stylists, and performed a valuable mission in bringing a breath of culture and philosophy into the haunts of their fellows in coffee-houses and clubs.

It was about 1730 that Samuel Johnson began his literary career, working first on the *Gentleman's Magazine*, and concocting Parliamentary reports. The model of *The Spectator* inspired him to the unsuccessful publication of *The Rambler* and *The Tatler*. His " Rasselas " was not particularly popular, and the " Journey to the Western Hebrides " is passed over by Boswell. His most solid and valuable works are, perhaps, his Dictionary, and " The Lives of the Poets," undertaken when he was over seventy years old ; but considered in relation to the works of the group which surrounded him, he was never a writer of the first rank.

It was more, perhaps, in his rôle of literary pontiff that Johnson's influence was valuable. Writers such as Fielding and Goldsmith belonged to his immediate following, as did also Sir Joshua Reynolds and Sir William Chambers. Gibbon was introduced once into the coterie, but he and the Doctor took an immediate dislike to one another and the experiment was not repeated. Thanks to a pension from the Crown, Johnson had arrived at a position of comparative security after long years of labour as a hack journalist, during which he had known the pangs of hunger and neglect. His power of concentration best fitted him to be a critic, and it was in this connection that his influence was felt and his leadership acknowledged.

Johnson's conversation was brilliant and erudite, but it needed some measure of resistance. His most constant admirer and biographer, Boswell, a man many years his junior, knew how to draw him out and make him shine. Reynolds could prompt him in matters of art and Sir William Chambers in architecture. Goldsmith was both his *protégé* and his butt, in the latter rôle often encouraging his brilliance. But in spite of his small shortcomings and vanities, Johnson above everything aimed at truth and the unmasking of pretence. He was recognised as the foremost critic and censor of his age, and there can be no doubt that these qualities fitted him admirably for the task of his life.

At the time when Johnson was still literary high priest, Adam Smith was publishing his great work, " The Wealth of Nations," and a score of minor poets were flogging the rhymed couplets of Pope. The great political writer and thinker, Burke, stands apart from them. His was an eminently practical mind, and it is not surprising that he mistrusted what were then considered the advanced teachings of Rousseau. He believed in an evolutionary theory of Government and administration and loathed the new republican spirit then gaining ground.

Goldsmith was one of the most brilliant members of Johnson's group. His Irish temperament was at once his strength and his weakness, and he was as ready to depreciate his own abilities as to indulge in ridiculous boasting. He was a seer and a humorist, and we notice particularly the easy detachment which enabled him to produce " The Citizen of the World," a daringly original survey of the social conditions of the time. It was more than a mere whim that caused him to make the chief figure a Chinaman. His famous play, " She Stoops to Conquer," which provided Sheridan with a model on which to base his technique, and the celebrated " Vicar of Wakefield," are the works by which he is chiefly remembered nowadays. Goldsmith, like Johnson, had known the bitterness of neglect and disappointment, and had served his apprenticeship in Grub Street, producing histories and compilations that are still distinguished by delicacy of style and language.

The historian Gibbon, however, was not subjected to these early struggles. The son of a country gentleman in affluent circumstances, the principal discomfort of his youth was a term of service in the militia, of which he has left us an entertaining account in his memoirs, which are among the most fascinating human records that the century produced. Gibbon was essentially cosmopolitan, an inveterate traveller and a splendid linguist. His first book was in fact written in French and published in France, where he always enjoyed a considerable reputation.

Gibbon was deeply interested in theological subjects, and in his early youth, while still at Oxford—a university which he detested—had been converted to the Roman Catholic Church. His father promptly packed him off to Geneva, where an enforced stay in the family of a Lutheran minister brought him back diffidently to the Protestant fold. But not for long ; for by his maturity he was a convinced agnostic, though this he never dared avow. His vast life work, " The Decline and Fall of the Roman Empire," though abounding in inaccuracies in the light of later scholarship, is among the most splendid works in English literature.[1] This book, which for some reason has a reputation for dullness, is one of the most lucid, entertaining and witty in the English language, and a masterpiece of sustained style. The celebrated attack on the Church in the portion dealing with the rise of

[1] George III., it is said, once evinced a desire to meet the historian, who was brought into his presence, but the monarch's only remarks were, " Scribble, scribble, scribble, Mr Gibbon ! " and then, after a pause, " Ha, ha, ha ! "

Christianity caused a considerable controversy at the time, and Gibbon retired to the shores of Lake Leman for the rest of his life, where he lived in comfortable affluence with a friend, though he died in London at the house of his old friend Lord Sheffield.

The crowd of minor poets of this time regarded Pope's verse somewhat as the clergy might regard orthodoxy. But these smaller men little realised that classicism in literature had reached its zenith and was about to give way to something new. We can discern the first glimmerings of romanticism in the poetry of Gray, and in the literature of the second half of the century there are several streams observable converging to the same end. Individualism becomes more apparent, and this is well illustrated in the case of the poet Burns, who, of Scottish peasant stock, raised his native style of lowland song to the heights of pure poetry. His natural and striking genius was of the soil, disdaining pedantry and gay in the face of obstacles. His gifts were of the nature of the new Romantic movement, and his poems did much to influence the development of later lyrical poetry.

In William Blake we find the innovator, the profound and solitary genius out of accord with the spirit of his time. Blake was a seer and visionary with glittering imaginative powers that are equally evident in his long mystical poems, his lyrics and his strange drawings which have in them more of the true Gothic spirit than all the jejune trappings of the Gothic revival. The case of Blake is too strange and too complicated to be discussed fully in these few pages. As can be readily understood, he was totally misrepresented and neglected during his lifetime and practically unknown to the public at large. It is only of recent times that his strange genius has come into the full recognition it deserves.

Apart from poetry and historical and speculative writing, the chief literary innovation of the Georgian period was the novel. It takes its place as a successor to the works of the Restoration dramatists who passed with the death of Vanbrugh. The narrative style adopted by Defoe in " Captain Singleton," " Moll Flanders " and " Robinson Crusoe " had paved the way for further developments, and a growing eagerness became evident on the part of the public to be told a plain tale in direct language that mirrored contemporary life. Apart from Gay's "Beggar's Opera," which was first staged in 1727, the theatre had become increasingly dull, and there was no new and daring effort, little wit and little tragic writing of importance to occupy the attention of a public that was

PLATE XCII.

A Group of the Cowper Family. Notice the type of instrument.
From a painting by John Zoffany.

A Walnut Spinet of the First Half of the Eighteenth Century, inscribed "Joseph Mahon, London."

PLATE XCIII.

Bookseller and Author.

Drawn by H. Wigstead.

Mr and Mrs Garrick entertaining Dr Johnson to Tea.

By John Zoffany.

growing tired of being amused by foreigners. Defoe's narrative whetted the public appetite, but it was not until Richardson and Fielding entered the field that the novel begins developing on modern lines.

Richardson's "Clarissa Harlowe" opened up a new era. He had first adopted the method of telling his story by means of letters in his "Pamela," and this method he continued. His books had an immediate success and paved the way for the works of Fielding, who set out to tell a story as it had never been told before. There is something of the attitude of the benevolent judge in the way he seems to preside over the children of his fertile imagination. "Tom Jones" is a lengthy work dealing with purely topical events and purely representative characters. The coarseness and brutality of the times are dealt with in a candid and often outspoken way, and he is far from irritating when he digresses to allow his characters to step aside and reappear refreshed. Fielding devised the structure of his books almost entirely from the material provided by the social fabric of his time. Such characters as Squire Western and Blifil were taken direct from life, and the action of the book has something of the inevitable regularity of an eight-day clock. Fielding had a host of followers, noteworthy among whom Smollett adopted practically the same method of narration. This method is pursued throughout the century till we find a mass of copious romances and serials, now practically forgotten, at the close of the period making way for the works of Jane Austen and the Brontës and the romantic novels of Walter Scott.

One writer, however, Laurence Sterne, deserves more than a passing reference. This curious clergyman produced books which are among the most entertaining of the century. Packed with wit and erudition, often not a little coarse, his "Tristram Shandy" seems to mock the current form of the novel. "The Sentimental Journey," a description of a tour through France, is equally diverse and entertaining, and both books commanded a considerable success at the time, and are read to-day.

There is little space here to touch on any but the most considerable figures in Georgian literature. The small poets, pamphleteers and lampooners who fill the century must remain untreated; poets such as Gray and Thomson can be given little but a passing reference. The great school of Romantic poetry, that of Byron, Shelley, Keats, Wordsworth and Coleridge, is of the next century, which also saw the founding of the formidable literary reviews. We can only briefly mention such dilettanti as Beckford and Horace Walpole, whose lives and works stand as a valuable index to the changing spirit of the times.

Throughout the century the publication of books was in the hands of the actual booksellers, and these, if we are to take the opinion of Pope in his "Dunciad," were, at the beginning of the period at any rate, hardly distinguished by taste, discrimination, or even common honesty. Publishing was, indeed, a dirty enough game, with its record of piracy, plagiarisation, scandalous and disgusting lampoon, and miserable neglect and underpayment of genuine talent, as is instanced in the case of Johnson. Nevertheless Pope, despite the fact that he was a Catholic and a hunchback, could, by the brilliance of his youthful virtuosity, immediately establish a reputation for himself at a very early age ; but it was easy at the same time to find some one to publish a disgusting personal attack on the young poet mainly at the expense of his physical defects. The rising man of talent had, indeed, to have a thick skin to get him through the mean attacks of Grub Street, and had at the same time to be something of an adept in paying it back in its own coin. Pope's magnificent pulverisation of this nauseating province in eighteenth-century life, "The Dunciad," is, if it sometimes descends to rather murky levels according to modern standards, one of the greatest fighting satires in the English language.

The author had always to find a patron of some eminence and importance to whom he would address his work in a fulsome page of dedication. This patron's influence would help to swell the list of subscriptions, for the work was invariably subscribed before publication. With the coming of the Amateurs, and the increase in taste among the upper classes, however, a writer might often find a real patron of learning and discrimination, and not merely a self-satisfied puppet to be flattered and cajoled.

Nevertheless, despite the disadvantages and indignities which so often attended the life of a man of letters in the eighteenth century, real talent very seldom failed to find its ultimate recognition. The reading public, though certainly smaller than it is to-day, had a very appreciably higher standard of taste. Poetry and literature were almost a necessity of life to the Georgian Englishman, and a writer even of humble origin could claim the public attention and rise to considerable eminence by the sheer force of original talent.

INDEX

A

Adam, Robert, 45, 68, 72, 110, 114, 117, 126, 132, 137, 140, 144, 150, 176; characteristic work of, Plates LXXII., LXXVI.
Adam, the brothers, and style, 99, 100, 119, 122, 133, 151
Addison, Joseph, 7, 19, 21, 22, 181, 187, 189
Advertisement, methods of. *See* Trade Cards
Agriculture, 2, 35, 61
Aldrich, Dean, 178
Amusements. *See* Sport and Pastimes
Anson, Admiral, 40
Anti-gallican Society, the, 136
Apothecaries, 65
Archæology, interest in, 11, 133
Archery, 75, Plate XLIII.
Architecture, in London and provinces, 10, Plates I., VIII., XXI., XXIV., XXII., XXXIII.; Inns, 34, Plate XXIV.; influence of agriculture, 36; naval, 42, 43, 64, Plates XXVII., XXVIII., XXIX., XXX.; shops, 72-73, Plates XXXIX., XL.; general state of, 97-115; town-planning, 102-104, 117 ff.; country-houses, 104-107, 117; domestic interiors, 130-133
Arkwright, Sir R., 4, 61
Army, the, 50-54
Arne, Dr, 179, *180*, 181
Arnold, Samuel, 182
Art, general state of, 13
Ascot races, 84, Plate XLV.
Astley, John, 164
Atterwood, Thomas, 182
Axminster, 17

B

Bach, J. S., 179
Bach family, 182-3
Bacon, ——, 171, Plate LXXXVI.
Bagnigge Wells, 20, 68
Bagshot, 34
Bakewell, 36

Ballad opera, 179
Ballooning, *82*
Bank of England, 101, 117, 126
Banks, ——, 171
Barcheston, 146
Barnet, 168
Barry, Elizabeth, 176
Basket-making, 62, Plate XXXV.
Bath, 10; pump room, Plate VIII., 20, 103; entrance, Plate VIII., 110, 116
Battersea, 68, 143
Bear baiting, 74, 80
Beckford, William, 7, 12, 193
Bedford, Duke of, 30, 36
Bedford Level, 35
Bedfordshire, 62, 66
Bedlam, 95
Beer, 28
Belfast, 4, 145
Belton Hill, 131
Bentham, General, 39
Bernini, 98
Berridge, John, 55-56
Bersham, 61
Betterton, Thomas, 174
Betting, 79, 84
Billiards, 75
Bilston, 143
Bird, Francis, 170
Birmingham, 3, 4, 68, 70, 71, 113, 142, 146
" Black Boy," 19, Plate XIV.
Blackheath, 34
Blake, William, 12, 159, 167, Plate LXXX., 168, 192
Blenheim Palace, 98, 105, 130
Bonomi, 126
Bookbinders, 65, 156-157
Bookselling, 194, Plates XXXVIII., XCIII.
Boswell, James, 190
Boughton, Northants, 105
Boulton, Matthew, 144
Bow china, 152, 154, Plate LXXVII.
Bowling, 84, 85, Plate XLIII.
Boxing, 88-89, Plate XLIX.
Boyce, William, 182
Bracegirdle, Mrs, 176
Bradford, Plate XXXIV.

INDEX

Braziers, 4, 170
Bread, 28
Brettingham the elder, 110
Brewing, 67
Brickmaking, 68
Brickwork, 118-119
Bridges, 116, 117, 118
Bridgewater, Duke of, 12, 51
Brighton, 20 ; pavilion, Plate VIII.
Bristol, 3, 32, 62, 104, 117, 145, 146, 153, 155
Brocket Hall, 126
Broughton, Jack, 88
Buckinghamshire, 66
Building and building materials, 10, 112, 115, 116 ff.
Bull running, 90-91, Plate XLVIII.
Bunbury, Henry, 165
Burial Clubs, 16
Burlington, Lord, 99, 105, 109
Burney, Dr Charles, 181, 184
Bury St Edmunds, 86 ; Town Hall, 102, Plate LIII., 110, 112
Bushey, 85
Buteaux, Abraham, 150
Button-making, 70

C

Cabinet-making, 70-71, 136, 138
Calico-printing, 68
Call, Sir William, 126
Cambridge, 98, 121 ; Trinity College Gates, Plate LIX.
Campbell, Colin, 99 ; work by, Plate LI., 108, 109
Canals, 4, 61
Candles, 48, 65
Carey, Henry, 182
Caricatures, 11, 80, 81
Carlini, 172
Carpenters, 128
Carpets, 17, 148
Carr, Mr, of York, 117
Carriages, and coaches, 30, 31, 32, Plates X., XXII., XXIII., LIV.
Carron, 4, 142
Carter, Thomas, 182
Cartwright, 61
Castle Howard, 98, Plate LI, 105, 130
Caughley, 155
Ceilings, 126, 127, 131, Plates LX., LXI ; painted, 132, 133
Chairs, 138, Plates LXVI., LXVII., LXVIII.
Chamber music, 186
Chambers, Sir William, 34, 101 ; Court at Somerset House, Plate LII., 102, 119, 120, 125, 129, 133, 155, 190
Champion, Sir Richard, 153
Chandeliers, 141, 146, Plate LXX.
Chantrey, Sir William, 172

Chasing, 76
Chatham, 44
Chatsworth, 105
Chelsea china, 153
Cheltenham, 20
Chequering, 119
Chesterfield, Lord, 7, 75
Children, treatment for, 14, Plate IX. ; toys, 15, Plate X. ; in industry, 61 ff.
Chimney-pieces, 132, 133 ; Plates LXIII., LXIV., LXV.
Chinaware, 18, 152
Chinese influences, 136, 140
Chippendale and his style, 18, 70, 136, 137
Church, the, 54-60 ; architecture, 98, Plates XXXII., XXXIII. ; music, 178, 186
Cibber, C. G., 170, 176
Cipriani, 132, 133, 137, 165
Cirencester, 117
Classicism, 10, 11, 13, 133, 136
Clavichord, 184
Clifton, 20, 104, 111
Clergy ridiculed, 56, 57, 58 ; respected, 58
Clinton, 52
Clock and watch making, 17, 71 ; curious figures, Plate XX.
Clubs, burial, 16 ; coursing, 80 ; literary, 30 ; political, 29
Coaches and coach-makers, 8, Plate VI. ; 32, 65, 66
Coade's Patent Stone, 118, 120
Coal, 4, 17, 61, 62
Coalport, 155
Cockfighting, 74, 80, 82, Plate XLVIII, 89
Cock throwing, 89, 90
Coffee houses, 29, 30, Plates XV., XVI.
Congreve, William, 174, 187
Constable, John, 159, 168, 169, Plate LXXXV.
Cookworthy, John, 153
Cooper, Samuel, 158
Coopers, Plate XXXV.
Copley, J. S., 164
Coppersmiths, 70, Plate XXXV.
Cork, 145
Cornwall, 70
Corsairs, 41
Cornwallis, Marquis, 52
Costume, men's, 24, 25, Plate XVII.; women's, 23, 24, Plates XVII., XVIII.
Cosway, Richard, 166
Cotes, Francis, 164
Cotman, John Sell, 159, 168, Plate LXXXV.
Cotton, 4, 61
Coursing, 75, Plate XLII.
Cowper, William, 56
Cox, David, 168
Cozens, A. and J., 168
Crabbe, George, 3-4, 54, 57

INDEX

Cricket, 87, 88, Plate XLVII.
Croft, William, 181
Crome, John, 159, 168, Plate LXXXIV.
Cromer, 48
Crompton, 4, 61 ; his " mule," Plate III.
Cumberland, Duke of, 52, 54
Curriers, 64, 65
Cutlers, 68

D

Dance, George, *junior*, 101, 117, 133, Plate LIII.
Dancing, 91
Darly, Mathew, caricatures *after*, 6, 11, 100
Dayes, Edward, 165
Deane, Sir A., 42, 43
Decorative Arts generally, 134-157
Defesch, Mr, 182
Defoe, Daniel, 5, 112, 187, 189, 192, 193
Deism, 54
Deptford, 42, Plate XXIX., 44, 64
Derby, 18, 153
Devonshire, 4, 66
Dibdin, Thomas, 179
Dighton, Robert, *frontispiece*, 165
Distilling, 68
Dockyards, 42, Plate XXIX., 44, 45, 46, 64
Doncaster, 76
Door furniture, 142, 143
Downman, John, 166
Drama, the, 174-177
Drinking, 28, 57
Dryden, John, 187
Dublin, 104 ; the Four Courts, Plate LII., 111, 146
Duck hawking, 75, 76
Ducking, 90
Duesbury, 154, 155
Duncan, Admiral, 41
Dwight, 152
Dyers, 65

E

East Anglia, 4, 32
East India Company, 17, 18
Easton Neston, 105
Eddystone lighthouse, 45, 47
Edmonton, 20 ; Fair, Plate L.
Edridge, Henry, 165
Edwards, James, 157
Eggington Manor, 114
Embroidery, 25, 26, Plate LXXIV.
Enamelling, 143
Epsom, 20, 76
Evelyn, John, 140
Exeter, 104, 114
Export trading, 4, 71

F

Faber, 165
Factory system, the, 62
Fairs, 74, 91, 93, 95, Plate L.
Farington, Joseph, 168
Farmhouses, 36, Plate XXV.
Farquhar, George, 174
Feather workers, 66, 67, Plate XXXVII.
Felton, William, 66
Fiction, 193, 194
Fielding, Henry, 5, 7, 187, 190, 193
Finchley Common, 33
Fire engines, 16, Plate XI.
— grates, 64, 141, 142
— implements, 142
— screens, Plate XIV.
Fishing, 74, Plate XLIII.
Fives, 86, Plate XLVI.
Flaxman, John, 133, 144, 155, 171-172, Plate LXXXVII.
" Fly boats," 31
Food, 27 ; at sea, 40
Football, 85, Plate XLVI.
Footmen, 18, 19, Plate XIV.
Foulston, ——, 127
Fowling, 74, Plate XLI.
Fox, C. J., 29
Frederick, Prince of Wales, 83
French influences, 3, 10, 24, 102, 105, 130, 132, 134, 150
Funerals, 15, Plate XI.
Furniture, 17, 18, 134-142
Fuseli, Henry, 164

G

Gainsborough, Thomas, 159, 162-163, Plate LXXXI., 167
Gala days, 94, 95
Gamekeepers, 79, Plate XLII.
Gaming, 22, 23
Gandon, 101 ; the Four Courts, Plate LII., 120
Gardens, 106, 107
Garrick, David, 175, Plate XCIII.
Gay, John, 11, 175, Plate XC., 180, 181, 192
George III., 76
George, Prince (George IV.), 12, Plate VIII., 83, 84
Germaine, Lord George, 52
Gesso, 140-141
Gibbon, Edward, 11, 190, 191-192
Gibbons, Grinling, 124, 131
Gibbs, James, 7, 107, 116, 125
Gillray, James, 165
Girtin, Thomas, 159, 168-169
Glass, 123, 124, 144-146, Plate LXXIII.
Glass-cutting, 146
Glees, 182

INDEX

Goldsmith, Oliver, 14, 175, 187, 190, 191
Golf, 87-88
Goodridge, ——, 127
Gorhambury, 107, Plate LV.
Grafton, Duke of, 35
Gray, Thomas, 12, 192
Green, Maurice, 182
Greenwich, 20, 154; Hospital, 105
Greyhound coursing, 80, Plate XLII.
"Grog," 40

H

Hairdressing, 66, Plate XXXVII.
Hair powder, 66
Hales, Dr, 40
Hambledon Club, 87
Hamilton, Gavin, 164
Hampton Court, 130, 141; chandeliers, Plate LXX.
Hampton Wick, 85
Handel, G. F., 179-181
Hanging, 34
Hardware, 4
Hardy, Sir C., 41
Harewood, 137; salon, Plate LXVIII.
Hargreave, 4; spinning jenny, Plate III., 61
Harness-making, 71
Harpsichord, 17, Plate XIV., 183
Harrogate, 20
Harwich, 64
Hat-making, 62
Hawkers, street, 28, Plate XIX., XX.
Hawksmoor, Nicholas, 7, 99, 105
Haydn, Joseph, 179, 183
Haymen, street-scene, 22
Head-dresses, 24, 25, 66, 67
Hearne, Thomas, 165
Hepplewhite, George, 138
Highwaymen, 33, 34, 94
Hilliard, Nicholas, 158
Hogarth, William, 5; "Night" and "Morning," Plate V.; "Rake's Progress," 7; funeral cortège, Plate XI.; Plate XIV., 33, 158, 159, 160, Plate LXXIX.
Holbein, Hans, 158
Holkham, 119; ceiling, Plate LX., 131, 132
Holland, Henry, 101, 102, 107, 113, 118, 119, 126, 133, 172
Hollis, Thomas, 156
Home industries, 61 ff., Plate XXXV.
Hoops, 26
Hope, Thomas, 138, *139*
Hoppner, John, 159, 166, 168
Horse milliner, 71
Horse-racing, 83-84, Plate XLV.
Houghton House, 99; interior, Plate LI., 118, 131

Houses, 16, 18, 104-107, 130-133, 119, 172
Howard, John, 10
Hull, 64
Humanitarianism, 13, Plate VII.
Hunting, 74, 75, Plate XLI., 76
Huntington, William, 56

I

Ibbetson, J. C., 165
"Implacable," the, 45
Imports, 25, 28, 152
Industrialism, 3 ff.
Inns and taverns, 31; interior, 34, Plate XXIII., 35; signs, Plate XXIV., 95; windows, 122, 123
Insurance companies, 16
Invasion, risk of, 41
Ipswich, 33
Ireland, 4
Ironmongery, 142-143
Ironwork, 115, 120-121, Plate LVI., 129
Ironworks, 61, Plate XXXVI.

J

Jackson, William, 182
James, John, 107, 142, 125
Janssen, Theodore, 143
Jervis, Admiral, 41
Jewellers, *63*, 64
Jockey Club, the, 84
Johnson, Garrett, 140
Johnson, Samuel, 7, 8, 11, 30, 187, 190; in bookshop, Plate XCIII.
Johnson, Tom, 88
Jones, Inigo, 1, 6, 97, 102, 116, 118, 120, 130

K

Kauffmann, Angelica, 132, 133, Plate LX., 137, 155, 165
Kedleston, 107, 137
Kelly, Michael, 182
Kendal, 117
Kent, William, 7, 48, 99, 109, 112, 124, 131; influence on furniture, 134, 136, Plate LXVI., 137, 175
Kew, 19
Keys, 142
King, flying shuttle, 4
Kneller, Sir Godfrey, 158

L

Labeyle, 116
Lace-making, 66
Lacquer-work, 139, 140, Plate LXIX.

INDEX

Ladbrooke, Robert, 168
Lamérie, Paul, 136, 150
Lancashire, 4
Lawrence, Sir Thomas, 159, 166-167, 168
Leadwork, 121-123, Plate LIX.
Leamington, 20
Leather-work, 67, 157
Lely, Sir Peter, 158
Le Marchand, 170
Leoni, 99, 132
Leverton, Thomas, 133
Lighthouses, 46, *47*, *48*, 49
Lighting, indoor, 48, 141
Lillo, George, 175
Linen industry, 4 ; flax-spinning, Plate XXXV.
Linley family, 182
Literature, 187-194
Liverpool, 104
Locks, 142, Plate LXX.
London and environs, 3, 19
  Apollo Gardens, 20
  Bank of England, 101, 117, 126
  Barton Street, 103
  Bayswater Tea Gardens, 20
  Bedford Row, 110
  Bedford Square, 103, 133
  Bedlam, 95
  Belsize House, 94
  Bermondsey, 20
  Billingsgate, 27
  Bloomsbury, 19
  Bloomsbury Square, 103
  Bow, 18, 68, 152 ff.
  Burlington House, 109
  Canonbury House, 20
  Carlton House, 133
  Cavendish Square, 103, Plate LIV.
  Charlotte Street, 103
  Chelsea, 19, 152 ff.
  Chesterfield House, 110
  Chiswick, 28, 99, 105
  Clerkenwell, 31, 71
  Clifford's Inn, 103
  Craig's Court, 103
  Denmark Hill, house at, 115, 121, Plate LVI.
  Devonshire House, 99, 108, 119
  Enfield, 68, 78
  Finchley Common, 33
  Fitzroy Square, 117
  Fleet Prison, 15, Plate VII.
  Great Marlborough Street, 103
  Great Ormond Street, 103, 110, Plate LVII.
  Golden Square, 103
  Hampstead, 19, 20
  Hanover Square, 103
  Highbury, 68
  Highgate, 19, 20
  Holborn, 31, 32
  Hoxton, 85

London and environs—*continued*
  Hyde Park, 20
  Islington, 20
  Jermyn Street, 103
  Kensington, 19, 20
  Kingsland, 68
  Lambeth, 18, 20, 28, 68, 118, 123, 152
  Lansdowne House, 110
  Lincoln's Inn Fields, 102, 117
  Lindsay House, *118*
  Lord's Cricket Ground, 87
  Manchester Square, 103
  Marlborough House, *108*
  Marylebone, 19, 20
  Mayfair, 95
  Montague House, 108, *109*
  Muswell Hill, 78
  New River 17
  Newcastle House, 108
  Newgate Jail, 5, 101, Plates IV., LIII.
  Nine Elms, 28
  Norfolk Street, 103
  Paddington, 68
  Pentonville, 68
  Portland Place, 103
  Queen Anne's Gate, 110
  Queen Square, 103
  Ranelagh, 20
  Red Lion Square, 103
  Regent's Park, 111, 120, Plate LVIII.
  Regent Street, 103
  Russell Square, 103
  St George's Fields, 20
  St James's Park, 20
  St James's Square, 103
  St Paul's Cathedral, 98, 116 ; Chapter House, 118
  Schomberg House, 111, 163, Plate LVII.
  Sloane Street, 113
  Soho Square, 103
  Somerset House, 101, Plate LII.
  Southwark, 95
  Spencer House, 110, Plate LVI.
  Spitalfields, 25, 149
  Spring Gardens, 20
  Stepney, 154
  Tottenham Fields, 20
  Tower, the, 95, Plate XXI.
  Trinity House, 46, 48, 117
  Vauxhall, 18, 20, 21, Plate XCI.
  Westminster Bridge, 116
London Courant, The, 8
Longton Hall, 154, 155, Plate LXXVII.
Lunardi, 82, 83
Lymington, 64

M

Machine guns, *99*
Macklin, Charles, 176
Malton, James, 165, Plate LII.

Malton, 165, Plate LIV.
Manwaring, 18, 138
Margate, 20, 111
Markets, 8, 27, 28
Marlborough, Duke of, 50, 51
Marot, his influence in England, 134, *135*, 136
Marquetry, 140, Plate LXIX.
Marylebone Club, 87
Masonry, 116-118
Mearnes, the, 156
Medicine, 9, 10, 12, 14, Plate X, 40
Meissonier, 136, 150, Plate LXXVI.
Metalwork, 133. *See also* Plate, Pewter, Ironwork
Metal workers, 4, 64, 113, 136
Militia, 53
Milliners, 66, *67*
Milling match, Plate XLIX.
Milk, supply of, 28, Plate XX.
Mirrors, 18, Plate XIII., 123
Moor Park, 132, Plate XII.
Moore, Sir John, 50, 52, 54
Morland, George, 159, 167, Plate LXXX., 168
Morris, Joshua, 146
Music, 79, 176-186, Plates XCI., XCII.
Musical instruments, 183 ff., *184*
Mylne, Richard, 114, 117

N

Nash, John, 101, Plate LVIII.
Naval architecture. *See* Architecture, naval
Navy, the, 37 ff.
Needlework, 17, 148-149, Plate LXXIV.
Nelson, Lord, 41, 43
Newcastle-on-Tyne, 61, 64, 123, 146
Newmarket, 74, 76, 83, 84
Newspapers, 8, 9
Newton, John, 55, 56
Nollekins, Joseph, 171
Nonconformity, Plate XXXII.
Northampton, 117
Norwich Society of Artists, 168

O

Oldfield, Mrs, 176
Oliver, Peter and Isaac, 158
Openordt, 136, 150, Plate LXXVI.
Opera, 181
Opie, John, 159, 166
Oratorio, 181, 183
Orford, Lord, 80
Organs and organ music, *184*
Ormolu, 144, Plate LXXI.
Otter-hunting, 77
Oysters, 27, 28

P

Paine, James, 107, 117
Painting, 158 ff.; studio, *163*
Palladio, style and influence of, 13, 97, 98, 131
Paper-making, 68
Papworth, John, 127
Parisot, Pierre, 146, 147
Parker, Richard, 41
Partridge netting, 77; shooting, 79
Payne, Roger, 156, 157
Pechy, Dr, 14
Pedlar, Plate XX.
Penrose, G. and W., 145
Pepusch, Dr, 179, 181
Pergolesi, 126, 137
Peruzzi, 97
Peters, Matthew W., 166
Pewter, 18, 150
Pianofortes, 183
Pingo, Thomas, 156
Pins, 68
Piranesi, 100
Plasterwork, 124, *125*, 126, *127*, 128, 131, Plates LX., LXI.
Plate, silver, 149-151, Plates LXXV., LXXVI.
Plays, 174-177
Ploughing, 36, Plate XXV.
Plymouth, 44, 45, 153, 155
Pollard, James, 33
Pope, Alexander, 6, 7, 106, 187-189, 194
Porcelain, 17, 151-155, Plates LXXVII., LXXVIII.
Portsmouth, 44
Potteries, 18
Printing and printers, 65, Plate XXXVI., 68, *69*, *188*
Prior Park, 107
Prisons, "gaoler's coach," 9, 10; the Fleet, Plate VII., 60; convict hulk, Plate XXX.
Punishment, 8, 9, 10, 40, 53, 78
Purcell, Henry, 178, 179

Q

Quin, James, 176

R

Racing, 74, 76, Plate XLV.
Raeburn, Sir Henry, 166, 168
Raikes, William, 60
Ramsay, Allan, 159, 164
Raynham, 132
Regency, style and effect of, 36, Plate XXV., 111, 133, 143
Revivalism, 9, 54, 55, Plate XXXIII.

INDEX

Reynolds, Sir Joshua, 11, 26, Plate XVIII., 30, 159, 160-162, Plate LXXXI., 163, 167, 190
Richardson, Samuel, 187, 193
Richmond, 19, 20, 114
"Riding the Skimmington," 91, Plate XLIX.
Riots, 3, Plate IV.
Ripley, ——, 119
Roads and travelling, 4, 8, 9, 19, 27, 30, 31, 32, Plate XXII.
Rockingham, Lord, 35
Romanticism, 12
Romney, George, 26, Plate XVIII., 159, 163-164, Plate LXXXII., 167
Rope-making, 62, Plate XXXV., 68
Roubilliac, 170
Rowlandson, Thomas, 159, 165, Plates VII., XXIII., XLV., LXXIX., 168, Plate LXXXIII.
Royal Academy, 11, Plate LXXXIII.
"Royal George," the, 43, Plate XXX.
"Royal George," the second, 44
"Royal Sovereign," the, 45
Rubens, Sir P. P., 158
Rudyard, Sir John, 46, *48*
"Rule Britannia," 181
Rysbrack, 170, Plates LXXXVI., LXXXVII.

S

Saddlers, 65, 71
Saffron Walden, 68
St Leger Sweepstakes, 84
Salisbury, 110
Samplers, 149
Sandby, Paul, 165
Sanitation, 3, 5, 12, 14, 16
Saunders, Paul, 146
Scheemakers, 170
Schools, 15, Plate IX., 56
Sculpture, 154, 170-177, Plates LXXXVI., LXXXVII.
Sedan chairs, 32, Plate XIX., 100
Servants, domestic, 18, 19, Plate XIV., 124, 151
Sheffield plate, 150
Sheraton, Thomas, 18, 138
Sheridan, R. B., 11, 29, 176, 182
Shipbuilding, 43, 44, 45, 64
Shoes and boots, 27, 65
Shooting, 75, Plate XLI., 78
Shops, 72, *73*, Plates XXXVIII., XXXIX., XL.
Shovell, Sir Cloudesley, 46
Siddons, Sarah, 176
Silk, 25, 27, 65, 149
Skating, 93
Skittles, Plate XLIII.
Slating, 120, Plate LVIII.
Smart, John, 166
Smeaton, John, 46, 48, *49*

Smith, Adam, 190
Smith, Edward, 172
Smithery, 64, Plate XXXVI., 121
Smollett, Tobias, 187
Soane, Sir Soane, 101, 102, 117, 120, 126,
Soap-making, 65
Society, 2, 4, 7, 13, 14 ff., 20, Plates XV., XLV.
Soho works, 144, 150
Sonata, 179
Song-plays, 182
South Sea Bubble, 23, Plate XVI.
Southill, 107, 126, 172
Spectator, The, 189
"Speeding," *81*
Spengler, J. J., 155
Spinet, 184, 185
Spinning, 62, Plate XXXV.
Sport and games, 8, 19, 20, 35, 74-96, Plates XLIII., XLIV., XLVI., XLVII., XLVIII.
Staffordshire, 18
Stag-hunting, Plate XLIV.
Staircases, 128, 129, 131, 133
Stamford, 90, Plate XLVIII., 110
Stanfield, Clarkson, 46
Stanstead, *106*
Stark, James, 168
Steam-engine, 45, 62, 144
Steele, Sir Richard, 30, 187, 189
Stepplechasing, 84
Stephan, Pierre, 155
Sterne, Laurence, 187, 193
Stevens, Francis, 182
Stoke Edith, 131
Stonebridge, 145, 146
Storace, Stephen, 179
Strawberry Hill, 132
Stucco, 119, 120, 129
Swaffham House, 80, 115, Plate LV.
Swift, Jonathan, 7, 187, 189
Symphonies, 183

T

Talman, 105
Tapestry, 146, 149, Plate LXXIII.
Tatler, The, 189
Taunton, 62
Taylor, Sir Robert, 107, 112, 119, 125, 171
Theatres, 101, 174, *175*, Plates LXXXVIII., LXXXIX., 177, Plate XC.
Thornhill, Sir James, 131
Thornton, Bonnall, 122
Tijou, Jean, 121
Tiling, 119-120, Plate LVIII.
Tin mining and plating, 68, 70
Town life, and houses, 5, 19, Plates IV., V., 108-110, Plates LIV., LV., LVII., LVIII.
Town-planning, 102-104, 120

Trade, 61 ff.
Trade advertising, 14, 15, *63*, *67*, *147*, Plates IX., X., XI., XX.
Troops, 12 ; troopships, 53
Tunbridge Wells, 20
Turner, J. M. W., 46, 168, 169

U

Uniforms, military, 53, Plate XXXI.
Upholsterers, 17, 136

V

Vanbrugh, Sir John, 1, 6, 44, 98, Plate LI., 99, 105, 117, 122, 130, 174, 187
Vandrebanc, John, 146
Van Dyck, Sir A., 158
Vandyke, Peter, 164
Vernon, Admiral, 40
"Victory," the, 43, 56
Viols and violins, 186
Virginals, 184

W

Waldenbury, 114
Walls, decoration of, 17, 129, 131, 132, Plate LXII., 146, *147*
Walpole, Horace, 7, 12, 14, 76, 132, 193
Walpole, Sir Robert, 3
Warbrook, 107, 125, 141, 142
Wardour Castle, 107
Ware, Isaac, 110, 112, 119, 125, 136
Warfare, naval, 38 ff., *39*, Plate XXVII., 42, 43, Plate XXVIII., 45, 46
Warwickshire, 4
Waterford, 45
Watt, James, 61
Waxworks, *95*
Weaving, 61, Plate XXV.
Webb, John, 97, 130
Webb, Samuel, 182
Wedgwood, Josiah, 100, 155, 172
Wellington, Duke of, 50, 54
Wesley, Charles and John, 54-55
West, Benjamin, 164

Westmacott, Sir R., 172
Weymouth, 20, 111
Wheatley, Francis, 165. 168
Wheelwrights, 67
Whitaker, John, 157
Whitbread, Samuel, 29, 36
Whitefield, George, 54, 55, Plate XXXIII.
Whittington, 146
"Wick," the, 114, *115*
Wilberforce, Samuel, 56
Wilson, Richard, 160, Plate LXXXIV.
Wilton House, 130
Wilton, Joseph, 171
Windows, 122, 123, 128
Windsor, 20
Wine, 28, Plate XXI. ; cooler, 17, Plate XII.
Wing, John, 117
Winstanley, Henry, 46
Woburn Abbey, 114, 126, 172, *173*
Woffington, Peg, 176
Wokingham, 91
Wolcot, John, 58, 59
Wolverhampton, 142
Wood, John, 103, 107
Woods, various, in use, 137, 138
Woodwork, 128-129, *128*, 130
Wool, 4, 62, 65
Woolpit, 68
Worcester, 153, 155
Wren, Sir Christopher, 97, 102, 108, 112, 116, 117, 118, 119, 121, 130, 131, 174
Wright, Joseph, of Derby, 164, Plates XXXVI., LXXXII., 168
Wrotham Park, 107
Wyatt, James, 117, 133
Wycherley, William, 187

Y

Yarmouth, 64
York, Duke of, 52
Young, Arthur, 35

Z

Zoffany, Johann, 159, 164, Plate XCII., 167
Zucchi, 132

www.ingramcontent.com/pod-product-compliance
Ingram Content Group UK Ltd.
Pitfield, Milton Keynes, MK11 3LW, UK
UKHW021314180426
11947UKWH00015B/1224